THE UMBRELLA MURDER

THE UMBRELLA MURDER

The Hunt for the Cold War's
Most Notorious Killer

ULRIK SKOTTE

WH Allen, an imprint of Ebury Publishing
20 Vauxhall Bridge Road
London SW1V 2SA

WH Allen is part of the Penguin Random House group of companies
whose addresses can be found at global.penguinrandomhouse.com

Plate section photographs: 'Commuters in London' © Evening Standard/Stringer/
Hulton Archive/Getty; 'Bulgarian defector Georgi Markov' © PA Images/Alamy Stock
Photo; 'Micro-Ball' © Keystone Press/Alamy Stock Photo; 'Gullino with dog' courtesy
of Ulla Knigge; 'Dead drops', 'Mondial business cards', 'Gullino's diary', 'Scotland
Yard folder' and 'Gullino 2021' courtesy of Ulrik Skotte; 'Franco and Bent at work',
'Franco portrait', 'Gullino's house' and 'Attic room' from Franco Invernizzi's personal
collection, courtesy of Helene Invernizzi and Bent Staalhøj; 'Gullino at
Copenhagen Central Station' courtesy of Bent Staalhøj.

First published by WH Allen in 2024

www.penguin.co.uk

A CIP catalogue record for this book is available from the British Library

Hardback ISBN 9780753560167
Trade Paperback ISBN 9780753560174

Printed and bound in Great Britain by Clays Ltd, Elcograf S.p.A.

The authorised representative in the EEA is Penguin Random House Ireland,
Morrison Chambers, 32 Nassau Street, Dublin D02 YH68.

Exactly thirty years have passed from the first step to the final one. I extend my gratitude to the Invernizzi family for our enduring collaboration, and heartfelt thanks to my wife Diana for understanding that this story needed to take precedence over many other things.

CONTENTS

PART ONE – WATERLOO BRIDGE

PART TWO – THE ARCHIVE

PART THREE – MANHUNT

CAST OF CHARACTERS

DENMARK

Ulrik Skotte – journalist and television producer

Franco Invernizzi – filmmaker and campaigner

Francesco Gullino – petty criminal and (at one point) chief suspect in the investigation into Georgi Markov's murder

Helene Invernizzi – Franco's wife

Poul Erik Dinesen – Danish intelligence officer

Pia Birgitta Møller – Danish intelligence officer

Jørgen Jakobsen – Copenhagen lawyer representing Francesco Gullino

Bent Staalhøj – filmmaker and longtime collaborator with Franco Invernizzi

Lukas – our researcher

Frederik – our director

Anders – our cameraman

BULGARIA

Todor Zhivkov — longest-serving Eastern bloc dictator and leader of the People's Republic of Bulgaria, also known as 'Number One'

Christo Fotev — poet and friend of Georgi Markov

Vladimir Kostov — journalist and dissident who left Bulgaria and was attacked in Paris shortly before Markov's death

Ljubomir Konstantinov — one of the men asked to kill Georgi Markov

Kalin Todorov — Bulgarian journalist

Bogdan Karayotov — examining magistrate in Sofia tasked with investigating Markov's death

Rikke — our photographer in Bulgaria

Viktoria — our translator in Bulgaria

SOVIET UNION

Oleg Kalugin — senior KGB intelligence officer

Sergei Golubev — senior KGB intelligence officer specialising in 'wet jobs'

Yuri Andropov — KGB chairman who later became leader of the Soviet Union

ITALY

Andrea Speranzoni – lawyer, researcher and historian

Guido Salvini – prominent judge who investigated the 'Gladio' network and other aspects of the 'Years of Lead'

LONDON

Georgi Markov – author, activist and playwright

Annabel Markov – Georgi Markov's wife

Jim Nevill – the first Scotland Yard detective to lead an investigation into Markov's death

Rufus Compton – Home Office pathologist

David Gall – lead scientist at Porton Down working on the Markov case

Christopher Bird – the second Scotland Yard detective to lead an investigation into Markov's death

David Kemp – Scotland Yard detective who took part in both investigations into Markov's death

PROLOGUE

London, 11 September 1978

A man in his late forties with a strong jawline and wavy salt-and-pepper hair is strapped to a bed in St James' Hospital, London, with intravenous drips spooling out of him. The head of his bed has been raised until it is almost vertical, giving him something of a Christ-like appearance. His skin is puffy and red, and he has a faraway look in his eyes. His voice is broken and hoarse, making it hard to follow everything he says. But one phrase is clear, and he has been repeating it for most of the day:

'The bastards poisoned me.'

When the doctors and nurses push for more, he tends to talk about the KGB, a secret plot and a man with an umbrella. The hospital staff are used to this kind of thing. Patients on sedatives and painkillers often become disorientated or paranoid – if it isn't the KGB that's out to get them, it's the CIA, MI5, Elvis or the Loch Ness monster. But the senior doctor on duty when this patient was admitted heard something in his voice which gave him pause. He wrote down what the man said and passed it on to the police. He also took a sample of his blood in case a toxicological examination was needed at a later date.

Suddenly, the patient's condition deteriorates. He is hurriedly wheeled to the intensive care ward, his blood pressure falling fast, his pulse climbing. His kidneys are starting to fail. An electrocardiogram reveals major damage to his heart.

A new set of doctors diagnose pyrexia with septicaemia; a cocktail of plasma expanders and antibiotics is administered. Yet no one can agree on what is causing this unusual combination of symptoms. The most puzzling thing is the patient's white blood cell count, which is staggeringly high, higher than anything the doctors have seen before. And yet there is no trace of any bacterial growth in his blood. This man's immune system is fighting an attack which does not appear to exist, as if the attacker has simply vanished.

For a moment, the patient's condition stabilises and some of the doctors wonder if he is about to recover. Then everything changes.

The patient's wife, who had gone home for a few hours, receives a call from the hospital, telling her that her husband's heart is about to give out. She rushes back. As she walks into the cubicle and catches sight of him, she realises with a terrible finality that Georgi, the man she loves, her husband and the father of her young child, is about to die.

She urges him to fight. For her sake. For the sake of their young daughter.

'Yes, Mama,' Georgi says.[1]

She turns to look at the machine monitoring his heart. The line on the screen levels out. The nurses do everything they can to resuscitate him, but after an hour they stop. There is nothing more to be done.

Two days later, the news begins to spread around the world. Slowly at first, and then accelerating into a great, clamouring rush: Georgi Markov is dead.

PART ONE

WATERLOO BRIDGE

1

FRANCO

Copenhagen, February 1994

One evening, after work, I went to meet a man called Franco. I would be lying if I said I was excited about this, because it was cold and late and, deep down, I wanted to go home to my partner. But I had said yes, and it would be rude to let this man down. I had just started out as a journalist at DR, the Danish Broadcasting Corporation, and one of my colleagues had told me about Franco and put the two of us in touch.

Franco Invernizzi, to give him his full name, had been described to me as an anarchist, a filmmaker and someone who was sitting on 'the biggest story of the century'. I called him up and he told me to find him in Café Sebastopol, in the Nørrebro neighbourhood of Copenhagen. This was famous for being the sketchiest part of town, the kind of place you would try to avoid if you were driving an expensive car – or, late at night, any car at all. Less than a year before, a riot had broken out in Nørrebro in which local residents attacked the police with paving stones; several years earlier, they had used pipe bombs and Molotov cocktails.

I walked into Café Sebastopol and looked around for anyone who could be an anarchist filmmaker. The café was fairly new but had been decorated to look like a battered Parisian bistro. Almost

5

everyone I could see was dressed like an artist and, like me, in their early twenties. None of them met my gaze, apart from a middle-aged man over in the corner who had begun to stare at me with an energetic intensity, as if he was noting down every detail of my appearance for a report he planned to write. I moved towards his table. His clothes were faded but clean, his skin weathered and worn. His hair was a rusty red, flecked with grey, and he had a moustache. As I came closer, he seemed to pull away from me, as if he was having second thoughts about this already.

'Franco?' I tried.

'Sure.'

I sat down across from him. He had both of his hands on the table, in an almost regal manner. On one hand was an enormous gold ring with a lion motif, like something a biker would wear.

'I'm Ulrik,' I said.

'First,' he said, as if he had been interrupted, 'you need to tell me about yourself. I need to know who you are. Where you come from.'

I told him that I was new to Copenhagen, had spent most of my childhood on a pig farm in Jutland in the north of Denmark, and that I was now living in a cramped flat with my partner, who was six months pregnant. I was about to become a father for the first time. Oh, and I had just started out as a journalist at the national broadcaster, DR.

When Franco heard the name DR, he winced — as he did when he encountered anything he was not sure about or disliked because it rubbed up against one of his political beliefs. Franco, as I would find out, was wary of all national broadcasting organisations.

'I am working on the sports desk,' I added.

Franco screwed up his face again.

Most evenings, I went on, my job was to head out with a photographer and sound engineer and watch an ice hockey game or a football match, edit the footage, and write up a short report for that night's television news bulletin. This was one of my few nights off – which was why I had been looking forward to going home, though I did not tell him that. But I had a side interest, I went on, hoping this would draw him out. I liked reading about the Cold War.

Franco's face relaxed for the first time since I had sat down.

'I was wondering,' I started, 'if you can you tell me about your story?'

'All you need to know for now is that I have cracked the case. Every last detail.' He gestured at the folder sitting on the table. It was square and brown, had a catch, and was clearly important to him.

'At first I couldn't join the dots,' Franco went on, 'but now it makes sense, and once the truth is out, believe me, they will fall like dominoes.'

I had no idea what he was talking about.

'Who will fall?'

'I can't tell you here,' he said, with an admonishing grin. 'These walls have ears.' I looked around the café. Nobody seemed to be paying the slightest attention to our conversation. 'You can come to my house next week,' he went on, 'I will explain.'

Franco wrote down his address and left. I felt as if I had made it through to the next round of a job interview, but was not yet sure what the job entailed or who this man was I'd be working for.

The following week, I parked up outside Franco's home, an elegant Danish villa with a tiled Mansard roof and a small balcony from which he could observe the street below. I had assumed that Franco would be living close to the café where we had met, perhaps in a shared living space with a handful of fellow activists. But his home was miles away in Glostrup, a well-to-do suburb of Copenhagen. Nervously, I approached and rang the bell.

Franco came to the door and introduced me to his wife and teenage daughter, who were both on their way out, before ushering me into the kitchen. Everywhere I looked I could see newspapers and magazines, bits of camera equipment or the remains of his last meal. Franco seemed different today. He was more open than before and began by talking a little about himself. Although he didn't say as much, the implication was that if I was ever going to understand the story he wanted to share, I first needed to understand him.

Franco's family had moved to Denmark from Italy when he was a toddler. His father had been a dairy farmer. 'The first to introduce Danes to gorgonzola!' he said with a half-chuckle. 'But he was more than a dairy farmer. He was like a showman. He told everyone at the dairy that the secret recipe for gorgonzola was locked away in his cabinet and nobody could see it. They became so frustrated that one day they broke in, but the cabinet was empty. Dad liked surprises.'

Franco attempted to follow in his father's footsteps, but soon realised dairy farming was not for him. Instead, he moved to Copenhagen, where he found himself drawn into radical politics. After growing up in a conservative, right-wing family, he moved as far as he could in the opposite political direction and joined an array of left-wing groups. At different times, he was anti-capitalist, anti-conformist, anti-fascist, anti-borders, anti-reactionary. Anti most things. Franco was out to take on the system and expose what he called 'the powers that be'. Early on in his political journey, he decided that his weapon in this struggle was going to be the camera and he became a filmmaker.

At this point in his monologue, Franco led me through to his study. Without pausing to draw breath, he reached over to his desk and picked up a piece of paper that he began to wave around before I could see what it said.

'Number one, this is my story. You understand?'

'But Franco, I still don't know what the story is.'

'I won't pay you for any of the time you put into this and I can't tell you anything unless you sign this agreement to say that you can't steal my story. I'll make the film. You make the book.' He paused for effect. 'If you dare!'

He gave a sort of inward-facing laugh.

'What do you mean?'

'Well, this story is dangerous. It's not like writing about a football match, or whatever it is you do. If you agree to this, you enter a new world. My world.'

He gave me the piece of paper.

For the first time, I stopped to ask myself if I was making a big mistake. I was curious to know more about Franco's story but I already had doubts about the man in front of me brandishing a confidentiality agreement. There was something about him that made me hesitate. Franco had said he wanted to collaborate and that this was the purpose of our meeting. But he did not feel like the kind of person who was comfortable in a team or was even capable of working alongside others. In that case, what did he really want from me? I simply did not know. And I still had no idea what the story was.

And yet, something about this had pulled me in. *The biggest story of the century*, that's what my friend had said.

I could always pull out later, I tried to convince myself.

Franco watched as I signed the document. He then inspected my signature as if it might be a forgery.

'There are many people who would like to have this story,' he said, half to himself. 'They want to steal it from me, you see. But I'm not going to let that happen.'

He took a series of deep breaths, like a footballer preparing to take a penalty.

'OK, so,' he began, rubbing the palms of his hands over the stubble on his face. 'Do you know about the Umbrella Murder?'

I had heard of it.

'The strangest murder of the Cold War,' Franco went on. 'A Bulgarian defector called Georgi Markov was killed on Waterloo Bridge in London with a poisoned umbrella. Everyone thinks it's the KGB. This happened fifteen years ago and is still a mystery. Nobody has been convicted for the murder and the killer is out there somewhere.'

'Sure, I remember hearing about it.'

'So,' Franco continued, 'I know who did it.'

'What do you mean?'

'I know who killed Georgi Markov.'

'So do I. It was the KGB, wasn't it?'

Franco's eyes widened in frustration.

'You don't understand. I know who killed Markov. I *know* the killer.'

'OK.'

'He's a friend of mine! The guy who killed Georgi Markov has been living in my house.'

'The actual murderer?'

Franco was beside himself now.

'That's only the start.'

'Why haven't you told the police? Shouldn't this man be in jail?'

Franco shook his head, like a teacher dealing with a student who had missed the first few months of term and was never going to catch up.

'He won't go to jail,' he said. 'That's the point. *That's the secret.*'

Franco's face was alive. His body seemed to fizz with the meaning of the words that had just left his mouth.

I thought about everything I had learned about journalism since joining DR, from how to write up reports for separate broadcast slots through to sentence structure, clarity, investigative techniques and the ethics of journalism. There had been a lot to take on, and I was still learning, but if there was one thing that my new colleagues stressed above all others, it was this: if someone tells you something, you need to work out how and why they came to believe that. Put another way – always challenge your source. So I knew what they would ask me if I were to tell them about this meeting – which, of course, I could not, because of the agreement I had just signed. They would want to know if Franco was for real. Or was I the audience in an elaborate performance that he was staging for his own benefit?

At times, Franco had the otherworldly air of a fantasist and I had begun to wonder if he was making the whole thing up. Or maybe Franco was the victim here. Perhaps the friend who had been living in his house was an impersonator, who wanted the world to think that he was the Umbrella Murderer, when in fact he was entirely unconnected to it.

But what was driving Franco on? More importantly, why was he telling me this, and what was his attachment to this story?

I had been there less than an hour but I was starting to feel like I was already out of my depth, and that working with Franco would not be the best career move. I had made a good start at DR and was on course to take up a permanent staff position. I needed this to happen. I had promised my partner that this new job was the start of a more serious and responsible chapter in my life. More than ever, my mind was on the future and earning enough money to move us out of our tiny ground-floor flat. Franco's story was only going to be a distraction.

It was also light years away from what I knew. My journalistic beat was predictable and safe. I had never thought of myself as someone who investigated political murders. Franco claimed to have identified a killer: someone who had killed in the past and might kill again. This story belonged to a world that was erratic, mysterious and dark – the opposite of pretty much everything else in my life at that moment. But that was exactly why it intrigued me. And if Franco was telling the truth, then he might be about to solve one of the twentieth century's most famous cold cases. This could be the biggest story I would ever work on.

As I left Franco's house that night, I told him that I would think about it. I drove home and told my partner a little about Franco before changing the subject swiftly. Lying in bed, I wondered what to do. At the very least, I told myself, before starting to drift off, I would find out everything I could about the Umbrella Murder. I would see if Franco's story checked out before telling him that it was not for me.

2
AN UNEXPLAINED DEATH

London, September 1978

On 12 September 1978, a high-ranking Scotland Yard detective walked into a cavernous room in Bow Street police station, in central London, and told everyone to gather round. His name was Commander Jim Nevill and he ran the Metropolitan Police's Anti-Terrorist Squad, previously known as the Bomb Squad. He had film-star good looks and always came into work looking sharp. Nevill's father had been a tailor and Nevill seemed to have inherited from him an instinctive understanding of how a suit should hang. He also had the rare ability, one that elevates some detectives to the top of their profession, to radiate calm under pressure.

During the so-called Balcombe Street Siege, three years earlier, Jim Nevill had negotiated with gunmen from the Irish Republican Army (IRA) who had taken hostages and were asking for £20,000 and safe passage to Dublin. He persuaded them to hand themselves in for nothing and the siege ended without loss of life. There were more IRA attacks in the following years and Nevill was often the officer chosen by the police to go in front of the cameras and reassure the people of London that the danger had passed — even if, as they knew, it had not. Nevill was a popular figure, experienced and capable. But his new assignment, in

September 1978, was completely different to anything else he had taken on before.

Once he had everyone's attention, Nevill began to explain what was going on. Their job was to investigate the unexplained death, the previous day, of a Bulgarian émigré called Georgi Markov. The working assumption was that foul play had been involved.

What did they have so far? That was the bad news. Almost nothing. No murder weapon, no witnesses, no list of suspects and no motive for the attack, if that's what it even was. Georgi Markov had not been in perfect health at the time of his death, Nevill explained, so there was also a chance that his death was the result of an underlying medical condition and, therefore, not actually a murder investigation. Nor had any detectives been able to speak to the victim during his final days in hospital because the doctors did not feel, at the time, that he was well enough to be interviewed. All the information they had was second hand.

But in all this uncertainty, one clue stood out. Markov had told one of the doctors that while he was crossing Waterloo Bridge, he had bumped into a man with an umbrella and, at the same time, he had felt a sharp sting on his leg. When he later took down his trousers to look at his skin, he noticed a small red mark, like a pin-prick. He showed this to a colleague but they agreed that it was probably nothing to worry about.

The post-mortem on Markov's body was now underway, Nevill told the detectives, and he would find out the results later that day. In the meantime, their job was to find out everything they could about Georgi Markov, what had happened to him as he crossed Waterloo Bridge and who the man with the umbrella could have been. This incident was alleged to have taken place in the middle of the day, so there must have been witnesses. But they had to move fast.

The detectives got to work. A police draughtsman made a detailed plan of the area between Waterloo Bridge and the Strand, where the attack was thought to have taken place. Police photographers went out to take pictures of the area. Nevill had another team work up a timeline of the events leading up to the alleged attack. Everyone else in the incident room was told to get out there and interview as many of Markov's friends and colleagues as they could. It was essential to speak to them now, while their memories were still fresh.

For some of the people who were approached by the police in the hours that followed, it was still too soon to talk about it all. One of Georgi Markov's closest friends, Todor Lirkov, was so upset by what had happened that he had drunk himself into a stupor and was initially unable to help. Others, fortunately, were more lucid and spoke at length about the man Georgi Markov had been. Witty and charismatic, they said, as well as 'flamboyant' and 'talented', something of an 'extrovert' and 'without doubt a "character"'.[1] It was also reported that, even though he was only recently married and had a two-year-old daughter, Markov had a 'reputation with women'.[2] Here was a possible line of inquiry – his death might be linked to a secret love affair and a jealous husband.

Another clue lay in the items found by the police in Markov's clothes. When he was admitted to hospital, he had in his pocket a mass of betting slips. In the hours before the alleged attack, Markov had placed bets on no less than fifteen different horses. His colleagues at the BBC World Service confirmed that he was known to gamble and would often slip out of the office to place another bet or check the latest odds. Perhaps Markov had been murdered in relation to a gambling debt?

Nevill's detectives went to the two betting shops where Markov had placed these bets, one in Clapham, close to his home, the other near his workplace. The staff in both remembered him well, describing him fondly as one of their most regular customers. But they were not aware of any large debt.

There was also a chance that Markov's death could be linked to politics. Jim Nevill was told that at the time of his death, Georgi Markov had been working on a satirical novel called *The Right Honourable Chimpanzee*, in which a chimp becomes the British prime minister. Perhaps someone had heard about this and become so worried about this book, and the reputational damage it might cause, that they had taken steps to silence the author.

Or could Georgi Markov's death be connected to Bulgaria, the country he had left almost a decade ago? At one stage, Markov had been one of Bulgaria's most celebrated authors, before falling out of favour with the ruling communist regime and defecting to the West. Although he had begun a new life in the United Kingdom, he remained an active part of a wider community of Bulgarian émigrés in Western Europe. His death might, for all Jim Nevill knew, be linked to an underground feud between rival Bulgarian diaspora groups, such as the Bulgarian Liberation Movement, the Bulgarian Social Democratic Party and the Bulgarian Social Democratic Union. In that year alone, there had already been four attempted political assassinations in London. This might have been another, successful one.

Or was someone back in Bulgaria behind this murder? Perhaps they had taken offence at something Georgi Markov had either written or said – one of his articles, books, plays or broadcasts – and made arrangements for him to be killed by an umbrella-wielding assassin. The problem with this theory was the timing of it. Markov had left Bulgaria nine years ago. So why kill him now? It did not make sense.

Jim Nevill and his team of detectives discovered a lot about Georgi Markov on the first day of their investigation. If he really had been murdered – and they were keeping an open mind on this – then they had a list of possible motives. Even if none of these stood out as the obvious reason for his death, they had made a start.

More importantly, they had an idea of roughly what had happened to Markov on the day of the alleged attack. The story they pieced together went roughly like this:

On the afternoon of 7 September 1978, Georgi Ivanov Markov, aged forty-nine, says goodbye to his wife and child and goes to work as usual. He leaves his vehicle – a green Simca van with a cream-coloured top – in a car park on the south side of the River Thames near Waterloo Bridge. He then crosses the river and walks to Bush House, about half a mile away, where he works for the Bulgarian Section of the BBC World Service.

Markov completes his first shift of the day and has a break until the next one begins. He wanders off to the betting shop to place a few bets and, at around six o'clock, he goes back to the car park on the other side of the river. His plan is to move his car closer to Bush House because by that time of day there are more parking spots available.

Georgi Markov walks south across Waterloo Bridge, with the Houses of Parliament and Big Ben away to his right. It's an overcast day but warm. He has almost reached the south bank of the Thames when he feels a prick in his right leg. He looks down and then up. A man is bending down to pick up the umbrella which he appears to have dropped.

For a moment, their eyes meet.

'I am sorry,' the other man says, in an accent that is not British. This stranger then hails a taxi that happens to be passing by. Markov will later say that the man who dropped the umbrella had trouble communicating with the driver, perhaps because of his accent, but the driver accepts his fare and the cab pulls away.

Markov thinks little of this. Just one of those things. There was a spot of rain earlier in the day and so there's nothing unusual about a man carrying an umbrella. The sting must have been a coincidence.

Georgi Markov finds his car and drives back to Bush House, where he completes his next shift. He also takes a moment to look at his leg. He can see on his thigh some kind of sting but is not worried by this.

The next morning, Markov falls ill. His wife, Annabel, takes his temperature and sees that it's 40 degrees Celsius. She calls up the BBC to say that he can't come in to work today. Her husband then looks at her and says, 'I have a horrible feeling this may be connected with something which happened yesterday.'[3]

Georgi Markov is taken to hospital. Three days later, he dies.

There is a moment in everyone's career, no matter what line of work you're in, when you get the feeling that you might be in over your head. Commander Jim Nevill was immensely experienced. But most of that experience involved robberies, kidnappings and IRA bombs. This new case was more mysterious and subtle than anything he knew, and the biggest problem he faced was just how little evidence there was.

Towards the end of the first day of the investigation, Jim Nevill left the incident room and made the short journey south to the Battersea mortuary, where he was due to find out the results of the post-mortem examination. Markov's corpse had been inspected that afternoon by Dr Rufus Crompton, the Home Office pathologist. Once Crompton had finished his examination, he washed up and went through to speak to Jim Nevill. His verdict was that Georgi Markov had died of acute toxaemia, meaning his death was related to the presence of bacterial toxins in his blood. He *might* have been poisoned, Crompton said, but he could not be sure. The problem, he went on — and it was a big one — was that he had been unable to find traces of any specific poison in Markov's body.

This was a major setback for Nevill, who had been hoping for something more definitive. But Crompton had not finished. There was something he had noticed on Markov's body which he had been unable to explain and which might shed light on what had happened to the victim. Nevill listened carefully. Crompton had observed a tiny puncture wound on Markov's right thigh – the pin-prick that Markov had complained about to the doctors when he was admitted to hospital, four days earlier.

The medical staff had x-rayed the area on Markov's leg but they had not seen anything abnormal. Crompton did not have an x-ray machine in the mortuary to check that they had not missed anything, but he thought it was possible that they might have done, and that beneath Markov's skin there might be some tiny foreign body, one that was so small it could have been missed in an initial x-ray. He had been about to cut into the small wound but decided against this. He wanted someone with more expertise to open it up – a specialist who knew about toxins, pathogens and exotic poisons.

Rather than cut into the puncture wound on Georgi Markov's right thigh, Crompton had sliced out a large block of flesh that contained the wound. For comparison, he had removed a similar lump of tissue from the other thigh and had sent both off for further examination to one of the most secretive buildings anywhere in the world.

Few visitors were allowed inside the Ministry of Defence's Chemical Defence Establishment (CDE) at Porton Down. Fewer still understood everything that went on inside. Porton Down had been set up by the British government during the First World War, after the German Army started to use chemical weapons on the Western front. A small group of scientists was given the job of protecting British soldiers against these chemical attacks, while also developing their own deadly weapons for offensive use. Some of these gases were later deployed on the battlefield. In the last two years of the conflict, chemical weapons were used by both sides on a horrific scale and were responsible for more than 90,000 deaths and over a million injuries (including those received by a young Adolf Hitler).

Research at Porton Down continued in the years after the war, albeit on a much smaller scale. Several decades later, in the wake of the Second World War, the focus had moved on to treating victims of chemical attacks and rare infectious diseases. But Porton Down suddenly became controversial in the 1960s when it was reported that a British serviceman had died there after coming into contact with a deadly nerve agent called sarin. A scientist also died after becoming infected with *Yersinia pestis*, the plague bacterium.

The news inspired marches in London and calls for this research establishment to be closed. But Porton Down remained open. The government decided that the risks of running this facility were outweighed by the benefits, which included a rapidly improving understanding of lethal pathogens, such as anthrax, Ebola and a string of sinister-sounding nerve agents. If Georgi Markov had been poisoned, there was a very good chance that the scientists at Porton Down would be able to work out which deadly toxin had been used.

Dr David Gall was the most senior of the scientists to work on the Markov case. He and a colleague were the first to open up the package from Dr Rufus Crompton. After reading the note accompanying the two samples of flesh, they decided to start by examining the tissue from Markov's right thigh, the one with the puncture wound. Gall took up his scalpel and made a first slice into the flesh. He then turned away for a moment. When he looked at the sample again, he assumed that his colleague had stuck a pin into the tissue to hold it in place because he could see on the flesh what appeared to be the head of a pin. He tapped it with the end of his gloved finger.

Only then did he realise that this was not a pinhead but a tiny metal ball. It rolled off the flesh and landed with a 'plink' in the metal tray below. Naturally, Dr Gall was intrigued, and he examined this foreign object more closely. It was a silver-coloured pellet, which reminded him of the tip of a ballpoint pen or a decorative bead. Moving slowly, he placed it under a microscope. Now that he could see it in more detail, he noticed that it contained two miniscule holes that had been drilled at right angles to each other. The pellet had a diameter of just 1.7 millimetres. Each hole was 0.4 millimetres wide. When he held the silvery ball up to the light, Gall could see that one of these apertures was clear while the other one appeared to be blocked up – presumably with congealed tissue. He carried out further tests and learned that the pellet was made from platinum–iridium, an alloy often used for surgical instruments because it was so tough and durable.

But what had this pellet been doing inside Georgi Markov's right thigh? Gall carried out tests to find traces of toxins. This was the curious thing. He found nothing. Next, he carried out tests on the tissue surrounding the pellet. Again, he drew a blank. This was, Gall admitted, 'disappointing'.

But for Jim Nevill, and everyone in the incident room in Bow Street police station, the discovery of the metal pellet was the breakthrough that they had been hoping for. It appeared to corroborate Markov's story. Perhaps he really had been murdered by an assassin armed with a poisoned umbrella.

The scientists at Porton Down might not yet have found traces of a toxin but the tiny size of the pellet was hugely revealing. This spherical object was only capable of holding a miniscule quantity of poison, just 0.45mg. If Markov had been poisoned then the toxin must have been staggeringly potent. For example, it could not have been cyanide, as a fatal dose would need ten times the amount that this pellet could possibly hold. In fact, its dimensions ruled out most known toxins, apart from the nastiest ones around, such as abrin, ricin and various snake venoms. Very few people in the world had access to toxins like these and even fewer possessed the means to insert them into a tiny pellet and then seal the object up with some kind of protective outer layer that would melt once inside a human body. And of these, only a tiny minority were likely to have the means to inject a pellet like this into someone in a way that was so subtle and careful, that the victim would be unsure if they had even been attacked. Either the killer belonged to an extremely sophisticated terrorist cell or he had the backing of a foreign government that had a history of attacks similar to this one.

On 13 September, the day after Nevill began his investigation, the story of Georgi Markov's death appeared for the first time in the media. As far away as Papua New Guinea, it was soon being reported that a Bulgarian defector had been killed on the streets of London by a man wielding a poisoned umbrella, or 'brolly', as the English tabloids preferred to call it.

From a newspaper editor's point of view, this story was perfect. It had everything: as well as being packed with mystery and danger, it was easy to visualise, quick to summarise and, once heard, almost impossible to forget. Part of the intrigue at the heart of this story was to do with the mechanics of it all. How could you actually kill someone with an umbrella? Nobody was sure. Newspapers began to publish detailed diagrams showing what they believed to be the murder weapon, with cut-aways of a firing device concealed inside an umbrella. They looked real and accurate, but they were based on nothing more than fantasy and speculation.

What also made this story stick was the fantastically unlikely combination of the murder and its location. London, for so many people, was still a rainy city filled with men in bowler hats carrying umbrellas. If you had to connect the umbrella with one city in the world, it was always going to be London. Go back in history and you would even find that London was the birthplace of the umbrella as we know it. Back in the eighteenth century, umbrellas became fashionable after the pioneering English merchant Jonas Hanway began to use one to keep dry when it was raining.

The idea that anyone could have been murdered with an umbrella, of all things, in London, within sight of Parliament, was like hearing that a man had been clubbed to death with a Russian doll right outside the Kremlin. It sounded both absurd and uncanny, as if someone was trying to make a point. As many commentators pointed out in the mass of articles and editorials that accompanied the news, the fate which had befallen Georgi Markov sounded like something straight out of spy fiction.

Jim Nevill did not welcome the publicity. He was certainly not the kind of person who courted it or relished the idea of going in front of the cameras. But he recognised that this blaze of media interest could work to his advantage. His team was still desperately short of evidence. What he needed more than anything else was to find witnesses to the attack, for that's what it appeared to have been.

On the same day that the news broke, Nevill sent a team of policemen to Bush House, on the Strand, close to the location of the attack, where they conducted a 'stop operation' out on the street, asking every pedestrian and the drivers of passing cars if they had been in the area on the day of the attack and if they remembered a man with an umbrella. Nevill's team also put up posters close to Waterloo Bridge with pictures of Georgi Markov, in the hope that these might jog people's memories. Others went door to door along Markov's street in Clapham. There was a chance that the murderer, or one of his accomplices, could have been watching his house in the days leading up to the attack.

However, none of this produced any good leads. Nevill then turned his attention to the person who would presumably know more about this than almost anyone else, the potential star witness in this investigation: the taxi driver who had picked up the man with the umbrella and driven him away. If the police could find him, then they had a decent chance of tracking down the murderer.

Nevill's team visited almost every taxi rank in central London and asked if any of them had been out on Waterloo Bridge on the day of the attack. They placed advertisements in taxi driver journals and put out messages on the radio. London cabbies were known to help the police with criminal investigations, so it was probably just a matter of time before they found their man.

But this taxi driver seemed to have vanished. This opened up several other possibilities. One was that Markov might have misremembered this part of the story — unlikely, but not out of the question. Another was that the man who picked up the killer was not a licensed taxi driver, but part of an elite assassination team.

The next breakthrough in the investigation came from several hundred miles away, in France. A Bulgarian journalist called Vladimir Kostov, who knew Georgi Markov and, like him, had sought political asylum in the West, contacted the *Daily Telegraph*'s correspondent in Paris and said that he had an interesting story. On the afternoon of 13 September, just two days after Markov's death, Kostov told the journalist about what had happened to him several weeks earlier.

Kostov and his wife had been travelling on the Paris Metro when he noticed a man with a shoulder bag giving him strange looks. They got off at their stop by the Arc de Triomphe, and the stranger followed them off the train. Kostov walked to the escalator and was halfway up when he felt a sting in his lower back. He spun around. The man he had noticed earlier was passing by. Kostov looked up to see his face. Their eyes met, before the other man ran up the final section of the escalator and sprinted off into the crowd of tourists.

Kostov's wife pulled up his jumper and could see on his lower back what appeared to be a fresh insect bite.

Vladimir Kostov fell ill later that day. But his condition did not deteriorate in the way that Markov's had done. Instead, he went on to make a full recovery. Kostov had thought little of this episode until he heard about what had happened to his friend in London. Could the man who had brushed past him on the escalator be the Umbrella Murderer? Was Kostov the first target and Markov the second? More worryingly, who was next?

Given the global interest in the Umbrella Murder, this was a major story. Jim Nevill was one of the first to hear about it and soon had two of his detectives on a flight to Paris with instructions to find Vladimir Kostov and interview him. His men spoke to the Bulgarian for several hours and returned to London with a Photo-fit, or composite sketch, of the man who had passed Kostov on the escalator. They also had in their luggage a sample of Kostov's flesh. He had bravely agreed to let a doctor remove from his lower back the nugget of flesh that contained the unexplained insect bite. Hours after the detectives had made it back to Bow Street police station, this lump of human tissue was sent to Porton Down for further examination.

Dr David Gall began by slicing into the lump of Kostov's flesh, as he had done with the material from Markov's right thigh. What he saw next must have made him gasp. Hidden inside the flesh was another silvery pellet, seemingly identical to the one he had found inside the sample that came from Georgi Markov. Moving with extreme care, so that he didn't lose the pellet, he was able to measure its diameter. It was just 0.01 millimetres smaller than the other one. He could also see that the holes were in precisely the same location and were the exact same size and depth.

The two pellets were nearly indistinguishable in terms of their size and shape. But the pellet which had been removed from Vladimir Kostov contained a tiny quantity of toxin and the remains of a wax coating. Gall's guess was that this protective outer layer on the Kostov pellet had not dissolved as it was supposed to. As a result, most of the toxin inside had not entered Kostov's blood stream, which was why he was still alive.

On 29 September, Jim Nevill held a press conference. He told a room full of journalists that the death of Georgi Markov was now being treated as a murder. He talked about the two pellets that had been found inside Markov and another Bulgarian defector called Kostov. He also released photographs of these silvery balls.

One of the reasons for sharing this information, Nevill said, was that 'making it public may encourage others who have similar pieces of metal inside them to come forward'. The other was that it might quell some of the feverish media speculation about the so-called Umbrella Murder. Instead, it became more intense. Over the next few days, dozens of new articles were written and published about the case. There were questions in Parliament and even a request from the leader of the opposition, Margaret Thatcher, for a private meeting with Markov's widow.

The *Daily Mirror* wondered if the pellets were radioactive. The *Guardian* thought they might contain 'the relatively rare disease known as melioidosis'.[4] A *Daily Mirror* correspondent believed the silvery balls probably carried 'a deadly shellfish poison that can kill instantly and leave no trace'.[5] The *Daily Telegraph* described a virus which must have been fired from an umbrella weapon operated by compressed air.[6] The *Evening Standard* trumped them all, claiming that the assassin had used a 'cancer gun' to fire radioactive, cancer-causing pellets made of gold.[7]

Jim Nevill's press conference also had the effect of focusing a lot of attention for the first time on Bulgaria. Most British people knew next to nothing about this Eastern European country, only that it was a totalitarian state with close ties to the Soviet Union as well as being a cheap place to go for a package holiday. These trips were not always a success. Arthur Scargill, the trades union leader, had recently gone to Bulgaria for a break. When asked by a reporter if he was enjoying himself, he said: 'If this is Communism, they can keep it.'

Now Bulgaria was in the news for a very different reason. The 'Bulgarian Umbrella' entered the lexicon. An umbrella shop in Paris put up a sign in its window saying: 'sale of umbrellas to Bulgarians prohibited'.[8] Then the story took another unexpected turn.

Just days after Nevill's briefing to the media, another Bulgarian who had been working for the BBC in London was found dead in equally puzzling circumstances. 'Has the Poison Brolly Killer Struck again?' asked the *Sun* — and many others.[9] The man who had died was Vladimir Bobchev, a Bulgarian who had defected back in 1971 before finding a job working for the BBC Youth Department. Some of his colleagues suspected him of secretly reporting to Bulgarian intelligence, but that was just a rumour. Bobchev appeared to have died after falling down the stairs of his East London house. But given what had happened to Georgi Markov, this sounded deeply suspicious. The coroner concluded that Bobchev died after breathing in blood from the broken nose he probably sustained as a result of his fall. But was he pushed or did he slip? And why, as it was later alleged, did the police find two glasses in the sink, both entirely free from fingerprints?

Jim Nevill had to work it out. In the end, he decided that Bobchev's death was most likely an accident. He had been wearing worn carpet slippers and it seemed most probable that he had slipped on the wooden floor.

The death of Vladimir Bobchev made the Umbrella Murder frontpage news yet again. Who was the killer? Where were they going to strike next? A stream of articles compared the situation once more to the plot of a James Bond novel. Political commentators demanded a response from the Bulgarian government. They were angry about the idea of a Bulgarian killer being allowed to roam around London, seemingly able to murder at will. Georgi Markov was a naturalised British citizen who had been killed in broad daylight within sight of Parliament. There had to be some kind of retribution or justice. An apology. Or at the very least an acknowledgement of what had happened.

But the British government did not demand any of these things of their counterparts in Sofia, and the Bulgarian ambassador to Britain was not summoned to the Foreign Office to be given the diplomatic equivalent of a rap over the knuckles. This was mainly because Commander Jim Nevill and his team of detectives had still not found evidence of an actual, verifiable link between Georgi Markov's death and the Bulgarian state. Everything they had so far was circumstantial and speculative. Whoever was behind this murder had gone to enormous trouble to cover their tracks and had done so meticulously.

On the frosty morning of 14 October, the body of Georgi Markov was buried at the Church of St Candida and St Cross in Whitchurch Canonicorum, a village in Dorset, close to where his wife Annabel had grown up. Pockets of mist clung to the edge of the churchyard as his coffin was lowered into the ground. For a moment, the only sounds were the muffled sobs of his friends and family, and the occasional caw of a rook in the trees beyond the graveyard.

Some of the mourners came from Annabel's family, but most of the men and women standing close to the freshly dug grave were Bulgarian émigrés who had come down to Dorset from London. As they made their way out of the churchyard after the service, they were quietly joined by plainclothes detectives from London.

Jim Nevill had sent some of his men to mingle with the guests at the funeral in the hope of finding out more. Once they had explained who they were and what they were doing, the detectives showed mourners the Photo-fit sketch that they had put together with the help of Vladimir Kostov of the man who had attacked him in Paris. Their theory was that this was the same man who had killed Georgi Markov. They were hoping that someone at the funeral might recognise him.

None of them did. Back in the incident room, in London, Nevill and his detectives went through a list of every Bulgarian national to have flown out of Britain in the days after the murder. They also looked at the names of those who had applied for visas to enter both France and Britain in the months before the attacks. The man they were looking for must have visited both countries during this period. But for one reason or another, each of the names that came up could be ruled out as a possible suspect and soon they were back to where they started.

Jim Nevill seemed to have gone as far as he could in his hunt for Georgi Markov's killer. Officers at MI5, Britain's security service, had also been involved. They weren't able to solve this puzzle either. More than a month after the murder had taken place, Nevill was nowhere near being able to make an arrest. He did not have the murder weapon. Porton Down had not yet identified the poison inside the pellet. The identity of the killer was a complete mystery. The best that Nevill could do was say that the assassin might have been a dark-haired man who spoke English with a foreign accent, but even that was a guess.

Nevill had been given a huge team of detectives and all the resources he had asked for. It was hard to see what else he could have done or to pinpoint any mistakes that he had made. The killing of Georgi Markov was beginning to look like a perfect murder.

3

THE ITALIAN

Copenhagen, March 1994

Two weeks after meeting Franco in his house and hearing that he
knew the man who had killed Georgi Markov, I went to see him
again. As I left my flat, I saw that I was running late. I tried to call
Franco to let him know. But when I picked up the phone, a strange
thing happened. All I could hear was a loud hissing sound, like a
storm at sea, and I wasn't able to make any calls. The telephone
had never been broken like this before. I made a mental note to get
it fixed when I came back, ran to the door and drove at speed to
Franco's place.

'There you are,' Franco said, welcoming me in. 'My wife is
at work, so we have the place to ourselves. Come in, come in. I've
made coffee.'

There was a boyish excitement about Franco; he had a more
playful energy than before. Walking into his home, I could see the
familiar piles of papers everywhere. But this time, I recognised some
of the cuttings as ones that I had found in my research over the last
few weeks. Looking more carefully at the articles lying around, I
could see that Franco had written notes on some of them. Everything
looked chaotic, but I soon realised that it was a deceptively organised type of chaos. Perhaps the same was true of Franco. I still didn't

know him very well, but that day he began to remind me, for the first time, of other creative people I had come to know in Copenhagen.

In this, and in so many other ways, Franco and I were very different characters. He was someone who liked to be surrounded by a jumble of information and ideas. I preferred a little more order in my life. We also came from different generations – I was in my twenties; he was in his fifties (making him the same age as my father). But as I began to drink the coffee he had made, I felt as if I was starting to understand this man and began to believe that our shared interest might one day bridge the gaps between us.

'Well, what do you say?' Franco said. 'Are you in?'

I paused.

The day after Franco had told me that he knew who killed Markov, I had gone into work at DR as usual, but that afternoon, I'd taken a moment to visit the library we had in the office. This was where you would usually find older DR journalists quietly researching documentaries they were working on. As I worked in Sports, I rarely had any excuse to be in the library. But in the days that followed, it began to feel like home. Every spare moment I had, I would slip back in and order up books or scour newspaper databases in the hope of finding out more about the Umbrella Murder. I found reports from around the time of the murder and a series of articles that had come out much more recently, in 1993. It was as if the story had come back to life after more than a decade in hibernation. These more contemporary reports in the Danish media were mysterious. They hinted at the identity of the killer without naming him. The other thing I found strange about them was that the journalist gave no sources, as if he was getting it all from one person who did not want to be named.

Something about the scale of this story began to make everything else I was working on feel either small or borderline irrelevant. I could feel it slowly taking hold of me and, at the same time, the doubts I initially had about Franco were moving to the back of my mind. Even when I was out reporting on a football match, my mind kept wandering back to the scene on Waterloo Bridge. One of the reasons I wanted to solve this mystery was, if I'm honest, because nobody else had. I had been a journalist for less than a year. Successfully figuring out the Umbrella Murder was the journalistic equivalent of climbing Mount Everest and I wanted to be part of the team that reached the summit. There was something intoxicating about the idea that Franco and I – the struggling filmmaker and the rookie journalist – might be able to succeed where Jim Nevill and Scotland Yard, MI5 and all the scientists at Porton Down had somehow failed. I wanted to keep going mainly just to see if we could actually do this. But I wasn't yet ready to say that to Franco.

'I have a few questions,' I told him.

Franco looked puzzled.

'Before I decide if I want to be a part of this, can you tell me more about this man, the one you say killed Georgi Markov.'

'OK,' Franco said, waving his arms in a welcoming gesture. 'Just ask.'

I took out my pen and paper.

'So, where is he now?'

'Good question. He used to live with me, but now he's wandering around. Probably in Hungary, where he lives most of the time, or in Germany, maybe the Czech Republic. He's a nomad. We talk every week and he's in a new place every time. He has a satellite phone. He's one of these people who's always on the move.'

'But you still have contact with him, right?'

'Yeah, yeah. But it's mostly me who calls him.'

'What do you talk about?' I asked.

'Small talk. I can only speak to him about the Umbrella Murder when he wants to and when he brings it up. Otherwise, I try not to mention it. I don't want to push him away.'

'How did you first meet this man?'

'First tell me if you're in.'

I thought for a second.

'I'm in.'

Franco smiled. 'This changes everything, you know? Maybe they will start watching you.'

'What do you mean?'

'Surveillance. Following you around. Listening to your telephone.'

'Really?'

'Yeah, I'm being monitored. I'm sure of it. Perhaps they will be interested in you. Perhaps they have already begun.'

I thought back to the strange noise on my telephone earlier that day.

'What's his name?' I asked.

'Who?'

'This friend of yours. The one you think is the Umbrella Murderer.'

'I can't tell you yet. But he's Italian. In the media, he's been called "F. G." Let's just call him, I don't know, "The Italian".'

'But I've signed your paper, so you can tell me in confidence.'

'The Italian.' Franco gave me a firm look.

'Okay. The Italian. And how did you meet the Italian?'

'I met him eight years ago. Lots of us Italians in Copenhagen know each other. We meet up to talk and eat, we try to help each other out. One day, back in — when was it? — back in 1986, I had a call from a friend, a restaurant owner in Frederiksberg. He asked if I would come over for lunch, to meet a friend of his. Why's that, I asked. Oh, he said, this guy has a favour to ask of you.'

'This friend is *The* Italian?'

'They are both Italian.'

'But *The* Italian.'

'Oh, sure. His friend is *The* Italian. So I went to my friend's restaurant. Lo Stivale. And this guy is waiting for me there. He's got jet black hair and waspish eyes. Average build. He's skinny and quiet.'

'This is the guy? The one who killed Markov?'

'Wait.'

'OK, so what were your first impressions of him?' I asked. 'The Italian.'

'I didn't like him,' Franco said, without hesitation. 'Maybe he didn't like me. But I didn't want to be rude. We were in my friend's restaurant, I was doing him a favour, so we did what Italians generally do.'

'Which is?'

Franco looked confused, as if everyone knew the answer.

'We talked first about the football, women and food, and then politics.'

'Why didn't you like him?'

'I could tell his political views were the opposite of mine. He was from the right. I remember he said some unusual things.' Franco did a croaky impression of this other man speaking: 'The weakest people are not that weak. The Mafia does not exist. There will always be corruption.'

'What was the favour he wanted?'

'That came later,' Franco said, looking thoughtful. 'After that first meal, we met up again.'

'I thought you said you didn't like him.'

'I was being polite. He wanted me to come and see his horse. He had this horse in a fancy stable outside Copenhagen. We drove out there one day, me and the Italian. He rode around a bit, wearing these black jackboots. He looked like a proper German junker! He even walked differently in those silly boots. I just read the newspaper. He was a good rider, though. I remember that.'

'Then you said goodbye?'

'No,' he paused. 'We had dinner that night.'

'With the guy you don't like.'

'It's hard to explain. You're right, I didn't like him. But there was something about him that I couldn't figure out and I *wanted* to. If that makes sense. When I got home that night, I joked to my wife that I had just met an Italian spy. That was the impression he gave. He was like someone who had a secret. At the same time, I enjoyed talking to him. I didn't agree with him but he knew a lot about Italian history, and we had a few things in common.'

As Franco kept talking, I became increasingly amazed by how much they had in common. The Italian had grown up in a village just outside Turin, in northern Italy, that was very close to where Franco was born. They were similar in age — although Franco was seven years older — and both men had spent their teenage years in strict boarding schools run by monks. I could begin to see how they might, in a foreign city, find themselves drawn to one another.

'When did the Italian move to Copenhagen?' I asked.

'He first came over in the early 1970s,' Franco began, 'but the authorities kicked him out. Something about his personal papers not being in order. Then he came back and began to run a little shop selling Chinese clothes and cheap Russian hats. After that, he started a business buying furniture and cheap paintings from Denmark and Sweden. Simple stuff. A deer standing next to a lake, flowers in a vase, that kind of thing. He would sell these on to clients in Germany. Scandi design was in fashion, so he made some money. Then he teamed up with a Danish guy to open a framing shop. But he got bored. So, he became an art dealer instead.'

'OK. What kind of art?'

'He told me that mainly he bought old paintings from flea markets and auctions, and sold them on in Germany. But he was big time. He was selling work at Sotheby's and Christies, even

Bruun-Rasmussen.' This was Denmark's best-known auction house. 'Suddenly, he's rich. He moves into a new place, he buys himself a new car. He gets a horse.'

'That's a lot of money.'

Franco's eyes lit up at this, like we were both in on a secret.

'Maybe too much, right? Too much, too fast. That's what I was thinking at the time. But I didn't know what could be behind it. Maybe he's not making all this money from art, and the art is some kind of cover? When I asked him about why he has so much money all of a sudden, he was evasive. I could tell that he did not want to talk about it. He said he was just selling to people in Germany and because they had lost so much during the Second World War, everyone there wanted to buy, so it was easy. Then he would change the subject.'

'You think he was lying?'

'I don't know. Maybe something about this story was not right.'

'Did you see a lot of the Italian?'

'Not much. I probably met up with him no more than five or six times.'

'And what about the favour?'

'Oh yes! The favour. This guy asked if he could store picture frames in my basement. *Why can't you pay for storage?* That's what I'm thinking. But he wants to use my house.'

'And you said yes?'

'Why not? I said yes.'

Something about this sounded wrong or confected. Perhaps Franco was being selective about his memory of meeting this man. I couldn't be sure. There seemed to be a gap between how he claimed to see the Italian in the early days and the details of the story. Either he was trying to hide something significant in their relationship or he had simply misjudged this man and wanted me to think that he had got the measure of him right at the start.

'So you didn't see much of him after he moved his frames into your house?'

'I saw him sometimes,' Franco said, sounding reflective. 'He would sometimes come round to my house and pick up a frame or drop one off. We got on OK. But we were not close friends.'

'But Franco, I still don't see what this friend of yours has to do with the Umbrella Murder.'

'Nor did I,' Franco said, 'until one night, last year, he called me up at home and asked to come round. That's when everything changed.'

This call had happened just over a year ago, in February 1993. Franco could tell right away that something was wrong. The Italian was on edge. He asked Franco if he could come round to pick up one of his frames, but Franco had friends round for dinner that night, so he told him to call back another time.

The next day, the Italian rang again. Franco was free and said he was welcome to drop round. A minute later, there was a knock at the door. It was the Italian — who must have called from a phone booth across the road.

'When he arrived,' Franco told me, 'he pulled me down to the basement. But not to pick up a frame. It was about something else. He was very nervous. I took him up to my living room and sat him down. In the same chair you're sitting in now,' Franco pointed at me. 'I told him to calm down, that everything was OK, and he could tell me what has happened. He said he'd been accused of something terrible. "Slow down," I said to him. "Tell me everything, from the start."'

The Italian's story began several weeks earlier. He had been at home in Nærum, north Copenhagen, when he heard a knock at his door. He thought it was Jehovah's Witnesses, as they had been in the area that day. Instead, he opened the door to a man and a woman, both smartly dressed and official-looking. The woman introduced herself as Pia, from the police department's G Division. The man said his name was Jimmy.

Pia asked if she and Jimmy could come in to ask a few questions. The Italian said he had nothing to hide and welcomed them in. Pia found a place to sit, which, Franco told me, would have been hard because his home was a mess and was filled with old frames, unwashed dishes, cigarette butts, dust and grime. The Italian's financial situation had changed a lot, in a short space of time, and he was now living in squalor. Pia and Jimmy found somewhere to sit and they ran through a list of questions about his business dealings, why he had so many foreign bank accounts and which countries he had visited. Then Pia asked if he knew anything about weapons, drugs or espionage.

The Italian was taken aback. He was not a criminal, he told her. He was an art dealer. Yes, he had fallen on hard times. He was no longer a wealthy man. But he was offended by the suggestion that he was some kind of criminal. Where had she got this idea from?

Pia would not say. Instead, she moved on to the money he owed to *Told & Skat*, the Danish tax agency. These two had evidently done their homework. She hinted that they could make this tax bill go away if he cooperated with them in full.

But he *was* cooperating with her, he insisted.

Pia asked him if he had ever had dealings with the police in other countries, and if he had visited Syria, Greece, France or Bulgaria.

Yes, he told them, he had been to Bulgaria several times, including a recent five-day trip.

For what?

'A ladies trip,' he told her, which was his way of saying he had gone there to pay for sex.

The conversation then took another unexpected turn. Pia and Jimmy began to hint that there were people out to get him and that they were the only ones who could protect him.

The Italian was baffled. Why would anyone be after him?

Several days later, Franco's friend went to the regional court in Lyngby for a hearing in relation to his house. Because the Italian had failed to keep up with the instalments on his mortgage, the judge ruled that his house would soon be sold off in a forced auction. He staggered out of court knowing that he would soon be homeless. His world was falling apart. The comfortable life he had once enjoyed was a thing of the past. But as he left the building, he saw Pia and Jimmy standing there in the cold, waiting for him.

The three of them went back to his house and the police officers quizzed him more about his past. They were even better prepared this time, and had brought with them several ring binders and plastic evidence bags. Franco's friend still couldn't see where this was going. But he did his best to answer their questions. Again, the conversation fizzled out and they said that they would be in touch.

Then several days later, he received a call from Jimmy, who said that they needed to have one final conversation. He told him to come to the local police station in Bellahøj on Friday at 10am. The interview would take place in room 220A.

On 5 February 1993, as instructed, this Italian art dealer, who was close to financial ruin, arrived at Bellahøj police station. He told Pia that he had come because he believed in Danish democracy, and he trusted her and Jimmy to be honest and fair.

Pia thanked him for that and said that there had been a small change of plan. They were going somewhere else. She led him down to the garage of the police station, and drove him to the Københavns Politigård, about fifteen minutes away.

This is the iconic Copenhagen police headquarters that pretty much everyone in Denmark knows because it appears in so many Danish television crime dramas. It's a fierce-looking building with a neoclassical façade and windows that only open inwards, because the architects wanted the building's outward expression to remain the same at all times, like a fearsome police interrogator. Beyond there is a much softer-looking courtyard, circular in shape, which feels like a sanctuary. Pia led him across this space to the building opposite, and up to the top floor where Jimmy was waiting for them. Except he was not really called Jimmy.

Jimmy was in fact Poul Erik Dinesen, an intelligence officer for Denmark's intelligence agency, Politiets Efterretningstjeneste (PET). Dinesen told the Italian that he was not under arrest and was not obliged to say anything. The reason they had called him here was that a pair of British detectives from Scotland Yard had flown over to Denmark in the hope of having a chat with him. Dinesen recommended that the Italian speak to them. Yes, it was up to him. But if the Italian refused to be interviewed by the two Englishmen, then Dinesen could have him arrested and a Danish judge would then decide if he should be flown to the United Kingdom to answer the questions from Scotland Yard. Speak to these detectives now of your own accord or risk being extradited to London. That was the choice.

The Italian still did not know what these men wanted but he told Dinesen he was happy to answer their questions. As he had said from the start, he had nothing to hide. He followed Dinesen and the woman who had been introduced to him as Pia – Pia Birgitta Møller, another Danish intelligence officer – into a large conference room.

He was feeling anxious by now, he told Franco, and was worried that this was some kind of trap. The room was dominated by a long, sleek table. It was empty apart from a huge double cassette tape recorder. There was no sign of the detectives, though. Pia offered him tea or coffee, and then gave him a few minutes to make himself comfortable. Once he was settled, she went to find the men from Scotland Yard.

The two detectives entered the room and sat down opposite the Italian. They introduced themselves and explained the purpose of this interview, and how it related to a murder investigation that had begun just over fifteen years ago.

4

BREAKTHROUGH

London, October 1978

In the days after Georgi Markov's funeral, Jim Nevill made another step forward in his investigation. Georgi's brother, Nikola, had told detectives about a friend of his who might have crucial information about the so-called Umbrella Murderer. This friend had been reluctant to speak to the police at first but had now changed his mind. Two of Nevill's detectives flew out to Bologna, Italy, where this friend was living, and sat down for an interview with him.

The friend's name was Dr Ljubomir Konstantinov, but he was known to everyone as 'Lubo'. Having once been a judge in Sofia, the capital of Bulgaria, Lubo had fallen out with a senior Communist Party official and subsequently left the country. He moved to Munich and started a new life as a stamp dealer. Recently, he had moved to Italy.

Less than a year ago, as Lubo told the two Scotland Yard detectives, he had been approached by a Bulgarian man with blond hair, who seemed to know a lot about him. This stranger understood that Lubo was a close friend of Georgi Markov's brother and wanted to know about Georgi's travel plans. Lubo told the blond-haired Bulgarian that he didn't know anything about where Georgi was planning to travel, and thought that would be the end of it.

But the Bulgarian came back to see him again. This time, he mentioned Lubo's sister, back in Bulgaria, and an outstanding fine that she had been unable to pay. Clearly, this man with the blond hair worked for the Bulgarian government. There was a way to make this fine go away, he told Lubo. All he needed to do was take a small phial of poison to Sardinia, where Georgi Markov was going on holiday, and slip it into his drink.

Lubo was appalled. At least, that's what he told Nevill's detectives. He was not an assassin and he was not going to murder the brother of his friend. Instead, he flew to London to tell Georgi Markov that his life was in danger.

This was the closest Jim Nevill and his team at Scotland Yard had come to identifying the Umbrella Murderer. If Lubo was to be believed, the plot to kill Markov originated in Bulgaria and its ringleader was the Bulgarian with the blond hair. Either this man knew the identity of the Umbrella Murderer or he might even have been the one who carried out the attack himself.

Then another suspect came into the picture: a Bulgarian called Dr Stantshulov, who had disappeared from his home in Munich at around the time of the attacks on both Kostov and Markov. Jim Nevill never liked to cut corners. He had got to where he was in Scotland Yard by pursuing every lead, no matter what. He sent two detectives off to Germany to find Dr Stantshulov and interview him.

The Bulgarian doctor denied any involvement in the attacks and even agreed to take part in an identity parade. Nevill arranged for Vladimir Kostov and his wife to be flown out to Munich where they inspected a line-up of Bulgarian men, including Dr Stantshulov.

Frustratingly, the Kostovs did not pick out Dr Stantshulov. Nevill was more or less back to where he had started. He could rule out both Stantshulov and Lubo as suspects. The blond-haired Bulgarian was a person of interest but he had long ago vanished behind the Iron Curtain.

What made the Umbrella Murder such an unusual case, and so completely different to anything that Nevill had worked on before, was that despite the global publicity – and by now the story had gone around the world many times – they had been unable to find any credible witnesses. Not even one. It was bizarre. This kind of media interest usually led to hundreds of people coming forward with memories of seeing or hearing something that would later unlock the truth. Something about the Umbrella Murder was different.

Several days after the identity parade in Munich, Jim Nevill told a journalist that unfortunately he still knew very little about the killer. He was probably 'a specially recruited assassin', Nevill said, who had been trained up long ago as a 'hit man' and given 'a list of defectors from Bulgaria whom he had to eliminate'.[1] But that was it. When Jim Nevill gave evidence at the coroner's inquest into Markov's death, in January 1979, he went on the record to say that his detectives 'still had no indication of who was responsible or how the pellet was administered'.[2]

The coroner ruled that Georgi Markov had been murdered and the cause of death was a poisonous toxin delivered by a small pellet. An umbrella *might* have played a part in his death but there was no evidence of this.

Markov's wife, Annabel, was one of those who thought that the umbrella was a distraction and had not been used to kill him. 'I got the impression, as he told me the story,' his wife later said, 'that the jab hadn't been inflicted by the umbrella but that the man had dropped the umbrella as a cover to hide his face.'[3]

In the popular imagination, however, there was no doubt at all that Georgi Markov had been killed with an umbrella. His murder had come to be seen as one of the most sinister and puzzling in recent history, and one that might never be solved. The truth about what happened was probably locked up in a Bulgarian government building. Nobody was going to solve this case unless the killer made a mistake and incriminated themselves, or the Bulgarian government decided to cooperate with Scotland Yard. Both seemed highly unlikely. When the story first broke, the Bulgarian Minister-Counsellor in London had 'stormed angrily round to the Foreign Office to deny his country's connection with Mr Markov's death'. He had warned that if media reports continued to make even the slightest connection between his government and this murder 'there would be "serious consequences" for Anglo–Bulgarian relations'.[4] Since then, state officials from the People's Republic of Bulgaria had continued to denounce media speculation about their involvement in Markov's death. Jim Nevill had sent the Bulgarian government a list of questions about the case but he had not received a reply – and nor would he in the months to come.

Jim Nevill's team was eventually disbanded. Very soon after that, Nevill underwent heart bypass surgery. Obviously the Markov case was not the only reason for his poor health, but the months that he had spent working on this investigation, almost certainly the hardest case he had ever been given, appeared to have taken a heavy toll on him. Trying to work out *who* had killed Georgi Markov, as well as *how* and *why* – and why there was no evidence at all – could feel, at times, like a Sisyphean struggle. No matter how long he spent on this, or how many people he had working for him, the answer was always out of reach.

Although the murder investigation remained open in the months after Nevill left the case, it was no longer being actively investigated. Annabel Markov began to piece her life together again while also raising their daughter. Inasmuch as she could, she tried to put what had happened behind her. Part of that process involved cutting off the possibility of finding the murderer. 'The killer had to be a Bulgarian assassin,' she told one reporter, 'who was then murdered to shut him up.'[5] In other words, there was probably no point looking for the murderer.

The pellet used to kill Markov went on display in Scotland Yard's collection of criminal artefacts, the 'Black Museum'. Every few years, a new theory would appear in the media about what had happened. But there was no fresh evidence and the case remained an enigma. It seemed as if the world would never know who had killed Georgi Markov.

Then, on 9 November 1989, eleven years after the Umbrella Murder, the Berlin Wall came down. The following morning, it was announced that Todor Zhivkov, the hardline dictator who had ruled Bulgaria for the last thirty-five years, one of the most grotesque of all the Eastern European communist leaders, had agreed to step down. Bulgaria was on the path to democracy. Freedom was in the air. Secrets were starting to leak out.

Several weeks later, Annabel Markov received an anonymous letter. It named a Bulgarian official she had never heard of as the man who had killed her husband. Researchers working on the BBC programme *Panorama* became interested in this case and soon had a new suspect, another Bulgarian official. They were pretty sure this man had carried out the Umbrella Murderer but did not yet have enough evidence to name him on television.

When the newly elected Bulgarian president, Zhelyu Zhelev, visited the United Kingdom, in early 1991, he made a point of visiting Georgi Markov's grave in Dorset. He told reporters in the churchyard that he would do everything he could to find those responsible for this murder.

Suddenly, after all this time, the truth seemed to be within reach. Scotland Yard assigned two detectives to the case. The man leading the new investigation was not Jim Nevill, who had retired after his heart surgery, but Detective Chief Superintendent Christopher Bird. He was supported by Detective Constable David Kemp, who had worked under Nevill on the original investigation. The two of them flew out to Sofia to meet Bulgarian officials and ask about the secret files that might reveal the identity of Markov's killer. However, their counter-parts in the Bulgarian police explained that most of the documents they wanted to see had been destroyed in the days after the fall of the Communist regime. It became clear to the detectives from Scotland Yard that there was something of a divide among the Bulgarian offi-cials they met: some did not want the truth about this case to come out, while others were much more open and wanted them to succeed.

One of the officials from this latter camp was Bogdan Karayotov, an examining magistrate in Sofia. He was leading a new Bulgarian investigation into Markov's murder. Although he had been unable to find any documents relating to the murder itself, he had located several folders dedicated to the agent who appeared to have been given the job of killing him. This agent had been given the codename 'Piccadilly'. The Bulgarian government was not willing to share any of these files with the British. But Karayotov was. He flew to London in 1992 with copies of these documents in his briefcase and showed them to Bird and Kemp.

For the first time since the attack on Waterloo Bridge fourteen years earlier, the British had a prime suspect. They had been given the name of someone who *might* have been responsible for the Umbrella Murder. But they also knew that nothing they had been shown by Karayotov could be used in court because they had seen this mate-rial on an unofficial basis. The suspect was alive and had never been charged. If they were going to mount a prosecution, they needed to find him and somehow persuade him to make a confession.

Bird and Kemp found out where their suspect was living and made arrangements to speak to him. After that, they flew to Denmark and on the morning of Friday 5 February 1993, they made their way to Københavns Politigård, the distinctive Copenhagen police head-quarters, where they were hoping to meet their man.

In the moments before the interview began, Bird and Kemp must have each experienced a flutter of nerves. This was a moment they had been working towards for years. For Kemp, in particular, this would have had a special meaning. He had interviewed most of Markov's colleagues during the original investigation, fifteen years earlier, and knew this case better than anyone else at Scotland Yard. He had lived with the frustration of not solving the case first time round. Now he had the chance to put that right.

Pia Birgitta Møller, the police assistant, came in to tell him and Bird that their interviewee was ready. They then walked into the conference room and introduced themselves to the man they believed to be the Umbrella Murderer – Franco's friend, the art dealer he sometimes called the Italian.

Kemp reached out to the tape recorder and pressed the record button and Bird began to talk.

5

MISTAKEN IDENTITY

Copenhagen, February 1993

The name of Franco's Italian friend, the man now sitting in front of Christopher Bird and David Kemp, was Francesco Gullino. As the two British detectives introduced themselves in English, Gullino listened carefully. He then interrupted and asked them to write their names down in his notebook. Once they had done that, he asked for their telephone numbers. Already, Gullino was trying to take control of this situation.

'I'm not going to tell you about our reason for coming here,' Bird went on, 'because I'd rather that was part of the conversation.'

Francesco Gullino turned to look at Poul Erik Dinesen, the Danish intelligence officer, as if to make sure that this was OK.

Dinesen nodded.

'We want to talk to you about your past and your present,' Bird went on, 'and to understand a little more about your personality.'

Gullino repeated what he had been saying since he first encountered Dinesen and Møller – that he was an Italian art dealer, he had nothing to hide, had complete faith in Danish democracy and was happy to answer any of their questions.

'You were born in Bra, in Italy?' Bird asked.

'Yes,' Gullino replied.

'In 1946.'

'Yes.'

'Just so that I know something about your background, your employment history,' Bird went on, sounding friendly and bland, 'when did you leave Italy?'

Gullino spoke about some of the earlier parts of his life and how he had liked to travel from a young age. 'I think it's something to do with my nature,' he said, warming up, 'to keep on moving.'

Next, Bird moved on to Gullino's career as an art dealer, asking about the different countries he had visited for work. Gullino became more talkative and the conversation accelerated. He had been to France, he said, to Turkey, Italy. Germany hundreds of times.

'What about England?' Bird interrupted. 'You've not mentioned England.'

'Very little,' Gullino said.

'Very little,' Bird repeated. 'You've never lived in England?'

'No,' Gullino said. 'Never lived there, no.'

'What do you think of it?'

'Oh, it's a lovely country.'

'You like it?'

'Very much, yes. Very, very much. I would like to have more to do with England.'

They spoke for a while about the art market in England. For a moment, they sounded like a pair of world-weary art dealers as they agreed that too many antiques were being sold to American buyers these days. Bird then casually moved the conversation back to Gullino.

'So, what have you done in London — you've just visited on holiday or something?'

'No,' he said, 'I went to buy at Christies.'

'How many times have you been to England?'

'I think I've been twice last year,' Gullino said, meaning 1992.

'That was the only time I was in England.' Gullino then thought for a moment and seemed to remember something. 'I was in England,' he said, as if reaching for a memory. 'That was many years ago.'

'Was that on holiday, was it?'

'Yes,' Gullino said hurriedly. 'Yes, yes.'

Bird chose this moment to pause. He pulled out a packet of cigarettes before asking Gullino if it was OK for him to smoke. Gullino nodded. Bird lit up and took a drag. The silence seemed to unsettle Gullino, who filled it with a rambling speech about art and auctions houses. Bird watched him speak, noticing how he was eager to take the conversation away from England and the time he had spent there.

Looking down at his notes, Bird began to run through a list of countries that Gullino might have visited. He spoke as if he was talking to himself, mentioning Belgium and Holland, Austria, Spain, Yugoslavia, Greece. 'We've covered Turkey, didn't we?' Bird went on, still sounding distracted. 'Bulgaria?'

Gullino asked him to repeat the question.

'Have you been to Bulgaria?'

'Yes.'

'When was that?'

'Er ... I used to be there when I was in Turkey.'

'Right,' Bird continued, absent-mindedly. 'Where else have I forgotten ...'

'Romania,' Gullino suggested.

'Romania. Yes, thank you.'

'Not an interesting country.'

'No,' Bird agreed, before changing tack. 'I'm particularly interested,' he said, 'in whether you were in London in 1978.'

The year of Georgi Markov's murder.

'28?' Gullino asked.

'1978.'

'Oh, if I could,' Gullino began, sounding hesitant, 'if I could play something in that year.'

For the first time in the interview, Gullino's language started to fail him.

'If I could,' Gullino repeated, stopping mid-sentence. 'If I could find something of that year.' He wanted one of the detectives to jog his memory with something that had happened in that year. Bird decided to jump in.

'In September of 1978, a Bulgarian émigré by the name of Georgi Markov was murdered.'

Gullino made a 'hmm-hmm' noise.

'Do you remember that?' Bird asked

'In September '78?' Gullino checked.

'1978.'

Silence.

'No,' Gullino answered, 'it doesn't tell me anything.'

'Does the name ring a bell?'

'No, no.'

'You've never heard of the name Markov?'

'No.' Gullino sounded quizzical. 'Marko?'

'Markov. M, A, R, K, O, V.'

'Hmm,' Gullino went on, as if musing to himself. 'September '78. You would like to know where I was in September '78?'

'Yes,' Bird replied. 'I said just now that I'm interested in where you were and then I've mentioned that' – the murder of Georgi Markov – 'because that was an event that occurred in that year. It was reported in the newspapers as the Umbrella Murder.'

'Yes,' Gullino said with a more hopeful air, as if something was coming back to him.

'Do you remember?'

'Yes.'

'The man being stabbed with a poison umbrella,' Bird tried.

'Yes, yes, yes. But I don't know. You say '78, but that's, I agree with you, but I could have said '84 or '71.'

'Do you remember the murder that I'm talking about?' Bird asked more firmly.

'I think I have seen it, something on television or in some newspaper.'

'Quite possible, yes. What I'm interested in is if you were in London in 1978 and you've told us that you were in London quite a few times.'

'Yes.'

'We'll just leave it there for a second. Does the name Markov mean anything to you?'

'No.'

'Only when I first mentioned it,' Bird said, 'you seemed to go rather quiet.'

'Yeah,' Gullino said.

'Your face was expressionless,' the detective went on. 'As if you'd got a sudden shock. Perhaps I misinterpreted you but there was a distinct change in the characteristics of your face.'

The mood in the room had changed. There was no more of the friendly back-and-forth. It was as if both sides were now ready to get down to business.

Gullino asked Bird if the visits from Pia and Jimmy over the last few weeks were to do with the Umbrella Murder.

Bird said that they were.

'And there's nothing else, it is only that?' Gullino asked, a new hardness in his voice.

'That's what I'm dealing with,' Bird replied. 'Do you know anything about that murder?'

Gullino paused.

'No,' he said at last. 'I didn't know why it happened.'

'When I mentioned that name,' Bird said — Markov's name — 'the expression on your face changed.'

'I couldn't see it,' Gullino replied.

'No, but I could from where I sit.'

'OK.'

'And I thought that was significant to me, having sat with you for two hours, the expression on your face was noticeable. Which perhaps indicated to me that you did know the name Georgi Markov. Do you understand?'

'Yes.'

'And yet, you say you didn't know the name.'

'No.'

'Now, I find that difficult to believe.'

There was a new menace in Bird's voice.

Gullino hit back. He said that his reaction was not to Markov's name but to the idea that they thought he might have been involved in this man's murder.

'I would suggest you're being untruthful,' Bird said. 'I think that you know more about Markov than you're prepared to say at the moment. That's my interpretation.'

'Because of my expression,' Gullino said.

'Well, for one reason, yes.'

'It's also for some other reason,' Gullino began, starting to laugh, 'if you came all the way from England to here.'

'Let's continue and just explore your contacts with Bulgaria,' Bird carried on. Gullino had said that he had only ever been there for a holiday or if he was driving through to get somewhere else. 'I feel that you're not being honest and that your association with Bulgaria is more than that. And again, you're showing the same features in your face as—'

'Oh, do I?' Gullino laughed, still wanting to feel that he was in control.

'—as when you reacted to the word Markov.'

'Hmm.'

'You're rubbing your chin. You're decidedly nervous.'

'I was also nervous before.'

Bird decided to move towards his big finish. Glancing down at the papers on the table, he began, 'Have you ever worked for the Bulgarian government in any capacity?'

'No,' Gullino replied.

'Have you ever received money from the Bulgarian government?'

'No.'

'Are you sure you're being truthful about that? This is quite important.'

'Yeah.'

'Really being truthful?'

'Yes.'

'Have you ever signed any papers on behalf of the Bulgarian government?'

'No.'

Time for the reveal. Bird produced from a folder in front of him a typed-up document which had a signature at the bottom. He laid it on the table in front of him and began to read out loud. Kemp watched the reaction on Gullino's face.

Two days later, when Francesco Gullino sat down with Franco and his wife, Helene, he described this piece of paper that the British detective had produced as the most extraordinary thing he had ever seen in his life. Someone, he told Franco, had mocked up a declaration of allegiance to the Bulgarian intelligence agency and had signed it in *his* name. Gullino's. This piece of paper made out that he was a spy!

'I, Francesco Gullino, born in Bra, 50 kilometres from Turin,' the British detective had read out, 'do freely declare in accordance with my moral convictions and my political beliefs to fulfil in all honesty and to the best of my ability any tasks set to me by the Bulgarian State Security Service.'

The strangest part of it all, Gullino told Franco and Helene, was that someone had found a way to forge his signature. Obviously, Gullino told the two detectives from Scotland Yard that he had never seen this document before. It was like something from outer space. But it was as if they could not hear him. They insisted that it was genuine, even though he kept telling them it was not. They said that he was being untruthful, that he was a Bulgarian spy and so on. Each time, Gullino came back with the same response. He had been set up. *He* was the victim. Somebody was trying to frame him. Think about it, he said to the detectives. It just didn't make any sense. How could he be a Bulgarian spy?

Gullino carried on with the rest of the story.

After the detectives had shown him the declaration with his signature at the bottom, they produced four passports, two Swiss and two Bulgarian. Each contained another man's name with Gullino's photograph and date of birth.

More forgeries, Gullino said.

Next came the part of the interrogation that made Gullino laugh, only because he felt that the British, or whoever was behind this, had gone too far in their deception. After putting away the Swiss passports, Bird said that he knew the codename Gullino had been given by the Bulgarians. Scotland Yard thought that when he wasn't dealing in antique paintings he was an international man of mystery by the name of 'Agent Piccadilly'.

'It's very funny,' Gullino said to Bird. After all, who would call their agent 'Piccadilly'? It was like something out of a spy novel.

Bird then said that someone else would like to speak to him, and in walked Bogdan Karayotov, the magistrate leading the Bulgarian investigation into the death of Georgi Markov, accompanied by a translator. Once Karayotov had sat down and introduced himself, he asked Gullino if he had ever been held in a Bulgarian jail. He was also curious about whether he had ever been to Rome.

Gullino said that he had never seen the inside of a Bulgarian jail and while he had been to Rome at various points in his life, he couldn't remember the last time he went. Karayotov made some notes, thanked him for his time and left.

Bird then turned to Poul Erik Dinesen, the Danish intelligence officer who had been present since the start of the interrogation six hours ago. He asked to speak to Gullino alone. Dinesen agreed and the tape was turned off.

At this point, according to Gullino, Bird became much more direct.

'Don't you regret working for these people?' he allegedly asked. 'Why did you do it? Money? Ideology?'

Bird said that he wasn't interested in what he might have done in Denmark. That was between him and the Danish authorities. His only concern was the Georgi Markov murder. Personally, Bird went on, he was not sure if it was Gullino who had killed him, but he had no doubt at all that he was somehow involved, and he needed him to come to London to clear up the whole matter.

'Let's solve the Umbrella Murder,' he had apparently said to the Italian art dealer.

Gullino told Bird that while he wanted to help, they had the wrong man.

By that point, it was almost 8pm. The interview had run its course. Bird told Gullino that he had no more questions but would like his help with one final thing. He asked Gullino to give a sample of his handwriting.

Gullino agreed and wrote out the entire alphabet. First in lower case letters, next in upper case. Bird watched in silence, before giving him an anodyne text to copy out. Next, he asked him to write:

'I have received 1,000 English pounds.' Finally, he asked him to write the word 'Piccadilly'.

Bird looked at Gullino's writing and compared it to the document he had brought with him – the declaration that Gullino was alleged to have signed all those years ago. A smile worked its way across his face. He looked up at Gullino.

'With these,' he allegedly said, according to Gullino, 'I can have you hanged.'

Bird and Kemp gathered up the eleven tapes they had used during the interview as well as the evidence they had brought with them from London and left the room. Gullino was now alone with Dinesen, who explained where things stood. He was planning to charge Gullino with espionage under Paragraphs 107 and 108 of the Danish Penal Code. The maximum sentence was twelve years in prison.

But the documents that had been shown to him were forgeries, Gullino said.

Dinesen insisted that they were genuine. He asked Gullino to sign a piece of paper to confirm that he had been charged, adding that he would formally contact the Bulgarian government to ask for the original documents, without which he did not have a case. For now, he concluded, Gullino was free to go, but if he decided to leave the country then he must let him know first.

Gullino was then taken away to have his photograph and fingerprints taken, before being driven home by the police.

It was over. Gullino could rest and try to make sense of what had just happened. One thing was clear: he needed help. He could have turned to any number of different people in the hours that followed, but he chose Franco.

6

JAKOBSEN

Why did Gullino go to Franco, of all people, in February 1993? It was not as if they were close. He must have known that Franco didn't really like him, or at least sensed that they were enormously different people. According to Franco, they had very contrasting temperaments. Franco was someone who liked to dominate a conversation, while Gullino was quieter and more watchful. Franco had a large network of acquaintances and contacts in Copenhagen. Gullino had a much smaller circle. Franco was from the left, Gullino was from the right. Gullino was single. Franco had been married three times (his most recent wedding had been attended by both of his former wives, which said something about him: you could get annoyed with Franco and realise that you were better off apart, but it was hard to feel permanently angry with him, and want to cut him out of your life entirely once you had let him in).

Nevertheless, the two men appeared to have been drawn to each other, as if by forces outside of their control.

When Gullino first explained what had happened, Franco was confused and did not know what to think. It was not every day that someone he knew would come to him and say that he had been mistaken for a highly trained assassin. But as the night wore on, Franco started to get his head around what had happened and a narrative took shape in his mind. Although he had doubts about it, he managed to convince himself that his friend had been framed. He had been stitched up by a foreign intelligence agency or a secretive criminal gang that was out to protect the true identity of Georgi Markov's killer.

Why did Franco believe this? In part, because he had read about this kind of thing so many times in the past. His first film, which he completed back in 1975, told the story of the CIA's secret involvement in Italian politics during the turbulent post-war years. Franco knew from his research how far some intelligence agencies could go when they wanted to cover their tracks. So Gullino might have been set up. Franco did not know who was involved – it could be British intelligence, the Danes or a conspiracy between them; perhaps it went all the way back to the Bulgarians. The CIA probably had a hand in it as well. But on account of Franco's background, he was at least willing to believe that Gullino was the victim of a conspiracy.

While Franco was often suspicious of people outside his circle, once he had decided that someone was OK and let them in, he often showed his affection by showering them with gifts. That was his love language. Franco would go out of his way to load up his friends with food and drink, advice, introductions to other friends of his or camera equipment (Franco always seemed to have more of this than he could use). To those he liked, he was always generous – too generous, his wife would say.

A part of him had always been intensely loyal to his friends. Once he had decided that he was on your side, that was it. He would do everything he could to help. Franco began to feel a crusading need to stand up for his friend.

He thought about how they could fight back. Was it even lawful for these British detectives to interrogate a Danish citizen here in Denmark? Probably not.

But there was another side to Franco's reaction, one that he did not volunteer at first and took longer for me to understand.

Franco had also spotted in his friend's predicament an opportunity for himself.

At one point in their long conversation on that February night, Gullino had asked Franco if he was still making films. This was not the first time they had spoken about this. Several years earlier, Gullino had suggested to Franco that he make a film about the Kurdish minority in Turkey. He had said that a rich Swiss friend of his was willing to pay for it. But that had come to nothing.

Was Franco still making films? Well, he had recently worked as a director of photography on other people's films, but it had been almost ten years since he had directed or written one of his own. He had been looking for the right subject and so far it had eluded him. At the same time, Franco held a deep belief that one day he would make a film of coruscating brilliance, a masterpiece that would expose some of the political conspiracies he had heard about over the years, and be talked about for years to come and studied in film schools. It would be his legacy. But until then, he had not found a story that seemed to be good enough.

Franco told Gullino that, yes, he was still making films.

'Maybe,' Gullino said that night, after describing his interrogation, 'you could make one about me.'

Just like that, Franco had his subject.

Gullino had planted in Franco's mind the seed of an idea that would grow and grow. Franco knew what he was going to do. He would make a film about the story of this impoverished art dealer, an Italian immigrant who had been set up and framed for one of the most outlandish murders of the Cold War. Franco buzzed with excitement at the thought of this film.

But for now, he needed to focus on helping his friend, who was facing many years in jail. He realised that there were several things he could do to assist Gullino. The first, he decided, as the conversation continued, was to find him a lawyer.

Gullino disagreed. He did not think he could trust a lawyer.

Franco noticed how pale he looked in that moment, and how his previous sarcasm and assertiveness had disappeared. Already, Franco was starting to observe his friend with something other than compassion. If he was going to make this film, he needed to see Gullino with a certain curiosity and detachment. He needed to be two different people at the same time – the filmmaker and the friend.

Although Gullino thought hiring a lawyer would only make things worse, Franco disagreed. A lawyer was essential, he said. It was their only hope. At some point in this conversation, Franco began to talk about the situation as a problem that they shared. He needed Gullino to see this as a joint ordeal: a burden that Franco was willing to shoulder alongside Gullino. They talked until dawn, by which point Gullino agreed that they needed a lawyer. The next day, Franco got to work.

'I sprang into action,' Franco told me. 'I called up my network of contacts to find a lawyer. The name that came up a lot was that of Jørgen Jakobsen.'

Jakobsen may not have been the best lawyer in Denmark but he was easily the most famous. He was someone who seemed to love publicity. He had an outsized personality and a long history of standing up for those on the fringes of society. During the Second World War, Jørgen Jakobsen had fought for the Resistance at a time when, on account of his having a Jewish father, he would have been sent to a Nazi concentration camp had he been caught. After the war, Jakobsen joined the Communist Party for a short time and became a lawyer. He took on some of the most controversial and challenging cases of his time, representing everyone and anyone, whether they were a Soviet spy or a Danish artist trying to make a film about the sex life of Jesus Christ.

Jakobsen was seventy-three by the time Franco contacted him, and was no longer in his prime. But he agreed to listen to what Franco had to say. Franco explained: his art dealer friend, Francesco Gullino, had been accused of something that he did not do.

What?

The Umbrella Murder.

Jakobsen's reaction was not what Franco had hoped for.

'He laughed,' Franco recalled, 'dismissing the tale as a bad spy movie.'

Franco pressed on — that was his way — until Jakobsen gave in and agreed to meet the pair of them.

Later that day, Franco and Gullino made their way to Jakobsen's office, located above a café on a busy shopping street. They were told by a secretary to wait for a few minutes, which gave them a moment to take in their surroundings. Jakobsen had done up his office to look prestigious and serious, which probably suited his sense of self. After a short wait, Franco and Gullino were led into an oak-panelled office filled with legal texts, awards and photographs. Behind an enormous desk in the middle of the room was the man himself, Jørgen Jakobsen. He was wearing bi-focal glasses and had to tilt his head back to properly see his visitors, which only added to the feeling Franco had that Jakobsen was already suspicious of them.

'So,' Jakobsen began, 'let's hear the story.'

This was the first time that Franco and Gullino had spoken to someone about what had happened, so Franco might have waited for his friend to speak, given that he was the one who had been interrogated and was now facing a lengthy prison sentence. Instead, Franco took control of the conversation. He gave a detailed account of what had befallen Gullino. Franco had an excellent memory and an engaging way of speaking. He was comfortable holding a room. In the hour that followed, Gullino listened quietly as his friend described the terrible injustice he, Gullino, had been through. You would think that Franco was the one who had been accused of this murder.

Jakobsen listened carefully. He interrupted with questions and took notes until Franco got to the end of his story. Both men looked expectantly at the lawyer. Jakobsen's manner was gruff and direct. Franco said that he reminded him of a retired army officer. He was also hard to read, and Franco was still not sure what he made of this story.

'Sure,' he said. 'I'll take on the case.'

Franco was overjoyed. Gullino was more muted in his response.

Jakobsen pressed a button on his telephone and his secretary walked in. She set herself up at a typewriter over to one side and Jakobsen dictated a series of letters. His legal strategy would involve two lines of attack. The first was evidential; the second was procedural. One of the letters he dictated was addressed to the public prosecutor of Copenhagen and the chief of the Police Intelligence Service. Using the sternest possible language, Jakobsen explained that he was representing Francesco Gullino and demanded to be sent copies of the materials shown to his client during the interrogation. He also wanted to hear the taped recordings of their conversation.

Jakobsen then dictated a letter asking for authorisation to take on this case on a *beskikkelse* basis – meaning the state would cover his costs. Next, he began a letter addressed to the minister of justice and the president of the Copenhagen Municipal Court. He suggested that parts of Francesco Gullino's treatment may not have been lawful. For example, why had there not been a lawyer present when Gullino was questioned in his house? Was anyone tapping the landline in his home? If so, did the police or PET apply for the correct court order? Jakobsen also wanted a court hearing to rule on whether Gullino's fingerprints and handwriting had been taken in a lawful manner.

Franco could feel his mood lift. Gullino might avoid jail after all. A high-flying lawyer like Jørgen Jakobsen would never take on this case unless he thought that he could win.

Once Jakobsen had everything that he needed, he asked the two men how they would like to be contacted. Franco and Gullino looked at each other and agreed that Franco would be the point of contact for Gullino. From that moment, every letter from Jakobsen's office regarding this case would be sent to his house.

Franco left Jakobsen's office feeling a new sense of hope and optimism. He was also excited about his film. Even if he did not know what the new few months would bring, he was going to have excellent access to the subject of his new documentary.

The two men were still walking away from Jakobsen's office after their meeting when Gullino turned to Franco and said that he was worried about going home.

Franco asked what he meant.

'I don't feel safe in my house anymore. Whoever is behind all this probably knows where I live.'

Franco agreed.

Gullino then looked at him again. 'It won't be for long,' he said, 'but can I move in with you? Only until I have worked out where to go.'

7

THE GUEST

Copenhagen, April 1994

It had been several weeks since I had first gone to Franco's house and he had started to tell me the details of his relationship with Gullino. There was far too much to squeeze into a single conversation and we agreed to meet up again. That wasn't enough, either, and very soon we were having regular sessions in Café Sebastopol, the place where we had first sat down opposite each other.

Usually, we would meet at about ten in the morning. My shift at DR began at midday, and it was a short journey there from the café. Franco was working nearby in the Copenhagen Citizens' House, where he taught unemployed people how to make films. As he put it, most of the people he was teaching had little interest in filmmaking and couldn't care less if he was there or not. Franco made no secret of the fact that he disliked his job. But it paid his bills and allowed him time to spend on the thing that really did matter to him and had all but consumed him – the case of Francesco Gullino and the Umbrella Murder.

'The last I heard,' I began, stirring my coffee, 'Gullino had asked if he could move in with you.'

'Right. We were walking away from Jakobsen's office and it came out of nowhere. I mean, what could I say? I still did not know him. I wasn't sure what he had done. A part of me thought that he was innocent, and I had to defend him. But I was also starting to have my doubts. Maybe he had killed this man with an umbrella and was part of the KGB. I can't be sure. Now he wants to move in with me. But it's not just me, you see. It's my wife as well. My wife and I would be sharing a house with this guy, as well as food, electricity, heating. I mean, Ulrik, what would you do? Would you let someone who could be a KGB man sleep under your roof? But I had no time to think. The hardest thing was that I could not ask Helene if she was happy for him to stay with us.'

I had met Franco's wife, Helene, a few times by now and was beginning to get a better understanding of her relationship with Franco. She once told me that when she first met Franco, the connection between them was instant. 'Like this,' she said, snapping her fingers. Helene had been a social worker at the time. The Franco she met back then was a passionate Italian filmmaker and political activist. She fell in love with his energy, his curiosity and his drive. She liked that he seemed to know everyone in their circle and that he was fearless. But she also liked the more idiosyncratic side of him and his sometimes eccentric way of doing things.

Early on in their relationship, Franco had called her up to say there was something he needed to tell her. He sounded worried. She went round to see him, convinced that he was going to say he was already married or he needed to call things off. Franco sat down and told her — in the low voice he reserved for grave subjects — that she needed to know before they went any further that he had a secret. He had dentures.

Helene adored Franco but she knew, like everyone who was close to him did, that his judgement was sometimes off. He did not always recognise when somebody was using him and was occasionally too quick to dismiss a potential risk or danger. In their marriage, she had become a counterbalance to Franco. She was the more critical one. She had a better nose for people. In other words, she was the one who was best placed to work out if Francesco Gullino was the kind of person they should be inviting into their house to stay with them. But she was not there when the prime suspect in the case of the Umbrella Murder asked the question. Franco made the decision on his own.

'I told Gullino that we would be very happy to offer him a room,' Franco said, 'and later that day I drove him over to his house so that we could pick up a few of his things.'

After that, they went to Franco's place and Gullino made himself at home. He spent the first night on Franco and Helene's couch and once they had cleared out the spare room on the top floor, he moved in there. They had someone else staying up there, and the two guests shared a bathroom.

Franco went to sleep that night wondering what he had done. He knew that he had lured the subject of his documentary into his house, giving him the kind of access that could turn this film into an award-winning tour de force. But he also recognised that he might have just asked a killer to live with him and his family.

One of the first things Helene noticed about living with Gullino was that his room in the attic of their house was always a mess. She could see on the floor a carpet of books, papers, maps and half-drunk bottles of Coca-Cola. On his desk, he had a typewriter, a hole punch, a stapler and a large radio. There was also hair gel, a brush to polish his leather shoes and a set of weighing scales by his bed. It turned out that Francesco Gullino always weighed himself in the morning. All perfectly normal. But then there were the objects that stood out. She noticed a large antenna that he had brought with him, the kind of thing that would allow you to listen to radio broadcasts from all over Europe. Helene also became familiar with the satellite phone that Gullino carried around with him in the house. It was huge and he often took calls on it. If she asked who was calling, he would say it was to do with his business as an art dealer. If she pushed for more, he said something about friends of his in Sicily. Only later did she become aware of the various passports he had in his room, including at least one with a false identity.

You learn a lot about someone when they come to live with you, especially their temperament and mood. Francesco Gullino could be sunny and light, and at his best he was fun to be around. If he was in a good mood, he would bounce into the living room and suggest to Franco and Helene that the three of them go on a road trip to Germany, Czechoslovakia or Hungary. When? Now! He was clever and able to laugh at himself. But he was only relaxed around Franco, and if he was left alone with Helene his charm seemed to melt away. There was also a caginess to this man and his mood could change without warning.

Helene noticed as well that when the doorbell rang, Gullino would quietly retreat to his room and wait until the visitor, or whoever it was at the door, had left. If he heard an unusual sound in the street outside, he had a way of breaking off from what he was doing to listen. His whole body would become tense, until he had judged that the danger had passed and he could relax.

The other thing that Helene picked up on was harder to pin down – when Gullino spoke to her there was something strange in his tone. She had met men like him before and began to feel that he was not someone who had ever had much respect for women. That suspicion seemed to be confirmed by her discovery of the photographs.

Among the belongings that Francesco Gullino moved into their spare room was a small cardboard box filled with pictures. All of them were of women and they seemed to have been taken by Gullino himself. The women were either wearing not very much or were naked. Very rarely, Gullino also appeared in the picture – always fully clothed. The women posed inside cars, on top of them, inside a photographic studio, or they were outside in a wood or a field. One day, Gullino showed these photographs to Franco, telling him that this was what he liked to do in his spare time. He paid women to pose for him, he said. It was a hobby. Nothing more. Some people collected stamps, while he took pictures of women he called his 'girlfriends'.

For Helene and Franco, these photographs pointed to a darker and more predatory side to this softly spoken art dealer. One of Franco's teenage daughters from a previous marriage, Stina, regularly came to stay in the house. She always slept on the ground floor, so was never close to Gullino. But Helene began to feel uncomfortable about her being around him.

Helene brought this up with Franco. Even if Gullino was entirely innocent, and this was nothing more than a case of mistaken identity, she felt that her husband was allowing himself to be used by their guest. The longer he stayed, the more suspicious she became of him. Who was this man, and why had he chosen to stay with Franco, someone he did not know well?

I was also puzzled by this and asked Franco about it on one of my visits to his house.

'I don't know why he asked to move in with me,' Franco said. 'Maybe it was because I was so different from him. Perhaps he did not trust the people in his own circle. Because you should know that Gullino and I don't agree on much. Our political views could not be more different. He's a fascist, for sure.'

'Really?'

'Without doubt.'

'How do you know?'

Franco looked a little sheepish.

'I went through all of his things,' he said eventually. 'When he was away, I looked through everything in his room. One time, I brought my cameraman and we photographed it all.'

'What did you find?'

'Oh my God ... Wait there.'

Franco left the kitchen and returned a few minutes later with two books, one blue, the other red. He put them in front of me with a flourish, before sitting back down at the table with a triumphant look on his face.

The title of the red book was *Min Kamp*, Danish for 'My Struggle', and the blue book was the same text but in the original German: *Mein Kampf*, by Adolf Hitler. Gullino owned two editions of the Nazi leader's extreme manifesto. I picked up the Danish edition and flicked through the pages. It was strange to hold this book in my hands and to think that Gullino might have pored over the same pages, and perhaps found in them some kind of intellectual sustenance. Or was there a more innocent explanation? Both books had been printed before the Second World War and were collector's items.

'Gullino was a businessman,' I told Franco. 'He was always buying and selling antiques. Maybe he bought these because he knew he could sell them on at a profit?'

Franco smiled, before scuttling out of the kitchen again and returning with a calendar.

'*Calendario, Benito Mussolini*,' it said on the cover. 'Price 5,000 Lira.' This was not a collector's item. It was a calendar for modern-day fans of Mussolini, the Italian dictator and founder of Fascism. Franco showed me the pictures inside. For each month there was a different black-and-white photograph of the Italian dictator looking pompous and self-absorbed.

'I also found more of his photos of women,' Franco continued. 'One of them was, well, it was very strange. It showed a woman dressed up like a Nazi with a swastika flag. So, yes. I think Gullino's a fascist.'

'But was Helene right in what she said? Do you think he was using you?'

'Well, I did a lot for him in the early days. I took him into our home, our family home. I found him a lawyer. I drove him around in my car. I looked after his legal affairs. I became his spokesperson, really. Maybe he saw me as some kind of life insurance and that's why he asked me to make a film about him.'

But slowly, everything changed. Gullino started to lose interest in the film that Franco was now excited about. On most nights in the house, Franco got out his camera, but Gullino always told him to put it away.

'Let's wait a little,' he would say. 'You, and only you, have the right to tell my story. You have my word on that. You can make the film. But only once the story becomes public.'

The longer that Gullino spent in Franco's house, the more this film seemed to become a point of contention between them. Sometimes Gullino accused Franco of filming him secretly without his permission. Franco always denied this, even though Gullino was right – Franco *had* begun to gather footage. Either he would record him with his camera or he used hidden microphones. Franco had always loved gadgets. He told me once that he was the first person in Denmark to get hold of a Sony Betacam. He also owned a Nagra SN, a state-of-the-art miniature tape recorder that was so small and easy to conceal it was said to have been popular with both the CIA and the Stasi. Soon after Gullino moved into his house, Franco began to use his tiny Nagra device to record their conversations.

One day, when I was in his house, Franco produced one of these tapes of him and Gullino chatting away. I put on his headphones and began to listen. The first thing I noticed was how bad the quality of the recording was, because Franco had kept the device hidden in his pocket. But once I had adjusted to that, I began to make out what was being said. The conversation I was listening to had taken place shortly after their first meeting with Jakobsen, the lawyer.

'I don't trust Jakobsen,' I could hear Gullino saying.

'What do you mean?' Franco replied, sounding hurt. 'He's doing everything possible to help you.'

'He's doing more harm than good. Why is he asking them about the fingerprints?' This was a reference to Gullino having his fingerprints taken after his interview. 'He should be making it all go away, not trying to get them to focus more on the fingerprints.'

Franco explained that Jakobsen was doing his job; he was trying to show that the interrogation had not been lawful.

'What he's doing is normal,' Franco said.

'In a case like this one,' Gullino replied, 'there's no such thing as normal.' Then in a quieter voice, almost to himself. 'I don't need a lawyer.' A pause, before he went on in a voice that sounded as if it was aimed mainly at himself. 'I need a miracle worker.'

'Jakobsen is just following the rules of the game.'

'Christ,' Gullino said, sounding deflated and at the same time exasperated, like he was the only one in the room who understood the situation. 'There are no rules in this game. The people who are trying to get me don't follow rules, they do what they like.'

'You might be right,' Franco said, sounding conciliatory.

'If this lawyer's as good as you say he is, he should know these things.'

'I'm not defending him,' Franco said. 'You're probably right. Change your lawyer if you like.'

'No, no,' Gullino said, his voice lighter. 'I'm not an anarchist like you, I'm not against the system!'

Franco laughed.

'But I think this lawyer has everything the wrong way round,' Gullino went on. 'You only work on these legal details *after* the case becomes public. Until that happens, the case is something else. It's chaos. It's like *La Divina Comedia* when he first visits the Inferno, but worse.'

Until I heard Franco's recording, I had Francesco Gullino down in my mind as a fascist and a pervert, and I was expecting, somehow, to find evidence of this in his voice. But listening to this audio made him come alive in a way which surprised me. I could feel my understanding of him shift. He sounded thoughtful and interesting. I was also struck, listening to him, by the authority in his voice; even when he was talking about the kinds of things that few art dealers would know anything about, like how a case such as this one 'should' work. Another thing that stood out was how much he seemed to loathe Jakobsen, someone who was trying to help him. This guy was on his side. Why was Gullino so suspicious of him?

What really surprised me, though, was the balance of power between Gullino and Franco. Listening to them speak, there was no doubt about who was in charge. Gullino was dominant, and Franco sounded submissive around him. This was the opposite of the Franco I had come to know, a figure who liked to remind me at every opportunity – and there were plenty – of who controlled our relationship.

After Gullino moved in with Franco, most nights they stayed up late in Franco's kitchen talking about how Gullino had been framed and speculating wildly about who was behind this.

Probably one of his business rivals, Gullino liked to say.

An art dealer he had upset.

Maybe someone in Bulgaria.

Franco still wanted to believe that his Italian friend was innocent. But the more time they spent around each other, the harder it was for him to maintain this idea. He realised that Francesco Gullino was not who he appeared to be. That did not mean that he had murdered Georgi Markov with a pellet-shooting umbrella device. He was still not sure if he was sharing a house with a trained assassin. But he had come to realise that there was some other side to Gullino, one that he had not yet understood, and that he had a secret life.

In ordinary circumstances, Franco might have told his guest to leave. If you think there's even a small chance that you have a murderer living with you, that's an understandable reaction. Franco was not one of Gullino's close friends and he could have come up with some lie about needing the spare room for something else. But what made this different, the factor that scrambled his decision-making, was that he had come to think of Gullino as the subject of his film, the film that was going to be his greatest achievement. Franco was trying to gather as much information about Gullino as possible. He needed him to stay, in spite of any personal danger to himself and his family.

Franco kept telling Gullino that he believed in his innocence, even as his doubts mounted and he began secretly trying to investigate who he really was. Franco had begun to lead two parallel lives. There was Franco the righteous friend, someone who would do anything to prove his friend's innocence. Then there was Franco the filmmaker, who knew that Gullino was hiding something and who was recording him on an almost daily basis without his knowledge.

He had so many questions about Gullino. Why did the British detectives think he was caught up in this? What was his relationship to Bulgaria? Was he really a victim of some international conspiracy? Franco also knew that it was on him to find answers to these questions. After all, he was the one who had invited him into their house. But this was going to be hard. Gullino gave away little and he seemed to hate being in one place for too long. He would often vanish for a few days before reappearing and suggesting that they all go out for a meal, one that he would always pay for.

Gullino had told the tax authorities at around this time that he had no money and was effectively bankrupt. He had recently been in court to hear that his house was probably going to be repossessed, leaving him without a home. But each time he came back from one of his trips he was flush with cash. Franco was intrigued by the source of this money. He was also confused about how easy it was for Gullino to come and go.

Dinesen, from Danish intelligence, had told Gullino that he was going to be arrested. At first, Gullino had been depressed about the future and was convinced that he would spend years in jail. Clearly something then changed. He began to travel freely. He had money. He no longer carried himself like a man facing a lengthy prison sentence but someone who knew that he would not be going to jail. Franco remembered Gullino, several months after his interrogation, going about the house humming, like a prisoner who has just had a reprieve. He was lighter and happier, and usually in a fantastic mood. Franco, meanwhile, was acting as if the world was on fire. He was calling up Jakobsen each day, doing everything he could to save his friend and the subject of his film. But the more Franco worried, the less Gullino seemed to care. Either he had come to some kind of arrangement with the Danish authorities, who wanted to charge him with espionage, or the case had fallen apart, or Gullino was simply innocent of the charges against him and he knew that he was able to prove this in court.

I began to feel certain that if I could meet Gullino for myself, I would come away with a sure sense of what he had done. On the face of it, of course, this didn't make any sense. How could I succeed where the two Scotland Yard detectives had failed? It was hard to explain but as Franco continued to speak about Gullino, I became convinced that I could work out whether he was innocent if I was only able to meet him. I didn't even think it would take that long. Ten minutes would do. I just had to be in the same room as him and able to observe his body language while he answered questions about Markov and the Umbrella Murder.

Franco had always said that he would introduce me to Gullino. He loved to dangle the prospect of this in front of me and watch the reaction on my face. I was beginning to think that there might be a part of him that enjoyed the hold he had on me. If I pressed Franco for a date for my Gullino interview, he always pulled back, like a matador swishing his cape out of the way. I had to be patient, he would say.

This story was starting to take over a part of my life. After only a month of talking to Franco about what had happened, I found it hard to get through a day at work without thinking about this case and slipping off to the DR library to carry out more clandestine research. I saw more of the staff in there than almost anyone else in our office. If nobody was around, I would carry on with the research at my desk. Sometimes I slipped into an empty conference room to make international calls to Bulgaria. If I saw someone coming, I would hang up the phone or sweep my research into the top drawer of my desk.

I was hooked. The question that had taken hold of me was the same one that had first consumed Franco: had Francesco Gullino killed Georgi Markov? Or was he the victim of an extraordinary conspiracy?

I had been pulled in by what Franco had told me about this man, but I also wondered if the intensity of my desire to solve this mystery was driven by anything else. I was about to become a dad, and a part of me knew that every spare minute I had should probably be spent looking into questions like which cot to buy, rather than trying to solve a historical murder. Instead of staying late at work each day, I should have been heading home early to be with my partner. Maybe by throwing myself into this, I was running away from the change that was coming in my own life. But even if I could sense that this was what was going on, that was not enough to change my behaviour. There was more to find out first.

It was obvious that Franco was reluctant to let me meet Gullino. I had to find out more about him myself. So far, I had focused on his life in Copenhagen. I had picked up as many details as I could about his career as an art dealer, the framing shop he had once set up and the lives of some of his friends. But there was more to this man than that. If I was going to unravel the mystery of who this elusive figure really was, I needed to look at his life in the years before he arrived in Denmark.

8

'A PLEASANT YOUNG MAN'

Bulgaria, 1970

One day in November 1970, a young Italian joined a queue of travellers waiting to cross from Bulgaria into Greece. He was twenty-four years old, a man still finding his place in the world. Ahead of him, he could see a lovely sweep of Greek countryside dominated by the snow-capped Mount Radomir, the highest peak in the Belasica range. We don't know what Francesco Gullino was thinking as he took in this landscape, but perhaps his mind had begun to move on to the next stage of his journey and everything that awaited him beyond that border — his arrival in Athens later that day, the fun he was going to have — accompanied by the satisfaction at having made some money over the last few days.

Gullino handed over his passport to the Bulgarian official, who did the usual passport-official thing of looking down at it and up at Gullino, down and up, searching for a discrepancy. Gullino had black hair which he liked to comb over to the right. His eyes were wide set, his nose long and smooth. He was not tall but not too short either. The Bulgarian official could see that the passport was in order. But he was curious about the number of stamps it contained and what this Italian had been doing in Bulgaria.

Gullino's reply was vague, something about passing through. The passport official decided to take a look at his belongings. So Gullino was removed from the line of people heading into Greece and his bags were inspected. It did not take long for a different Bulgarian official to find a small quantity of drugs. They also discovered some undeclared foreign currency. This was enough for him to be arrested. Gullino was told that he would not be continuing his journey into Greece and he was soon in the back of a police van being driven to Sofia.

Who was Francesco Gullino at this stage in his life? It depends on who you ask. He was a businessman and an entrepreneur – or a petty criminal, a grifter and, above all, a chancer. Gullino had spent most of the last two years floating around Europe, often buying items in one country and selling them in another on the so-called black market. His activities were either illegal or close to it. But he was careful. If he did commit a crime, he made sure that it carried a short jail sentence. Gullino had become good at this. He understood how to close a deal. He was light on his feet, had a keen sense of how much someone might be willing to pay for a particular item and could spot when something was being offered to him for much less than its market value.

The other thing about Gullino was that his only loyalty appeared to be to himself. On one of Gullino's first trips to Bulgaria, aged eighteen, he had agreed to help a young English couple smuggle a Bulgarian national out of the country. When they were all arrested, Gullino told the Bulgarian authorities everything and gave up the names of those he had been working with.

On his arrival at in the central police station in Sofia in November 1970, Francesco Gullino was transferred from the police van to an interview room. He was already in trouble for the currency and drugs discovered by the border official. But Gullino was now also accused of having brought a second-hand vehicle into the country and selling it off in parts, which was against the law. Gullino made no attempt to lie his way out of this and admitted to what he had done.

Gullino was charged with illegal trading activity and smuggling contraband; he was told that the punishment could be up to ten years in jail. He could not afford a lawyer, so one would be appointed by the state. The charges against him would be brought formally in the next few days.

The Bulgarian investigator knew that the next step in this procedure was to contact the Italian Embassy. He had a duty to tell them that he was about to formally charge an Italian national with a series of crimes. But he decided not to do this.

Several days later, Gullino was taken out of his cell and introduced to a man who was silky smooth, worldly and full of charm. This Bulgarian explained to Gullino – in excellent Italian, one of several languages he spoke – that he had the power to make these charges against him disappear and to have him released from jail. But before he could do that, he needed to know more about him.

Gullino eagerly told his new friend about his past, his relations with his parents, his life until then and how he saw the world. He seemed to be holding nothing back, and doing everything he could think of to win this man over.

If that was the plan, it worked. Gullino was told that he was being transferred out of jail. From now on, he would be staying in a hotel, where his new friend would see him for further conversations.

The man who had suddenly come into Gullino's life as a saviour, father-figure and friend was an intelligence officer for Bulgaria's state security service. He worked for the First Main Directorate, which dealt in foreign intelligence. Part of his job was to recruit spies for foreign missions.

The first question this Bulgarian spymaster needed to ask himself when looking at a potential recruit was if he or she was sympathetic to socialism. In Francesco Gullino's case, the answer was easy. The young Italian could hardly stop talking about his enthusiasm for the cause and repeatedly told this intelligence officer of his heartfelt admiration for the Bulgarian socialist regime as well as his disdain for the more decadent life enjoyed by those in the West. When the Bulgarian official said to him, in a light-hearted way, that perhaps the regime could use someone like Gullino, he said at once that he would be willing to work for free, such was his admiration and respect for the Bulgarian regime.

But what could Francesco Gullino do to help Bulgaria?

Gullino gave the spymaster a long list of his acquaintances and friends who might one day be useful to Bulgarian intelligence, as if he had been expecting this question. There was a secretary he knew in the consular department of the Italian embassy in Ankara. A policeman in Turin. A Turkish friend who had recently been in Israel repairing military planes. A Belgian woman who was a chemical engineer and had left-wing views.

The Bulgarian spymaster was hugely encouraged by what he heard and asked Gullino to take the next few days to write up a more detailed account of his life. Reading through the document, several days later, this intelligence officer was blown away.

'He had a real understanding of life,' he cooed. Francesco Gullino 'was practical, resourceful and business-like. In addition to Italian, he also spoke very good French, English, to a lesser degree, Spanish and German.' He was, the officer went on, 'a pleasant young man' who had 'refined manners. He is familiar in great detail with the prices of all types of cars, old books and everything which might be bought and sold at a profit. He knows the extent of the laws and the extent to which he can transgress them without particular consequence for himself. He is not easily scared. He has a real appreciation of the circumstances around him. In conversations he is open and calm. One can talk to him frankly like a trading partner.' He was also someone who seemed to be able to make friends easily and had connections all over Europe.[1]

Intelligent, resourceful, comfortable with risk, sympathetic to socialism, courageous, good with languages, refined. Francesco

Gullino ticked every box for a Bulgarian spymaster looking to take on a new agent.

To a more cynical observer, he might be too good to be true. A little more probing into Gullino's political views might have shown that his understanding of socialism was limited for someone who claimed to be such a fan of the Bulgarian regime. But this particular Bulgarian spymaster had a quota to reach for the year and needed to recruit a certain number of foreigners.[2] Gullino was one of the most promising candidates he had come across in months.

On 6 April 1971, Francesco Gullino was given a piece of paper that contained a declaration of loyalty to Bulgaria's State Security Service. He was asked to copy it out and sign it. This document also stated that from that moment onwards he would be referred to in official government paperwork by his new codename: 'Piccadilly'.[3]

Bird and Kemp, the Scotland Yard detectives who interviewed him over twenty years later, were right. At an early stage in his life, Francesco Gullino was recruited as a Bulgarian intelligence agent with the codename Piccadilly. But was he effectively blackmailed into this? Gullino had been told that he faced ten years in jail unless he agreed to work for the Bulgarians. Most people in that situation would at least consider signing the piece of paper if it meant later being allowed to leave.

Before Gullino was sent anywhere, he was told to attend a Bulgarian spy school. Over the next few months, he was given a crash course in espionage. Gullino practised following people on the streets of Sofia without being seen. He learned how to tell if he was being shadowed. He was given instructions on how to use a 'dead drop' – spy jargon for a secret location that is known only to you and your handler where you can leave messages and secret material. He also learned the best way to make contact with his handler while on the move.

Gullino was soon given his first test. He was asked by his handler to report on the lives of various foreigners living in the capital.

The Bulgarians wanted to know more about what these men and women got up to, how they saw the world politically and any illegal activities in which they might be involved. But perhaps more than that, this task was about establishing Gullino's loyalty. The Bulgarians wanted their new agent to get used to spying on other people and, ultimately, betraying their confidence.

After two years of this, in 1973, Gullino was given his first international mission. Perhaps by this point he had come to believe in the Bulgarian government's socialist ideals and felt a real antipathy towards the West. Or he was a terrific actor and being sent out of the country was the goal he had been working towards since the day of his arrest. Maybe agreeing to be a Bulgarian agent was nothing more than a means of escape.

Gullino was told that his destination was Denmark. As instructed, he flew to Copenhagen. His handler made sure that he had money, and after a few false starts Gullino was able to open a small shop in the Danish capital.

Franco had been right to think that Gullino had a secret life. His houseguest had been recruited by Bulgaria's state security service and sent to Denmark as an undercover agent. But this did not prove that he was involved in the murder of Georgi Markov. If anything, the details surrounding Gullino's recruitment tended to undermine the whole idea. They pointed to the possibility that this new agent was going through the motions so that he could avoid being sent to jail. I knew that if I had been in his situation, a young man facing jail in a brutal police state, I would have been tempted to sign something that could lead to my release.

Or perhaps the question of whether Gullino's heart was in it was the wrong one to be asking. There was another clue which cast all this in a very different light. Even if the Bulgarian regime had wanted to kill Georgi Markov, it was hard to say if they were capable of carrying out an attack like the Umbrella Murder. There was one crucial detail which did not fit.

9

AN UNIDENTIFIED SUBSTANCE

Porton Down, October 1978

Dr David Gall was stuck. The leading scientist at the Ministry of Defence's secretive Porton Down facility was under pressure from Scotland Yard to supply more information about the pellet that had been used in the Georgi Markov murder. What the police really wanted to know was which substance had been used to kill him. That would make a huge difference to their investigation and might even lead them to the killer.

Gall had begun by looking for any trace of a toxin on the pellet they had found inside Markov's right thigh. Using some of the state-of-the-art technology available to him at Porton Down, he carried out a number of tests, but had found nothing. Nor was Gall able to detect any toxin in the surrounding flesh. But the idea that the pellet could have been empty was too strange to contemplate. Something must have been in there. Perhaps it had been absorbed by Markov's body in a way that left no trace.

The pellet found in the other Bulgarian defector, Vladimir Kostov, who had been attacked in Paris while travelling on the Metro with his wife, was more promising. When Gall had first inspected this object, he had seen traces of a substance inside. After carrying out several tests, he was able to conclude that this pellet had been filled with a toxin called ricin.

A surprisingly large number of plants naturally produce ricin, but usually in such tiny quantities that they pose no risk to humans and are not thought of as poisonous. There is one exception, however: the castor bean plant, *Ricinus communis*, which has been grown by farmers all over the world for thousands of years, and is cultivated today in countries such as Brazil, China and India. The bean from this plant – although technically it's a seed, not a bean – is harvested, heated up, crushed and pressed to extract castor oil, which can be used for treating skin conditions, as fuel for oil lamps or as a laxative.

The oil itself contains very little ricin but the spent remains of the castor beans – known as the 'cake' – are more dangerous. Up to 5 per cent of this leftover material is made up of the toxic protein molecule that constitutes ricin. This molecule contains two polypeptide chains. When separated, the chains are harmless, but when combined, as they are in ricin, they have a uniquely destructive effect on most mammals, including humans. The way they work is this: once the ricin has entered the body, the second of these chains – chain B – will latch on to a carbohydrate found on the outside of a cell membrane and effectively hold open the door so that the other chain – chain A – can enter the cell. Chain A attaches itself to the cell's ribosomal subunit, which would otherwise be producing crucial enzymes, and very soon the cell is dead.

What sets ricin apart from almost every other known toxin is its staggering potency. Pound for pound, it is more deadly than any nerve agent. You can fit on the head of a pin the amount of ricin you'd need to kill an adult human being. During the First World War, when the US Army investigated the possibility of using ricin as a chemical weapon, they decided not to go ahead, only because they would be unable to protect their own troops. What makes ricin particularly dangerous is that there is no widely available antidote.

As well as discovering ricin inside the pellet from Vladimir Kostov, Dr Gall had found ricin antibodies in the flesh surrounding this metal ball. He was confident that a small quantity of ricin had left the pellet, but Kostov's body then produced enough antibodies to defend itself from this attack which had allowed him to survive. It followed that ricin could have been used to kill Markov, given how similar the two pellets were, and that in Markov's case, all of the toxin had left the pellet.

This was Gall's theory. But he needed proof. He looked for historical accounts of people who had experienced the symptoms of ingesting ricin, to see if they matched those of Georgi Markov. But it turned out that there was no record of anyone in Britain ever having been poisoned with ricin. Either this was the first time it had occurred or in the past it had gone undetected.

Gall did, however, find several scientific studies that had tested the effect of ricin on small animals such as rats and guinea pigs. This gave him an idea. He decided to inject ricin into an animal that was about the same weight as Markov and observe its symptoms. He did some research into the weight of various farmyard animals before arranging for a healthy pig to be delivered to Porton Down. This unfortunate creature was then given the same amount of ricin that one of the mysterious pellets could hold and the scientists sat behind a glass screen to see how the pig would react.

'Nothing happened for about six hours,' Gall recalled. 'The pig was as right as rain. Then it obviously became a bit sick. At this time, its temperature was going up and so was its white cell count.' These were the same symptoms that had been observed in Georgi Markov. 'It did not vomit, but it was off its food.' Again, Markov had reacted in the same way. 'By the next morning it was obviously more sick,' Gall continued, 'its white cell count was still going up.' Later, 'a fever developed and the white cell count rose sharply'. Several hours after this, the pig died.

The similarities to Markov's symptoms were clear. Gall con-cluded that he must have been poisoned with ricin and passed on the news to Jim Nevill at Scotland Yard. This had a huge impact on the investigation. Very few countries in the world had both the ability and the desire to extract ricin from the 'cake' left over after oil has been taken from castor beans. Bulgaria was not one of them. Even if the original order to kill Markov had indeed come from Bulgaria, the use of ricin seemed to confirm that another country was either heavily involved in this attack or had carried out the whole operation itself.

10
LABORATORY 12

Moscow, 1918

Over sixty years earlier, on 30 August 1918, Vladimir Lenin was leaving the Hammer and Sickle arms factory in Moscow when he heard a woman call out his name. Her name was Fanya Kaplan and she was a twenty-eight-year-old from Ukraine. She belonged to a political party called the Socialist Revolutionaries, which had been outlawed several weeks earlier. The order for this to happen had come from Lenin, who had recently become leader of what would, in four years, be renamed the Soviet Union.

Kaplan called out again. This time, Lenin turned to face her. Kaplan then raised her right hand. Only at this point did it become clear to those watching this scene play out that she was holding a revolver — a FN Browning M1900, a semi-automatic pistol that was known for being easy to conceal. Kaplan fired the weapon three times. One bullet — possibly the first — ripped through Lenin's coat without touching him. The other two struck his body. One punctured his lung and ended up lodged next to his right collarbone. The third came to rest in the muscle surrounding his left shoulder blade.

Lenin fell to the ground, face down. It looked as if he had just been killed. But he was still alive and his minders bundled him into the back of his car and drove him to the Kremlin. One of the bullets fired by Fanya Kaplan was later removed in hospital, but the other was left where it was and remained there until Lenin's death, five years later.

Kaplan was arrested later that day. She confessed to her crime, but refused to name her accomplices. She was shot in the back of the head. Kaplan had hoped to kill Lenin and believed that his death could lead to the downfall of his political party. Although none of this happened, her attempt on his life would change the course of Russian history nonetheless.

Lenin's main response to this attack was to launch the 'Red Terror'. In the years that followed, thousands of people were labelled 'enemies of the state' and either imprisoned or killed. But Kaplan's attack affected Lenin in another way. As well as becoming more wary and suspicious, he developed a fascination for political assassinations and a new desire to be able to carry them out himself.

Lenin had been told by the police that the bullets used by Kaplan, including the one still buried inside him, had been coated in a little-known substance called curare. This is a paralysing agent derived from the bark of a vine that grows in South America and has an asphyxiating effect when mixed with blood. Brazilian Amerindians will sometimes daub curare onto the tips of their arrows and darts when out hunting their prey. Lenin was intrigued. He began to wonder if Russian assassins could do something similar, using poisons developed by the most talented Russian scientists to kill his enemies. But some of his opponents had managed to flee the country and found refuge in countries with which Russia had good diplomatic relations. He wanted these people dead, but understood the political cost of killing them openly. He became transfixed by the idea of using poisonous substances to murder his enemies in a way that could not be traced back either to him or to the Russian state.

Several years later, Lenin set up Russia's first ever poison laboratory. It was referred to by those in government as the 'Special

Room', the 'Special Bureau' or the 'Special Cabinet'. Later, it would be given a series of ever-more mysterious and sinister-sounding names, such as 'Laboratory No. 1', 'Lab X' and, finally, 'Laboratory 12'.

The challenge for the scientists inside the secretive Laboratory 12, part of Lenin's own secretariat, was to develop lethal toxins that had no taste, no smell and could not be detected in an autopsy. Most of their work was focused on manufacturing new versions of existing poisons. One of these was a novel form of cyanide. This could be sprayed as a mist and cause the victim to show all the signs of having had a heart attack. Another poison they developed could be applied to the bulb of a reading lamp. The idea was that it would remain inert until the light was turned on, once the target had sat down to read. As the bulb warmed up, the substance would turn into an invisible cloud of poisonous gas that was capable of killing anyone in the vicinity.

One of the first people known to have been killed using a poison developed inside Laboratory 12 was Alexander Kutepov, who had fought against the Communists during the Russian civil war. Another victim was Nestor Lakoba, who had fallen out with Stalin, and had poison slipped into his wine (the glass was handed to him by Lavrentiy Beria, future head of the predecessor to the KGB).

Assassinations like these became known in Russia as *mokroye delo*, or 'wet jobs'. The KGB even had a specialist unit, Spetsbureau 13, dedicated to these types of covert assassinations, that was known as the 'Department of Wet Jobs'. It relied increasingly on new poisons concocted inside Laboratory 12.

By the start of the Second World War, research inside Laboratory 12 had become even more elaborate and specialised. It had one department dedicated to bacteriological weapons and another focused on chemical poisons. This one was run by the Russian scientist Grigory Mairanovsky, a man known to his colleagues as 'Dr Death'.

Mairanovsky was a sadist. He took genuine pleasure in coming up with new and more sophisticated ways to kill opponents of the Soviet regime, a process that involved a certain amount of trial and error. Mairanovsky needed victims on which to experiment, and with that in mind had developed a close working relationship with the commandant of Lubyanka Prison, less than a mile from his laboratory, who supplied him with prisoners for his experiments. Mairanovsky's team did not share his sadism and found the sound of the prisoners' screams so upsetting that they purchased a radio set that was played at full volume during the tests.

'Dr Death' was fascinated by the effect of different poisons, including digitoxin and curare, and personally injected curare into the veins of Cy Oggins, an American-born Soviet agent who had been sentenced to death. Mairanovsky later looked into the possibility of using mustard gas in assassinations, concluding that it was no good because it would be picked up easily in an autopsy. He also explored the idea of carrying out extra-judicial killings using ricin.

In the years after the Second World War, this Soviet poison factory became busier than ever. Wolfgang Salus, former secretary of Leon Trotsky (who was himself murdered by a Soviet agent), was poisoned and killed by a mystery substance. Several years later, Lev Rebet, a Ukrainian anti-communist, died of a reported heart attack, but had, in fact, been sprayed in the face by a cyanide mist from Laboratory 12. Stepan Bandera was another Ukrainian who died in almost identical circumstances. The former KGB hitman and defector, Nikolai Khokhlov, was later handed a cup of coffee laced with a lethal dose of thallium. Again, Laboratory 12 had been involved. The Hungarian policeman Beal Lapusnyik was poisoned with dimethyl sulphate after defecting to the West. The dissident writer and Nobel-Prize-winner Alexander Solzhenitsyn was attacked in 1971 by KGB assassins using a poison gel thought to have contained ricin.

Seven years after the attack on Solzhenitsyn, Georgi Markov was killed with a poison that was almost certainly ricin. At that time, one of the only places in the world capable of producing ricin was Laboratory 12 in Moscow, paid for and controlled by the KGB. Dr Gall at Porton Down knew that, and so did the detectives at Scotland Yard. So, this being the case, the logical conclusion seemed to be that the KGB was likely to have been heavily involved in Georgi Markov's death.

But Scotland Yard was not so sure. Jim Nevill and his team of detectives had either heard or seen something that left them 'convinced', according to one report, that this murder 'was not ordered by KGB headquarters in Moscow'. They believed, instead, that it was the handiwork of 'junior agents in Bulgaria'. Nevill had been told that the KGB was 'furious at the assassination because the Russian secret police HQ was not consulted and the revelations have caused them acute embarrassment'.[1]

But if that was true, how on earth did the Bulgarians get hold of the ricin? Where did the pellet come from, and the umbrella allegedly used to fire it? More importantly, how did they instruct their man Francesco Gullino to use it – if that's what really happened?

11

DECISION

Copenhagen, June 1994

Four months after I had first met Franco and embarked on this strange journey, he was still refusing to arrange a meeting with Gullino. Perhaps he was exaggerating the access he had to this man. Although Gullino had used Franco's house as a base for several months in 1993, by the summer of that year he had moved on. I found out later that this was mainly because Helene had insisted that he leave. But Franco did not dwell on that. He liked to make out that he continued to be a gatekeeper to Gullino. He seemed to enjoy the hold he had on me and how much I wanted to speak to Gullino. Perhaps I should have done more to disguise my desire to meet his former houseguest and played it cool, but I've never been good at that. I was finding it hard to hide my impatience, and my desire to move this story along to some kind of resolution. The only way to do that, as far as I could see, was to keep pressing Franco for a date when I could meet the man thought to have been behind the Umbrella Murder. But so far, that had not worked.

Over the summer, my wife had given birth to our beautiful boy. A lot changed in the weeks that followed – though not in the way that some parents had assured me it would. I didn't feel like a new man. My world had not been turned upside down, but it was as if the music of my life was now being played in a different key. The way I thought about the future was different, and I was more alive to what my family needed and more protective than before.

I was still going to meet Franco at Café Sebastopol once a week. Each time, I'd walk in with the hope that this meeting was going to be different, that this time Franco would finally agree to let me meet Gullino. The trouble was, I never knew which version of Franco I was going to get. Sometimes I sat down opposite the Franco I found it easiest to talk to: persuasive, friendly Franco, someone who enjoyed discussing our shared obsession and the constellation of secret organisations that might be – or must be, according to him – caught up in this story. But there were other times when I ended up having a coffee with the other Franco: an irascible and prickly man who could become cross with me, and who treated me as the stiff from the mainstream media who was out to steal his story.

A new doubt had entered my mind, one that I couldn't shake off, no matter how hard I tried. The uncertainty I started to live with was less about whether I was going to meet Gullino, or if this Italian art dealer had killed Georgi Markov, but the possibility that by agreeing to help Franco I was putting myself and my young family in danger.

I remembered Franco saying soon after I met him that he might be under surveillance and that I could be too. I didn't think much of this at the time. Franco often said things like this. The way he saw it, everyone was out to get him.

'Can you prove it?' I had asked.

'Not yet,' Franco replied. 'But come on, think about it. This case is interesting to a lot of people.'

'Like?'

'All of them. Danish intelligence. PET and the military intelligence, FE. British intelligence. The Bulgarians.'

I had all but forgotten about this, until unusual things began to happen at home. I'd had the telephone line in our house fixed but it was still acting up. When my wife or I picked up the receiver, we now heard a soft buzzing sound in the background, one that had not been there before. It might have been simply a coincidence that this had started just as I agreed to help Franco with his investigation.

Then I became aware of the car that was often parked in the street outside our apartment. It was a green Ford Mondeo and was distinctive for several reasons. One was the pair of oversized aerials on the roof. The other was that every time I saw it, there were two men inside. They just sat there, apparently in silence. I found a place in our apartment where I could sneak a peek at them through the window without them being able to see me and noticed that the man closest to me kept looking over in the direction of our apartment.

In my relationship with Franco, he was supposed to be the suspicious one, while I took on the role of the sceptic. I was there to ask him for proof of whatever it was he was saying or to suggest a more innocent explanation than the one he had come up with. So my initial instinct, on seeing this mysterious car outside our apartment, was to tell myself that there was nothing strange going on.

That changed the day that I drove away from our apartment block and noticed the green car pull out from its parking spot and start to follow me. At first, I couldn't quite believe it. *Just a coincidence*, I told myself. *Nothing more*. I had been planning to drive into work but instead I turned left and went around the block, purely to see what the other car would do.

It followed me.

Driving in convoy, we then arrived back at my apartment.

This was like something out of a television spy drama. But not a very sophisticated one because these two weren't exactly making any effort to hide what they were doing. Even I could do a better job of tailing a car. Perhaps they wanted to be seen and that was the point.

Unsure what to do next, I drove around the block again. The green car did the same. In total, I went round our block three times that day, and only after this did the green car drive off.

Next came the break-in. Our apartment was on the ground floor, at street level, with a back door that opened onto a yard. The space was overlooked by so many houses and apartment blocks that it had never even crossed my mind that someone might try to gain entry. But one night, that's what happened. I had left the window by the door a little ajar – only a few centimetres – but someone who knew what they were doing had used a tool to break in.

That night, I was working late and was not at home when the break-in occurred, but my wife and our son were asleep in our bedroom. Luckily, they did not wake up. The intruder made their way through our apartment and went through some drawers and cupboards, but disappeared without taking a thing.

Of course, there was a relatively straightforward explanation. Break-ins were not completely unheard of in this neighbourhood. An experienced burglar might have found a way in, hoping to make off with some valuables, but run away after they were interrupted by an unexpected sound – perhaps our son crying.

Either that, or there was some truth to what Franco was saying. This intruder might have been given instructions to find out more about our investigation into Francesco Gullino. I had no idea.

My wife and I had become closer since the birth of our son. At that time, we were a small and happy family. Our son was not yet in his own room, so, each night, the three of us slept together in our bed. On some nights, we kept the curtains open. I remember lying there and watching our son while he slept, and how his eyes would sometimes blink open in the middle of the night. I would see him gazing out of the window at the night sky. More than anything else in the world, I wanted to keep him safe. I was also beginning to see that I needed to be more present in our family life, and that too much of the time I came back from work and was distracted. This amateur murder investigation that I had become a part of was taking up more of my headspace than I had anticipated, and now, with the break-in at our apartment, it seemed to be putting my family at risk.

When my wife had first said that this Umbrella Murder business seemed to be taking over my life, I had pushed back. But I was starting to see that there was something in this. She understood my interest in the story, and in the early days she shared some of my excitement, but increasingly, she was frustrated with the time I gave to it.

'It's just a hobby,' I'd say. 'Just for fun.'

But we both knew that was not true.

Soon, my friends were starting to react in a similar way. When I first told them about the story, their faces would light up. Usually, they'd say something along the lines of 'It sounds like a John Le Carré novel!' (It was always Le Carré. There are other spy novelists, I wanted to say.) But after spending a few months of digging into this story, I noticed a different reaction from the same friends. They would ask if I was still working on the spy story, but that was it, and after a few polite questions they'd move the conversation on.

I didn't blame them. Little had changed since I had started talking about this. But they were also reacting, I think, to the strength of the grip this story had on me.

My work was suffering as well. For almost any other young Danish guy like me, my job at Denmark's largest sports broadcaster was the stuff of dreams. I was being *paid* to watch football matches. The office was exciting. I loved the energy and the breakneck speed at which things tended to happen. Our daily editorial meetings were fun and the satisfaction I felt at the end of the day after producing two crisp minutes of sports news was immense. I was that annoying guy who genuinely looks forward to going into work.

But in every spare moment, my thoughts would boomerang back to Francesco Gullino and the Umbrella Murder. In my locker at work, I had secret folders for my research into Georgi Markov. As a disguise, the first few pages were to do with football. I couldn't get out of my head some of the things that Franco had said about Gullino. 'He's never what you think he is. He's a chameleon. A trickster. Like your old Danish god, Loki. He can be whoever he wants to be.' A part of me was desperate to find this man and confront him, but over the next few months, I realised that this was probably never going to happen. I had to let it go.

Eventually, I called up Franco and told him that we needed to talk. We arranged to meet the next day at his house.

It seemed that Franco could tell something was wrong from the moment I walked in. After we had sat down at the table in his kitchen, I explained that I had made my decision. I felt that we had taken the project as far as we could. I was out.

For a long time, Franco didn't say a word. He picked a spot on the table and stared at it with a strange kind of intensity, as if he had noticed something in there that he had not seen before.

'Yeah, yeah,' he finally said, still looking at the table. 'You can quit. I'll keep going.'

'It's been over a year now, Franco, and we're just not making progress,' I said, wanting him to agree.

But he didn't. Franco just sat there, looking downwards at an odd angle. Then he started to chuckle.

'I knew it,' he said.

'What?'

'That this would happen, that you would not see what's really going on.'

'Francesco Gullino killed Georgi Markov. You're making a film about it and I was going to write a book. That's what's going on.'

'No, I mean the bigger picture. Who Gullino really works for. You see, you have to keep asking yourself — why would a fascist like Gullino work as a spy for a communist regime?'

'I haven't a clue.'

'OK. I'll tell you what happened. Gullino is not what he appears to be, and that's because he started out as a fascist. After that, he was recruited by an Italian intelligence agency. They instructed him to go to Bulgaria and commit some minor crime so that he could be arrested. They did that because they knew he would be recruited. The plan worked! Then when Gullino gets into trouble for killing Georgi Markov, the Italians cut a deal with the British and the Danes. They want to protect their asset. And that's why Gullino will never be prosecuted! He's a double agent.'

It was a startling theory. But without any evidence I had no idea if there could be any truth to it. The trouble was, Franco would not show me the material he had gathered, because he could not bring himself to trust me or anyone else.

'Franco, you need to show me the evidence. Otherwise we're just going round in circles. We have endless meetings, but there's no output, no interviews, no written research. You're mistaking talk for work. And you still won't let me meet Gullino.'

Franco said nothing for a while.

'This kind of story takes time and patience,' he said, looking up at me for the first time. 'But if you want out, then off you go.' He rearranged himself in his chair. 'I'm not giving up.'

I could sense him adjusting to the new reality, in which he was once more the lone crusader in search of the truth, a role he had played for most of his life.

'I knew it would end like this,' he went on. 'This story is not just about uncovering what happened. It's about finding a way past all the people who don't want us to succeed. If you're someone who gets scared, then it's not for you. You need to be able to handle the danger and the risk. Otherwise, forget it. Go back to writing about badminton, or whatever it is you do.'

I looked down at my watch and saw that I was late for work. I said goodbye to Franco and ran out to my car. Once I was on my way, I realized that I might never see Franco again.

For the rest of the day, his words stayed in my mind and I couldn't help but wonder if there was something in what he said. Perhaps I was afraid. Maybe I had become too comfortable in the cosy world I had built for myself. But I had made my decision and it felt like the right one. My wife was relieved and, in many ways, so was I.

Two weeks later, my phone rang. It was Franco.

It was the first time we had spoken since I had said that I was out.

'I've made a decision,' he said, sounding energised and triumphant. 'I'm going to Bulgaria.'

'You're what?'

'I'm travelling to Bulgaria. I've arranged a translator and I have a camerawoman coming. A girl I know, who's going to drive us down. I've secured the equipment, everything. And I'm speaking to television stations about the story and one or two of the big magazines. Everyone is interested.' I had never heard Franco speak so fast. 'If Gullino won't take part in my film, then I will go to Bulgaria and find out everything about him myself.'

Then there was a pause. I wondered if the line had gone dead.

'You can come if you like.'

It was as if he was offering me a chance to redeem myself after what had happened before.

'You can set up some appointments for us in Sofia,' Franco went on. 'I'll do the same. Then we go to Bulgaria, we get something on tape. I make my film, you research your book and we can finish the whole thing off.'

The idea of bringing this story to an end was completely intoxicating, in a way that I hadn't expected. At the same time, there was no way I was going on a trip to Bulgaria with Franco. I had a baby to look after. My wife and I were saving up for a bigger apartment. I'd struggle to get the time off work. And why would I spend a week of my annual leave on a wild goose chase in the company of a conspiracy theorist? Going to Bulgaria was a terrible idea and just about the last thing I should do. But at the same time, it held out the promise of an ending.

I booked a flight from Copenhagen to Sofia. Then I went to tell my wife.

12

SOFIA

Bulgaria, 1995

Our trip to Bulgaria got off to a bad start. I had flown to Sofia,
where I was due to meet Franco, who had already driven down
from Denmark. I had no trouble spotting him as I walked into
the arrivals hall of the airport. There he was with his familiar blue
jacket, ironed trousers and, under his arm, the same brown document folder he carried around with him everywhere, as if it were his
own nuclear football.

'You're late,' Franco said, before leading the way to the car park.

We stepped out into a cold spring day. Piles of snow were
dotted around and in the distance I could see Franco's car, a Ford
Granada. But something was wrong. Men in leather jackets were
standing next to it, looking both pleased with themselves and somehow hostile. Once we were closer, I could see that one of the wheels
on Franco's car had been clamped.

As someone who had grown up in Denmark, one of the most
peaceful and law-abiding countries on earth, I assumed that Franco
had parked in the wrong place and this was a matter for him to
settle with the local traffic authorities. I looked around for some
sign of officialdom but there was none. The clamp belonged to the
Bulgarian men in leather jackets.

Franco's car might have looked scruffy back in Copenhagen, but out here in Sofia, among the ageing Ladas, Skodas and Trabants, it was like a visitor from the future.

'Deutsche mark,' one of the men said to Franco, rolling a thumb over his fingers.

Franco was not happy. He argued with them in Italian, as well as Danish and English. His cheeks flared up, turning the colour of beetroot, as he waved his arms about with force and feeling. The men smiled back at him. After an hour of this, Franco counted out forty Deutsche Marks, his car was unclamped and we set off for the centre of Sofia.

'Unbelievable,' Franco muttered, shaking his head. 'Of course, none of this would have happened if you hadn't decided to fly.'

'I can't get as much time off work as you. We've spoken about this.'

'You need to try harder. You need to be more committed.'

'Perhaps you can claim the money back as an expense?' I tried.

'What do you mean?'

'You said there were television programmes interested in covering this trip.'

Silence.

'I'm sure they'll pay for something like this. It wasn't your fault.'

'There was a lot of interest in this trip in the beginning,' Franco began, 'but the editors I saw said they were going to wait until we got back before going ahead with anything.'

As I later found out, Franco had pitched the story of our Bulgarian trip to a number of television news programmes, as well as to major newspapers and respected magazines. Everyone he spoke to was interested at first. They all wanted that first meeting. But once they had listened to him going on in his Franco-ish way about how this story was about more than Francesco Gullino, and how the Umbrella Murder was part of a conspiracy involving the

CIA, the KGB, Bulgarian intelligence, the Italian criminal underworld, the Danish PET and Scotland Yard – and how the man who
killed Georgi Markov was secretly being protected, for reasons he
had not yet worked out – their interest cooled and they backed
away from the story.

Franco could not help himself from making the story of
Francesco Gullino and the Umbrella Murder more complicated
than it needed to be, to the point where I had begun to wonder if
there was something else going on here, some kink in his psychology that prevented him from finishing this off. Perhaps the hunt
was always going to be more absorbing than the kill. Maybe his
quest to uncover the truth about Georgi Markov's death had taken
over his life to the extent that the thought of ending it was one
that scared him, and he kept looking for another layer of intrigue
as way of putting it off. Whatever the reason, the outcome was
that we had no financial backing for the trip, a detail Franco had
not shared until now. Everything was going to have to be paid for
by Franco and by me, and neither of us had budgeted for being
robbed at the airport.

We drove in silence towards the centre of Sofia, which gave me
a chance to focus more on my surroundings. The city I could see out
of the window looked almost nothing like the one I had glimpsed in
archive footage I had found at work, all of it filmed during the time
of the communist dictator Todor Zhivkov. Everything in those shots
looked intentional and calm, in a way that appealed to the mini-
malist in me. For a moment, it had made me question what I had
learned at school about countries like Bulgaria being dark dystopias.
But what I could see now, as Franco steered us towards our hotel,
was different. The traffic was chaotic and loud. The driving was all
over the place. Among the clapped-out cars we passed were carts
drawn by horses, mules or donkeys. The stucco plasterwork on the
older buildings was peeling off and the façades of the Stalinist blocks

— so modern and clean in the footage I had seen — appeared bleak and hard to love. Everything had a dishevelled quality, as if the city was recovering from a heavy night out. On most street corners, I saw men standing around in the cold, looking watchful. There were stalls selling cigarettes, nuts, shoes and anything else that was small and useful. Some buildings had queues outside but most were boarded up. The Cyrillic script on their signs added, for me, a sense of dislocation, until we passed a well-lit sign for KFC or an Audi showroom stuffed with cars that very few people could afford.

I remember the first time I had really wondered what life behind the Iron Curtain, in a country like Bulgaria, was like. It was during the 1974 football World Cup. My dad and I had set out to watch as many matches as possible on television. The one that captured my imagination was when East Germany played West Germany and won, thanks to a lone goal from Jürgen Sparwasser.

I knew nothing about Sparwasser or the country he came from. But I was intrigued. This country was described to me as being completely different to ours, and yet at the same time, it was so close. In the years after that, I noticed how athletes from East Germany always performed miraculously well in international competitions and seemed to be much stronger and more focused than our own. At the time, I had no idea about the doping programmes and was left with a vague sense that these people living beyond the Iron Curtain were doing something clever that we in Denmark were not. It wasn't that I admired countries like Bulgaria. I was young and didn't really know what they were. But I had a vague sense that their vision of how life should be was more radical than our own.

Franco parked up outside the Sheraton Hotel, an ocean liner of a building and the place he had booked for our stay. Leading me into the lobby, he told me cheerfully that it was also the most expensive hotel in Bulgaria. I was dazzled by the shiny marble flooring, chandeliers and luxury boutiques selling designer jewellery.

We seemed to be almost the only guests. The staff wore starched white shirts and black jackets, and treated us like visiting dignitaries, which embarrassed me. But Franco was enjoying this treatment. It seemed to suit his sense of who he was.

'Right,' Franco began, 'come with me. I want you to meet our team.'

He led me over to a sofa on one side of the lobby where two women were waiting for us.

Rikke was Danish, roughly my age and was going to be our camerawoman. She had shoulder-length red hair that she kept in a ponytail. Rikke was also tough. She came from one of the plain-speaking fishing towns at the northernmost tip of Denmark and seemed unfazed by everything. She and Franco moved in the same alternative film circles and somehow he had convinced her that this trip to Bulgaria would be a fantastic career opportunity for her. What Franco had forgotten to ask Rikke, in his excitement about having someone who was willing to join us, was if she had done anything like this before. (She had not.)

The other woman was Viktoria, who was going to be our translator. She had grown up in Bulgaria before moving to Denmark. Viktoria had glasses and a long fringe. She was more withdrawn than Rikke and harder to read. Like her, she had been persuaded by Franco that this trip would look good on her resumé and had driven down from Denmark with him. But even in that first meeting I could sense that this trip was not at all what she had expected and that she already had doubts about the whole thing.

Franco seemed oblivious and was already revelling in his role as undisputed boss and group elder – he was twenty years older than the rest of us. Once we had all been introduced, Franco ran through the plan for what we should do tomorrow. We had a list of interviews that he had lined up, including a childhood friend of Georgi Markov's and several former Bulgarian intelligence officials.

'How about you, Ulrik?' Franco interrupted himself. 'What have you set up?'

'I have been in touch with Any Krueleva, the Bulgarian official handling the investigation into Markov's death. Although I'm still not sure if she will speak to us.'

'And?'

'First thing tomorrow, we have an interview with Kalin Todorov.'

'Ah, yes,' Franco murmured his approval.

'Who's Todorov?' Rikke asked.

'He's a journalist who wrote a book about the Umbrella Murder,' I said. 'The only one that's ever been published in Bulgaria.'

'He will have the inside line on everything,' Franco added. 'We need to find out what he was not allowed to put into the book.'

Todorov's book had come out right after the collapse of the communist regime and had caused a sensation. It was the first time any Bulgarian author had tackled the Umbrella Murder head on. A number of other European authors had written about this murder, but what made Todorov's book different was the way he was able to bring Georgi Markov to life. He had done a great job of capturing the world in which Georgi had grown up, and had made a considerable effort to understand who this man really was. He had also spoken to a number of former government officials about the circumstances of his death. What had made his book so controversial when it came out was that Todorov had a very different explanation for Markov's murder, one that had not been heard outside Bulgaria until then. Tomorrow, I would be able to ask him about it.

I found it hard to sleep that night and for a while stared out of the hotel window at the streets of Sofia. In the blur of our journey in from the airport, I had lost sight of the fact that this was where Georgi Markov had lived for most of his life. I was surrounded by the same streets he had walked up and down and the same vast buildings that for so many years had formed a part of his urban horizon. Only later did I understand that the key to understanding what happened on Waterloo Bridge lay here, in Sofia, and that the story of the Umbrella Murder began long before Francesco Gullino became a Bulgarian spy.

13

GEORGI

Bulgaria, June 1962

It's a balmy summer evening, and we're in a smoke-filled restaurant in central Sofia. The room is full of poets, playwrights, writers and their hangers-on, and the doors to the street have been thrown open. You can hear the sound of intense conversation, with some light music in the background. This is the Journalist's Club, the place to be for anyone in Sofia who has ever thought of themselves as a writer. And yet, for reasons we'll get on to, none of the country's literary superstars are anywhere to be seen right now.

One of the young writers in the Journalist's Club right now is Georgi Markov. He's there with his friend, Christo Fotev, a promising young poet. Georgi is thirty-three years old. He is magically good looking, funny, and has a wry and inquisitive mind. He usually comes across as intoxicatingly confident, but tonight he's not his usual showboating self. Instead, a different side to him has come out, one that his friends don't often see. As evening gives way to night, Georgi Markov becomes increasingly nervous.[1]

A few streets away, the country's most celebrated writers have assembled in the headquarters of the Bulgarian Writers' Union, one of many buildings in the centre of Sofia to go up after the Second World War, when the city centre was flattened by a series of Allied bombing raids. The members of the Writers' Union are due to vote on whether Georgi and his friend Christo should be admitted to their union.[2] This may not sound like a big deal. But in Bulgaria at that time, becoming a member of the Writers' Union was a life-changing event. Georgi had been working towards this accolade with what he himself called an 'almost hysterical persistence and obsessive ambition'.[3] We know this because Georgi later wrote about this period in his life in a series of essays published after his death.

On joining the Writers' Union, you received a red membership card and a strange-looking grey suit to wear at official functions. And, more important than any of that, you were richer than before, and you could write with the confidence that comes from knowing that almost anything you produced was going to be either published or performed. The tricky thing was being elected to the union in the first place. Membership of the Writers' Union was not decided purely on literary merit or commercial success. It was also, as Georgi put it, a test of 'whether a given literary work served or could serve the current needs of Party propaganda'.[4] These criteria also applied to the author behind it. In other words, to become a member of the Writers' Union, you had to find a way to be seen by the ruling Communist Party as someone who could be trusted and who was ideologically sound, while at the same time being recognised by your fellow authors as a writer with integrity and wit, and one who might have buried in their work some fine layer of subversion. This was the paradox facing Bulgarian writers like Georgi and his friend Christo. They wanted to be asked to join the Writers' Union, but they did not want to be seen by their peers as mouthpieces for the communist regime.

Georgi had grown up about a half-hour drive away from the Journalist's Club, in a small house in Knyazhevo, a suburb of Sofia. He was the eldest of three and as a child was known for being an avid reader. He was ten years old when the Second World War broke out, which, in most people's lives, would be a seminal and traumatic moment in their childhood, the point at which everything changed. But for Georgi, the rupture in his early years came shortly after the war, when the Bulgarian monarchy was abolished and in its place came a communist republic. Georgi was seventeen at the time.

The new regime generated a lot of its vitality and momentum by creating an atmosphere of permanent crisis. 'Enemies of the people' were, the government insisted, trying to steal the socialist revolution. Anyone who had been part of the former government or had been given a position of authority was automatically singled out as a potential subversive. The same was true of their children.

Georgi Markov's father, Ivan, had been an army officer and in the eyes of the country's new rulers that made both father and son individuals who might not be loyal to the new regime. Aged twenty-one, Georgi was thrown into jail. In the jargon of the day, he had been imprisoned for 'political reasons' — code for having a parent who might have been connected in some way to the monarchy. During his time in prison, Georgi reached a conclusion about the Bulgarian government that stayed with him for the rest of his life. He decided that there was never going to be a popular uprising in Bulgaria. Instead, he wrote, 'Bolshevism will collapse under its own weight, from its vices, crimes and lies.' He was confident of that. 'But we'll have to wait a long time.'[5]

Sitting his jail cell, Georgi realised that if he was going to make something of himself in this new Bulgaria, then he needed to find a way beyond his past and the fact of who his father had been. Others from a similar background might have accepted their diminished status in this new society or left. But Georgi decided to stay and to do whatever it might take to flourish.

This was not the only thing spurring him on. Several years earlier, Georgi had caught tuberculosis, and spent the next decade of his life in and out of hospital. His poor health forced him to give up on his dream of becoming an engineer, and he spent a lot of time in bed, surrounded by disease and death. The experience of making friends in hospital who died at a young age changed something deep inside him. Having come so close to death, and surviving, gave him an almost manic urgency to make the most of his life, and to succeed.

Georgi began by writing articles for a satirical newspaper – but never being *too* satirical and always sidestepping controversy. He knew that different rules applied to him because of his father's military background. He still had to convince the Party that he was on their side. Next came a collection of short stories, which did well and again contained nothing that could land him in trouble. He followed up with *The Victors of Ajax*, a science fiction novel for children, and after that came *Between Night and Day*, another set of short stories.

Georgi's literary breakthrough came in 1962, ten years after he had started out as a writer, with the publication of *Men*, his second novel. This innovative work was awarded the country's most prestigious literary prize, which, for almost anyone else, would guarantee a place in the Writers' Union. But Georgi's situation was different, as he well knew.

In the years since he had ended up in jail, Georgi had found a way to get along in Bulgarian society without breaking any of the unwritten rules. 'We read newspapers without really reading,' Georgi said of those years, 'because we did not believe a word in them, and we learned the trick of talking to one another while saying nothing. Indeed, we took such pains to hide our own personal truth from others that sometimes we hid it even from ourselves.'[6] He experienced the same thing that so many artists living in a dictatorship will endure: a feeling of internal exile. A part of him was on show and was always ready to sing for his political supper. But the rest of him, his more critical self, was hundreds of miles away and had long ago left all this behind.

Back in the Journalist's Club, it's getting late. But Georgi and his friend Christo are not going home until they find out what's happened at the nearby Writers' Union. As the night wears on, they start to make fun of themselves for how tense they have become.

Georgi asks his friend if being elected to the Writers' Union will change his life.

'Well,' Christo says, 'the militia won't be able to arrest me after drunken brawls.'[7]

Both men tell each other it's absurd that they care so much about this, but they carry on in a state of nervy, drawn-out tension until shortly before midnight when an official from the Writers' Union walks into the restaurant. He looks around, catches sight of them and comes over to their table. He then lets them know what has happened.

Christo has been admitted to the Writers' Union, and so has Georgi, who has been elected as a full member.

'I nearly went out of my mind with joy,' Georgi wrote. 'Previously – and subsequently – I hated titles, laureates and awards because I believed that they were part of the corruption of Bulgarian art, but during that memorable night I was a victim of the general madness.' These two new members of the Writers' Union 'wandered all night through the streets of Sofia and it seemed to us that the world was ours'.[8]

In one sense, it was. Georgi had been catapulted into Sofia's high society. He was now part of what was known as the 'red aristocracy'.[9] He and his wife would start to enjoy privileges that were denied to most ordinary Bulgarians. He soon had a sinecure as an editor at a state-run publishing house, which guaranteed him a much larger salary, and he began to write in the knowledge that getting published was going to be easy.

Soon, Georgi could be seen driving around Sofia in the ultimate status symbol – a new BMW. Owning one of these was a huge perk. Georgi would invite friends of his over and take them out for a ride in the car; they would spend hours cruising around the ring road that surrounds Sofia, like an aeroplane locked in a holding pattern.

Georgi also had access for the first time to individuals at the top of Bulgaria's brutal communist regime. He was soon collaborating with a group run by a senior intelligence officer and was given permission to read secret files in the name of research.

But the higher you climbed in a society like this, the further you had to fall. The best way for anyone like Georgi to protect themselves and their family was, he explained, 'to become someone's protégé: everybody tried to take refuge under the wing of a powerful person whom he could serve.'[10] There were hundreds of 'little Stalins' in Bulgaria: senior party figures who would dispense favours and privileges to those who might repay them with loyalty and deference. But out of all the communist officials in Bulgaria there was one who outranked every other, and from whom all power in the nation seemed to flow. The man every Bulgarian writer wanted to have as an ally was the absolute ruler of Bulgaria, Todor Zhivkov, the mysterious and contradictory figure often referred to within the country as 'Number One'.

Two years after Georgi's election to the Writers' Union, he was invited to spend the day with Number One. He had been chosen, along with a handful of other writers and artists, to accompany Zhivkov on a climb of Mount Midzhur, one of the highest peaks in the country.

This was how Todor Zhivkov worked. Rather than terrify the country's intelligentsia, his strategy was to win them over. He showered the ones he liked, and thought might be loyal to him, with attention, praise and money.

The day began early. Georgi was picked up by a black Chaika, the distinctive limousine favoured by the country's Politburo. He had imagined, as he stepped into the vehicle and took the only seat left, that this would take him to a presidential palace where he would meet the country's ruler. Instead, as he looked around him, he saw that he was sitting directly opposite Bulgaria's terrifying dictator, Todor Zhivkov.

Georgi was fascinated. 'When one meets someone face to face whom one has seen before in a photograph, or on the screen, or at a distance, one almost always discovers some physical difference. At close quarters, Zhivkov's face appeared to me more symmetrical and even somehow more spiritual. At any rate, it was a very mobile face with an attentive self-confident air that I did not find disturbing. His eyes gave the impression of quiet energy and keen observation.'[11] Georgi also found, on the drive out to Mount Midzhur, that Zhivkov had it in him to be a surprisingly good listener. He noticed as well that you could rarely tell what he was thinking, which, for Georgi, had the effect of making him want to talk more. He was interested, too, by this man's lack of pomposity. Zhivkov could be well-mannered and spontaneous. From what Georgi saw in that first drive, this was someone who could laugh at himself, had an excellent memory and seemed to possess a natural intelligence.

After several hours in the limousine, this band of intellectuals, security guards and one Eastern bloc dictator reached the lower slopes of Mount Midzhur. Georgi had never been here before; the same was true for most Bulgarians. The entire area had been turned into a security zone due to its proximity to the border. This gave it the feel of a private wilderness that had been set aside for the amusement of Zhivkov and his guests.

Georgi began to walk with everyone else through a young beech wood. The air was damp from the recent rain. With no path to follow, Zhivkov strode ahead and everyone followed in his wake.

'We have quite a way to go!' he shouted over his shoulder, carrying on at an impressive pace.[12]

They climbed through the woods for about an hour, after which the trail moved through sloping grassland. The higher they went, the more spectacular the views became. In the distance, they could hear the sound of bells on sheep and goats, and, as the trek continued, with hikers moving at different speeds, gaps began to appear between members of the party. After several hours of walking, Georgi Markov found himself alone at the head of the group with the country's leader.

To begin with, the two men walked together in silence, before the most feared man in Bulgaria turned to Georgi and asked him what he felt was missing from Bulgarian literature.

'Passion!' Georgi replied, without really thinking about it. What he meant, he explained, was that most Bulgarian writers were much too worried about the need to please Party officials. Zhivkov was taken aback. But he listened to what Georgi said and then went quiet. Zhivkov remained a few steps ahead and seemed preoccupied. They climbed further and were soon making their way along a slender mountain path until the two men found their way blocked by a large puddle that was several metres wide.

They looked at each other.

'We'll have to jump!' Zhivkov said.

Georgi went first. He took a run at it and made it across safely. Zhivkov then jogged up to the puddle and leapt as far as he could. But he stumbled just as he took off and fell on his hands and knees in the muddy puddle.

'Suddenly he stood up,' Georgi remembered, 'looked at me, smiled and said in a very peculiar voice: "Well, you've probably never seen a *muddy* First Party Secretary before."'[13]

Georgi could not help but feel in that moment a great tug of sympathy for the mud-splattered dictator. 'Maybe I was exaggerating, but at that precise moment I felt that, for the first time, I was making real contact with him'.

Georgi would make other, more caustic observations about Zhivkov in the weeks after their trek, but in that moment, he was filled with nothing but positive impressions of the country's ruler, his new friend. He went home after this first meeting feeling 'elated'.[14] Zhivkov, it seems, felt much the same. Both men believed that they were at the start of a promising new friendship.

14

TODOROV

Bulgaria, 1995

After breakfast in our hotel, we set out to find Kalin Todorov, the former journalist who had written an acclaimed book about the death of Georgi Markov. Franco was at the wheel, and was being given directions by our translator, Viktoria, who had a map spread out over her lap. But the thing about Franco in a situation like this was that he would often be selective about which directions to follow. Viktoria would tell Franco quietly that he was taking us in the wrong direction or that he had missed a turning. I would repeat what she had said, sometimes in a less forgiving voice. Rikke would watch in silence.

Franco was mostly oblivious. Sometimes he followed our directions, other times he did not. He didn't seem to care. It was as if he had his own sense of where Todorov's house should be, which was more important than where it actually was. Making the job of finding Todorov's house even harder, many of the streets in Sofia had been renamed during the six years since the collapse of the communist regime. The signs on most of the roads which had once been named after either Lenin, Todor Zhivkov or the country's first socialist dictator, Georgi Dimitrov, had since been changed. But the signs were hard to find and the people we asked for directions did not always know which one was now in use. Then there were streets where the new name had not been accepted by the local population because they had a lingering affection for the former regime, leaving them caught in a nominal no-man's-land where nobody could decide what to call the road – which only added to our confusion.

We spent the next hour cutting back on ourselves, driving round in circles and occasionally shouting at each other, until, at last, we reached what we believed to be Todorov's house. The four of us clambered out of Franco's car. We were at the very edge of Sofia now. It was a long way from the tree-lined avenues of the city centre or the polished marble of the Sheraton lobby. The air smelled of mud and piss. Everywhere I looked were abandoned houses, gardens that had been overtaken by a wilderness of weeds, and temporary shelters fashioned out of corrugated iron. There were smudges of snow on the ground and, close to where we had parked, I saw three spent bullet casings on the ground.

I had never seen poverty like this. The contrast to what I was used to in Denmark was intense and so was my disappointment. When the Berlin Wall came down in 1989, I remember feeling both joy and a small regret at knowing that I would never see life behind the Iron Curtain for myself. This was my first journey into the 'other' Europe and I had been half expecting to find evidence of what had once been a socialist wonderland, in spite of everything I had been told in school. But what I could see now looked more like a post-apocalyptic wasteland.

Franco went up to the door of Kalin Todorov's house and we were soon being welcomed in. He had dressed up for our visit and was looking smart in a reddish turtleneck and a jacket. He had a tanned, clean-shaven face and oil-black hair that he'd brushed back over his scalp. He also had company that day. All the time we were there, three burly men hovered in the background. Todorov never introduced us to them and they rarely spoke, but they watched us carefully. I couldn't help but notice that two of them had handguns half-hidden under their clothes and that there was a weapon on the table by the door.

Franco had seen this as well and seemed a bit shaken.

'I had heard Todorov was less of a journalist these days,' Franco whispered to me, 'but I didn't know he had become a gangster!'

Franco and I chatted to Todorov while Rikke set up her camera for the interview. Our subject had a lot of questions. He wanted to know exactly what we were doing and was almost comically suspicious. He also had an accusatorial way of staring at each of us between questions, as if he was searching for something in our faces, some tell that would reveal an ulterior motive. Soon Rikke had everything ready, which was harder than I had realised because she had never done anything like this and not all of the equipment that Franco had lent her worked.

'Shall we begin?' Todorov asked.

'OK,' I started, looking down at my notes. 'Let's go.'

'Yes, let's go,' Franco said.

'Right,' I said, looking over at Franco. 'How about I start by asking my questions?'

'Yes,' Todorov joined in. 'Just one interviewer.'

We both looked at Franco.

'Fine,' Franco said and moved angrily to a chair at the back of the room.

'So,' I started, 'in your book, Kalin, you said that there was one detail everyone missed about Georgi Markov. We all know that he was a famous writer in Bulgaria and that he turned against Zhivkov after he left. But you have also said that while he was living here, Markov was working for Bulgarian intelligence.'

'Yes. Because he was.'

'Nobody else has said that.'

'That's because the other people who write about this are not from Bulgaria,' Todorov continued, in a deep drawl. 'What you need to understand is this. Todor Zhivkov was a very intelligent man. He was like a fox. He knew that in a country like this, you had to buy the intelligentsia. So, he paid them very well, and Georgi Markov was one of those he liked. Markov had a BMW! Only the people at the very top of society with special connections had one of these.'

Todorov went further. With Viktoria helping out when he could not find the right word, he told us that Georgi's BMW was the first one to be seen in Bulgaria, and that these cars could only be purchased by individuals connected to the Bulgarian security service. The way Todorov saw it, this BMW was basically proof that Georgi had been a spy. Todorov also explained the significance of his having a passport valid for travel all over the world. Again, this was not just unusual, it was a rare privilege reserved for those with deep connections to the machinery of state intelligence.

When Todorov interviewed a senior figure in the Bulgarian military, several years after the collapse of the communist regime, he was told that Georgi Markov had been recruited by Bulgarian intelligence in the late 1950s, shortly before he was elected to the Writers' Union, and that his task had been to report on fellow writers. The luxuries he enjoyed were a reward, Todorov was told, for the information he provided.

For Todorov, that was just the start of it. He was also convinced, amazingly, that Georgi Markov had been secretly working for MI5. Several years earlier, Todorov had spoken to a Bulgarian official called General Vlado Todorov (no relation).[1] This man claimed to have seen Georgi's personal file in the Bulgarian state archives. According to him, Georgi was a Bulgarian agent who had been sent to Britain. He had been given various jobs in London and he carried these out satisfactorily at first. But then he was turned by the British and started to work for MI5. Once the Bulgarians found out, they decided to have him killed.

This angle, if true, obviously cast Georgi's murder in a different light. It was less a case of 'paranoid dictator silences a distant critic' and more one of Bulgarian intelligence punishing one of its own after they had committed the ultimate act of betrayal. One Bulgarian agent – Gullino – might have been sent to kill another – Markov.

But this idea rested on the recollection of just one man, and I wasn't sure what to make of it.

Several hours after it had begun, Todorov signalled that it was time to end the interview. I was exhausted and hungry, and had lost track of time. Rikke packed up her camera equipment and the four of us left Todorov's house. The handgun we had passed on the way in was still sitting on the hall table.

Could Todorov be right? We had no way to prove it. For what it was worth, Todorov himself was adamant. He believed what he had been told emphatically. Although we did not have the evidence ourselves, it seemed at least possible that Georgi Markov was at one stage closer to the regime of Todor Zhivkov than he later chose to admit. On the way back to our hotel, I couldn't help but think of the fascinating account that Georgi had written of a meal he had with Zhivkov, just as their relationship had begun to sour.

15

DISSENT

Bulgaria, November 1968

On a miserable, wet evening, Georgi Markov went to see Todor Zhivkov once more – as he later recalled in an essay published after his death. It had been four years since their first encounter, and that night Georgi was due to have dinner in the Palace of Bistritsa, in the Rila Mountains, one of Zhivkov's country residences, several hours outside Sofia. But Georgi did not want to go and had spent most of the day thinking about ways to get out of it. One option was to stay at home and pretend he had simply forgotten about the dinner. But, as one of his friends warned him, this sounded improbable and would be seen by Zhivkov as a snub. He would be better off going.

Zhivkov was wearing relaxed holiday clothes as he came out of the palace to greet Georgi. Bulgaria's longest-serving dictator seemed especially pleased to see his guest, someone he had come to think of as a friend. He asked Georgi, with a smile, if he had ever slept in the bed of a king. No, Georgi replied – still unhappy about being there – he had not. Zhivkov beckoned to an aide and told him to have Georgi's things taken to the bedroom in which King Ferdinand of Bulgaria had once slept.

This was intended to lift Georgi's spirits. It did nothing of the sort. 'I could not help but reflecting how modestly the Bulgarian monarchs had lived compared with the "people's representatives" who succeeded them,' Georgi thought to himself, while looking around his bedroom for the night. 'I was reminded of the famous remark of a Politburo member about the former monarchy: "If only they had left us real palaces!"'[1]

Once he had unpacked, Georgi went downstairs to the hall where the meal was to take place. It was a tall-ceilinged space decorated with deer antlers. He looked at the seating plan and saw that he had been put next to Zhivkov.

In the years since their first meeting, Georgi had become close to the country's leader. He had even got to know members of Zhivkov's family, including Ludmilla, his daughter, who was now minister of culture. Georgi was often seen at dinners and banquets like this one and to anyone watching his rise in Bulgarian society, it looked as if he was a trusted part of the regime. But behind closed doors, his relationship with Todor Zhivkov had begun to curdle.

By this point in his career, Georgi Markov had become a superstar in the Bulgarian literary scene. Ordinary people would queue up to buy his latest book. His language had become more dynamic than ever and he was not afraid of taking creative risks. Opening one of his books was exciting because you didn't know where he was going to take you. His writing was fluid and bold, never predictable, always playful. But with that came the possibility of it being read in many different ways.

Georgi had begun to test the limits of what he could say in his work, and he was not alone in this. Other Bulgarian authors had become more daring. By the start of 1968, the arts in Bulgaria had begun to open up. An intoxicating new atmosphere was taking hold, one in which everyone felt that they had more intellectual freedom than before.

But later that year, after Soviet-led forces poured into Czechoslovakia to put down the Prague Spring, this stopped. A new artistic clampdown was underway and Georgi's most recent play, *Let's Go Under the Rainbow*, experienced the full force of it. The director, lead actors and even the set designer were told that the regime had decided they would never perform in the capital again.

Georgi was understandably upset. He felt this was an over-reaction and sent a copy of the offending script to perhaps the only man in Bulgaria who could reverse this decision. His hope was that Todor Zhivkov would take one look at the play and agree that it did not represent an attack on the regime. Rather than send Georgi a reply, Zhivkov invited him to this dinner in the Rila Mountains.

That evening, when Georgi sat down at the dinner table next to Zhivkov, he could see around him some twenty other guests — ageing generals, young poets, writers — and noticed that everyone was keeping half an eye on Zhivkov and what he was doing. When an aide came up to 'Number One' and began to whisper something in his ear, the rest of the table fell quiet.

Georgi was finding the conversation heavy-going until he remembered something he had been told earlier that day. 'Say something about shooting or tell a hunting story,' a friend of his had said, 'you'll see that after that they'll talk about hunting for the whole evening and forget you.'[2]

That's what Georgi did. It worked. Zhivkov launched into his favourite hunting tales and others cheerfully followed with their own accounts of shooting animals. 'I listened to amusing stories about the hunting exploits of various members of the Politburo,' Georgi remembered, 'about the passionate sportsmanship of a minister who had missed an important meeting, about an enraged boar who had been killed at the very last second, about the shooting of a man-eating bear and the tracking of an elusive stag.'[3]

Georgi was alive to the hypocrisy here. In schools all over the country, children were taught that hunting had been the decadent pastime of the despised feudal aristocracy, now ousted by the more egalitarian Communist Party. But hunting had since become the go-to hobby for members of the country's Politburo, a contradiction that nobody dared to point out in public.

Listening to Todor Zhivkov that night, Georgi felt that either he had misjudged this man at their first meeting or 'Number One' had changed completely. The new Zhivkov was hopelessly self-important, he wrote, and had 'a complete lack of understanding of complex phenomena and the impudence of a not very intelligent minor dictator'.[4] 'He had not read many books and his education was rather limited; even his vocabulary frequently showed the uneasy combination of simple peasant language and pompous phrases.'[5] 'In my opinion no one else in Bulgaria has had a more disastrous and destructive influence on literature and the arts.'[6]

Georgi also loathed the sight of Zhivkov trying to encourage his own hero-worship, because he knew that while Zhivkov longed to be loved, he simply was not; he had become a figure of ridicule. 'The whole country was inundated with jokes about Todor Zhivkov,' Georgi later said. 'He was invariably portrayed as common, uncultured and limited.'[7]

After several hours of hunting stories, a Party official rose to give a speech in which he tore into a well-known poet who had recently become critical of the regime. He slammed him as arrogant and ungrateful. Zhivkov interrupted to say that this poet 'should have been shot long ago!'[8]

'The very word "shot" sent shivers down my spine,' Georgi later wrote.[9] At last, he understood what was going on. There was nothing spontaneous about this speech. The whole thing had been worked out beforehand. It was a coded warning, a performance, and it was aimed at him. Georgi had received similar threats in the past, but none as strong as this.

Next, an accordionist was summoned who began to sing a medley of songs in praise of Todor Zhivkov and his efforts to defeat

Fascism. It was, Georgi wrote, 'musical torture'. But what surprised him, and left him more dispirited than ever, was how much pleasure Zhivkov took in this kind of sycophancy.

Several days later, Georgi went to see Zhivkov and asked if the director of his most recent play could be allowed to work again in Sofia. 'Number One' was in a forgiving mood and agreed to the request. He then showed Georgi a piece of paper which had recently come into his possession. It was a drawing which had been found in the house of a leading Bulgarian writer, someone who had once been close to Zhivkov. The picture seemed to compare the country's leader to a pig.

'That's what I am for you!' Zhivkov said to Georgi, lowering himself into his chair with a crumpled look on his face.[10] By 'you', he meant the whole literary establishment. Georgi had never seen him so upset. He had the expression of a man who had been betrayed by a close friend. Criticism from overseas or from those he did not know had little effect on him, but attacks from those he knew or had once been close to seemed to land like a savage blow.

Georgi's next play, *Assassination in a Dead End*, was set in a totalitarian police state not at all dissimilar to Bulgaria and was centred on the story of two people who plan to kill a dictator. His next play, *I Was Him*, openly made fun of the communist system. At its premiere, in June 1969, the theatre was filled with the sound of out-of-control laughter. During the interval, a furious colonel from the state security service went up to Georgi and told him, as Georgi must have thought he might, that this new play was unacceptable and could not be performed again without major revisions to the text.

Georgi could have done what he always did, which was to attend a meeting the next day in which a representative of the regime would go through everything that needed to be cut. He would then make the changes and present for approval a politically bowdler-ised version of his original script. Instead, he turned his back on the colonel and stormed out of the theatre. His blood was up. He might be in trouble now and he knew it. But a part of him no longer cared. In that moment, he had had enough.

When he told a friend about what had happened, the advice he received was clear: Georgi needed to leave the country for a short time. He knew that his friend was right, and resolved to go away for a few weeks.

'My mother and father saw me to my car,' Georgi wrote. 'I told them that I would see them in a couple of weeks' time. And I left. I got to the ring road. There had just been a spring thunderstorm and when the clouds cleared, the sky over Vitosha and its entire untamed verdure glistened and shone under the sun.' He carried on towards the border. He was leaving behind his home, his wife, and everything he had ever known. 'The car drove along the drying asphalt and everything around me looked so strange and indescribably beautiful. Pitilessly beautiful. As though nature had decided to show me the priceless riches of a land which I was doomed to lose.'[11]

Soon, Georgi was out of the capital, never to return. His thoughts moved to the curiously intense relationship he had had with its leader, and an idea began to form in his mind. One day, he would tell the world the truth about 'Number One'. He wanted to expose him for what he really was. But that could wait.

Georgi Markov presumably had no trouble as he crossed the border, what with his passport that allowed him the privilege of international travel. Just over a year later, at a similar crossing not far from this one, a young Italian called Francesco Gullino would be given significantly more trouble by the Bulgarian authorities.

16

BIG BROTHER

Bulgaria, 1995

The mood in the car as we drove back to the hotel after our interview with Todorov was an excited one. It felt as though we were starting to get somewhere. Franco, more than anyone else, was elated. At times like these I could forget that he was twice my age. I was amazed by his stamina. He was gripped by the idea that Georgi Markov might have secretly been a Bulgarian agent. We had read this in Todorov's book, but it felt more real now that the author had explained it to us. Was he right? I still wasn't sure.

It was entirely possible that a writer in Georgi's position, a member of the 'red aristocracy', would have been asked to supply information about other writers or at least to give his opinion of them. Perhaps this information was turned into intelligence. If he knew that this was happening, did that make him a spy? Was the BMW he had been seen driving really evidence that he had been a professional intelligence agent?

Not exactly. Owning a BMW might have *suggested* a link to the country's intelligence agency but was not proof of it. The idea that Georgi had been a fully-fledged agent sounded like a story that could have been put about in the years after his death as those in the Bulgarian intelligentsia tried to make sense of his murder. If his death could be explained by his having been an agent, then perhaps things were not as bad as they seemed. The thing that would have scared them more than anything else, as it scares most of us, was the idea of being killed for a reason that nobody can explain. If he had been a spy, then the whole episode made sense, and could be written off as spy business.

The strangest part of our interview with Todorov, however, came towards the end, but Franco had not seen it. I had moved the conversation onto the subject of Todor Zhivkov and asked Todorov a few questions about the former dictator.

Then Todorov interrupted me.

'You don't *know* Zhivkov,' he said to me. It was a curious form of words. He seemed to be suggesting that he, by contrast, did know him. 'He is a very smart, interesting and brutal man,' Todorov went on. 'Today, he just looks like an old man. Zhivkov would have known if Bulgarian intelligence had killed Markov. The Communist Party controlled intelligence.'

'How do you *know* Zhivkov?' I asked. 'Have you met him?'

Todorov thought for a moment before replying. 'Yes. I have met him.'

From the way he said this, it sounded as if he had nothing more that he wanted to say on the subject.

'Do you think it would be possible for us to meet him?' I asked, a little timidly. 'On this trip?'

Even as I said the words, I realized that this was a waste of a question.

Todorov shook his head.

'Zhivkov is under house arrest,' he said. 'He speaks to nobody apart from his family.'

Soon after that, we ended the interview and began to pack up our things. While this was going on, I saw Todorov take out a page from his notebook and write something onto it. He then folded the paper in half. While Franco was busy with something else, Todorov came over and handed me the paper.

'You're OK,' he said quietly. 'But him,' he nodded at Franco, then chatting to Rikke, 'he's a spy.'

I was too tired to take this seriously or to look at the paper, and shoved it into my pocket without thinking anything more about it. But as we neared the hotel, I looked at the note to see what it said. Todorov had written down something in Bulgarian, so I was staring uselessly at several lines of Cyrillic.

I thought about mentioning the piece of paper to Franco and the others in the car but decided to wait until we had got back to the hotel and I'd had a chance to have it translated by a member of staff.

Franco eventually found the hotel and once we had dropped our things in our rooms, we went out for our dinner. We ended up in the restaurant of another hotel, an enormous space that could have seated at least a thousand people. We were the only customers. They served the best goulash I have ever tasted. Long after we had finished eating, we were still talking about the interview.

'Todorov has opened up the whole case,' Franco began enthusiastically. 'Markov was working for the Bulgarians but then when he was in London he became a double agent. He agreed to work for the British. It's all starting to make more sense.'

'Although, Franco, that's not what he actually said.'

'It is.'

'No, Todorov said they had no proof that he was taken on by MI5, only that *one* person thinks he was.'

'Well, I do too.'

This was not the first time we had disagreed like this. Franco often failed to hear doubt or equivocation in somebody's voice, and found it easy to confuse speculation with fact. I remember thinking to myself when Todorov suggested that Markov had been working for MI5 that this sounded unlikely, along with the idea that he had been sent to London by the Bulgarians with instructions to infiltrate British society.

One problem was that he did not go straight to London from Sofia. Instead, he had spent almost a year living elsewhere in Europe before he travelled to Britain. It was difficult to imagine him spending so long crossing Europe if he really had been told by Bulgarian intelligence to make his way to London.

Other parts of his story were harder to interpret. Several months after he arrived in Britain, Georgi applied for political asylum. He described himself to the Home Office in London as a writer who had been denied the freedom to write about the communist regime in Bulgaria, and who had effectively been forced to leave the country. It's important to add that Georgi's departure from Bulgaria had not yet been denounced by the Party as a defection. Several months after he left Sofia, Georgi's Bulgarian passport was even extended for another year. This was presumably not something that would be done for a sworn enemy of the Bulgarian regime.

So, he did not appear to be a wanted man. But it was in Georgi's interests to portray himself to the Home Office as a literary freedom fighter, to be granted political asylum as such. The following year, he began to work as a freelancer for the Bulgarian section of the BBC World Service. This seemed to change everything for the Bulgarian regime, and from that moment onwards he was described by the Bulgarian regime as a 'non-returnee'.

The Bulgarian government's policy on 'non-returnees' was interesting. Rather than hunt them down, they looked for ways to lure them back. Deep within the Bulgarian state, a new file on Georgi was opened and he was given a codename. Others who had left Bulgaria and showed no sign of wanting to return were given pejorative monikers like 'Tarzan', 'Hyena' and 'Renegade'. Georgi was labelled *Skitnik*, Bulgarian for 'the Tramp' or 'the Wanderer', probably because he had spent most of his first year outside Bulgaria moving between different European cities. Perhaps this itinerant life was all part of his deep cover and perhaps he was still a Bulgarian agent – and this file and all the attempts to persuade him to come home were just a ruse. Much more likely, though, was that this was genuine, and Georgi Markov was simply a well-known writer who had left the country and decided to start a new life overseas.

'The Tramp' did well at the BBC World Service and was soon given a full-time position. Once he had settled in London, Georgi then started to moonlight for the Bulgarian section of a West German radio station called Deutsche Welle. He recorded for them a series of attacks on the Bulgarian regime. Again, not the type of activity you'd associate with a Bulgarian spy. Or had he been turned by this stage?

After Georgi criticized the regime on the radio, his parents were told that they could no longer leave the country. The police then went to what had been Georgi's house and destroyed his collection of books; they also went to the trouble of chopping up his writing desk. His wife, still in Bulgaria, was pressured into filing for divorce. Georgi was then tried in absentia by the Sofia City Court. One of the charges against him was that by working for the BBC he was guilty, under Article 108 of the Bulgarian Penal Code, of disseminating libelous propaganda on behalf of a foreign government. He was sentenced to more than six years in jail, fined 3,000 levs, and the belongings he had left behind in Bulgaria were confiscated by the state.

The BBC director-general, Charles Curran, complained to the Bulgarian ambassador when he found out about this. As far as he was aware, it was the first time that any government in the world had classed working for the BBC as a criminal act. In protest at what had happened, he refused to accept a forthcoming visit from a Bulgarian delegation.

Fast-forward several years and Georgi seemed to have reached a crossroads in his life. He had settled down in London. He was writing again – and writing well – and had recently fallen in love with a fellow author, Annabel Dilke. In 1975, they were married and the following year, they had a daughter, Sasha.

Georgi loved being a father and adored his daughter. He was safe. He was free. He had a young family. He could have turned away from the political situation in the country he had left behind and given himself over to the new life that had just begun. But he chose a different path. Georgi put himself to work on a series of new talks for the US-backed Radio Free Europe. This station had been set up in the 1950s to broadcast anti-Soviet material into Eastern bloc countries such as Bulgaria. The American government had poured millions of dollars into Radio Free Europe over the years, and in the early days there is little doubt that it had close ties to the CIA.

Another Bulgarian émigré who was also writing material for Radio Free Europe was Vladimir Kostov, the journalist who would have a ricin pellet injected into his back shortly before the attack on Georgi.

Working for a radio station with such close ties to American intelligence was a risk for Georgi. But more than his position there, it was the content of his broadcasts that really dialled up the danger. Starting in late 1977, Georgi delivered a series of eleven talks for Radio Free Europe. They were called, simply, 'My Meetings with Todor Zhivkov'. Very few exiles had come to know 'Number One' as well as he had, and none of them had his superb eye for characterisation. His talks were neither hysterical nor angry, and they contained light as well as dark, touching on Zhivkov's virtues as well as his vices. But they were ruthless and unsparing, and it was clear from the start that Georgi was going to hold nothing back. He called Zhivkov a snob, a minor dictator and a man with a feeble sense of humour. Worse, he said that he was forever being bullied by the Soviets and was unable to stand up to them.

By talking openly about Zhivkov and making fun of him, Georgi had smashed the greatest taboo in Bulgarian society. His talks were a sensation. 'Why do members of the Politburo miss meetings on a Thursday?' went the joke. 'To hear Georgi Markov on Radio Free Europe.'

Why did Georgi decide to give these talks? Kalin Todorov, the man who we had just interviewed in Sofia, was in no doubt that Georgi had been put up to them by someone working for British intelligence. According to Todorov, Georgi was under instructions from London to pump out propaganda against Todor Zhivkov and the Bulgarian regime. But if Markov really had been taken on as an agent working for MI5, or even MI6, this is about the last thing you could imagine him being encouraged to do. His case officer would be much more interested in protecting their asset. Asking him to make these broadcasts would only put his life at risk.

More likely, Georgi was experiencing a form of survivor's guilt and was unable to turn away from the hardships his fellow Bulgarians experienced while he was living in comfort on the other side of the Iron Curtain. These talks could even be seen as a sublimated form of penance for the privileged life he had once enjoyed in Sofia. Maybe he was driven on by the simple and noble desire that you find in the bravest journalists and whistleblowers to tell the truth and to shine a light on something that appears to be wrong, even if you know it will put your life in danger.

The four of us finished our meal in the deserted hotel restaurant and returned to the Sheraton. After agreeing to meet in the morning for breakfast, I told them that I had something to ask about at reception. I watched as the other three went up to their rooms. Once they were out of earshot, I felt around in my pocket for the crumpled piece of paper which Todorov had slipped into my hand before we left. I walked up to the main desk.

'Excuse me,' I said to the man at reception. 'Can you tell me what this says?'

I handed him the paper.

A strange look came over his face, one that was not like anything else I had seen since we arrived in Bulgaria. It was a mixture of fear and surprise, with a splash of confusion.

'This is the name of a Bulgarian person,' he began. 'And it gives directions for how to find this person's house.'

'OK. Which Bulgarian person?'

For a moment, it was as if he couldn't find a way to say the word which had begun to form in his mouth.

'Zhivkov,' he said at last. 'This paper has directions to the home of Todor Zhivkov.'

17

THE HUNTING RIFLE

My plan was to tell Franco about the piece of paper at breakfast and I was about to do that when he made an unexpected announcement. Maybe announcement is the wrong word, because that makes it sound like a statement directed at the whole group. What he had to say was not intended for Rikke and Viktoria, but for me.

'For the interviews today,' he began, his gaze fixed on the croissant before him, 'it's best that we go alone.'

'What do you mean?'

'I don't think we should bring too many people to these interviews.'

'So just one of us goes.'

'No, I think three.'

'OK,' I said, assuming he meant Rikke should stay behind. 'Just three.'

'I think you should stay in the hotel,' Franco said, aiming his voice at me, but not his gaze.

'Me?'

'Right.'

'But we need an interviewer *and* a back-up,' I tried, not yet ready to accept what Franco was saying. 'That's what we agreed.'

'The people we're seeing today are more sensitive,' he said, this time to his coffee cup. 'One is a former intelligence officer.'

But that didn't explain what was going on. The previous day, I had asked all the questions while Franco sat on the sidelines. I had unwittingly triggered the fear he so often had, that this story was about to be snatched away from him.

In that moment, however, sitting at the breakfast table, I hadn't worked this out. I felt a surge of anger and frustration, and a growing sense that I'd been duped. When Franco had called me, back in Copenhagen, and suggested that I come with him to Bulgaria, it sounded as if something had changed and that we were now equal partners in this enterprise. I flew out to Sofia thinking that we were two fellow detectives, brothers-in-arms, trying to solve the same case. At last, I thought, he had learned to trust me.

But no. Here he was, the Franco I thought I had left behind, desperately asserting his authority over me and doing everything he could to let me know that within our relationship, he was Number One.

Franco, Rikke, and Viktoria left the table quietly, and breakfast began to be cleared up around me. I wandered out to the hotel lobby. I had Zhivkov's address in my pocket but there was no point trying to find him myself. Without a translator, I was stuck. I sat in the lobby and watched the other guests walking past. I tried to imagine what had brought each of them here. Most looked like foreign businessmen who had come here to make a lot of money. What were we doing? Losing money. This whole trip was starting to feel like a long and drawn-out mistake – unless, I considered, I could find a way to interview Todor Zhivkov.

When I first met Franco, and began to research the Umbrella Murder, Zhivkov had been a remote part of the story, and not one I had thought about much. Yes, he had been consistently linked to this death. But there was no detail, no evidence, nothing to prove that he could have ordered this hit. Since then, however, new material had come to light.

In 1994, soon after I was first introduced to Franco, the former Russian intelligence officer Oleg Kalugin published a memoir in which he described the thirty-two years he had spent working for the KGB. In that time, Kalugin had seen it all. He had risen to the rank of general and been involved in hundreds of KGB operations. But only one of these, he claimed, had been a 'wet job', or assassination. That was the murder of Georgi Markov.

The story that Kalugin told went like this. Back in 1978, the KGB was contacted by the Bulgarian minister of the interior, Dimitar Stoyanov, who told them that his boss wanted someone dead. That someone was Georgi Markov. Stoyanov's boss at the time was Todor Zhivkov. Markov was then living in London and Bulgarian intelligence did not have the know-how to carry out an assassination in Britain. That was why they asked the KGB for help.

The KGB behaved towards Bulgarian intelligence like a much older brother. They looked out for their Bulgarian counterparts and saw them all as part of the same socialist family, but, at the same time, they were sometimes guilty of trying to keep the Bulgarians in a permanent state of dependency. They seemed to like knowing more than them and to enjoy being asked for help in situations like this. Kalugin remembered being summoned to a meeting of senior KGB officers in Moscow, where they began to discuss their response to this request from the Bulgarian minister of the interior.

It is telling that Kalugin had already heard of Georgi Markov. His friends in Bulgarian intelligence had described Georgi to him as 'a former close associate of Zhivkov's', and someone who had since become a 'nuisance'.[1]

'They want us to help them in the physical removal of Markov,' one of Kalugin's colleagues, Vladimir Kryuchkov, told the room, stressing that this request 'comes from President Zhivkov himself'.

'We sat there in silence for a few seconds,' Kalugin recalled. 'I will never forget the tidy euphemism Kryuchkov used for Markov's assassination — "physical removal", *fizicheskoye ustraneniye* in Russian. I felt a chill go down my spine, then thought to myself: "To hell with these Bulgarians. Let them do whatever they want to their political opponents. Why are they dragging us into this mess?"'[2]

The man who had called the meeting, Yuri Andropov, chairman of the KGB, couldn't work out what to do. He started to pace the room.

'I am against political assassinations,' Andropov muttered. 'I don't think it's the right way to deal with these problems. The time when this sort of thing could be done with impunity is past. We can't revert to the old ways.'[3]

Silence. Kalugin could hear the traffic beyond the window in Dzerzhinsky Square. This was a turning point. Georgi Markov's future, and maybe the history of Russian state-sponsored killings, had reached a moment of crisis. It was about to go down one of two very different paths. Either they would tell the Bulgarians that this was no longer acceptable, or they would do what they had done so many times before.

'It's Comrade Zhivkov's personal request,' Kryuchkov pushed back. 'If we deny him our assistance, Zhivkov may think that Comrade Stoyanov has fallen out of favour with us or maybe that his own reputation in the eyes of the Soviet people has been tarnished.' He went on, 'I repeat: this is a personal request from Zhivkov. We have to deal with the problem somehow.'[4]

'All right, all right,' Andropov said. 'But there is to be no direct participation on our part. Give the Bulgarians whatever they need, show them how to use it and send someone to Sofia to train their people. But that's all. No direct involvement.'[5]

The Russians got to work. First question: which KGB officer should be sent out to Sofia with the task of helping the Bulgarians put together a plan for killing Georgi Markov? Easy. There was only really one candidate for a job like this, and his name was Sergei Golubev. He knew more about 'wet jobs' than anyone else in the KGB, and probably the world. Golubev was an expert in assassination.

If anyone defected from the KGB, then Golubev and his team had the job of hunting them down. Golubev was told that Markov needed to be 'removed' in a way that could not be traced back to either the Soviet Union or Bulgaria. Nor did they want it to look like a murder. 'Even a despot like Zhivkov,' Kalugin wrote, 'didn't have the stomach to shoot someone in the head on a London street.'[6]

Golubev knew where to go first. On being given this job, he made an appointment to see a senior scientist at Laboratory 12, next to KGB headquarters. He told them that he needed a poison, and a means of delivering it, that would leave no trace and could be transported outside the country. The scientists talked him through various options.

Golubev flew to Sofia holding a briefcase that contained an array of toxic samples. He told his Bulgarian counterparts that there were three ways of getting the job done. The first was to murder Markov using a poisonous gel that had been developed inside Laboratory 12. It could be applied to any surface that Markov was likely to touch, such as the door of his car, or perhaps they could find a way to rub it onto his skin.

Another option was simpler and more old-fashioned – poison his food or slip something into his drink. Maybe both. As Golubev explained, the samples he had brought with him were unlikely to show up in an autopsy, partly because no one would be looking for them. In most parts of the world, those performing an autopsy will only test for obscure toxins if they have reason to believe that the deceased has been poisoned. It's hard to find something you're not looking for. Although Georgi's death would be sudden and unex-pected, Golubev's hope was that it would not be suspicious and nobody would think that he had been murdered.

If neither of these approaches worked, the third option – the riskiest and most technologically demanding – was to inject into Markov's flesh a miniature pellet containing ricin.

The Bulgarians discussed the various options. Was Zhivkov consulted at this point? Did his minions run through the different options and ask him if he had a preference? Kalugin did not know. All that he could say was that the KGB was told that the Bulgarians wanted to try the poison first.

Golubev had a fatal toxin couriered from Moscow to a Bulgarian agent operating undercover in West Germany. Georgi was often in Munich because this was where he recorded his broadcasts for Radio Free Europe (the ones in which he tore into Zhivkov). The Bulgarian plan was simple: add the poison to his drink while he was out in a restaurant or bar in Munich. The agent who received the poison was told to follow Georgi Markov around the city and wait for an opportunity to pour it into his drink.

But by this point in his life, Georgi had become extremely security conscious. He no longer ate out in restaurants or bars, and if going to a friend's house he would bring his own food and drink. He often changed his travel plans at the last minute and rarely told his friends where he was going. When travelling on the tube in London, he would wait for the train to come with his back against the wall, so that nobody could shove him onto the tracks. The Bulgarian agent in Germany could not find a way to poison him and was forced to give up. The first attempt on Georgi's life had failed.

The second was set to take place in Sardinia, where Georgi Markov was on holiday with his family. This time, Golubev, the KGB officer, supplied Bulgarian intelligence with a poisonous gel as well as poison. Originally, the job of murdering Georgi in Sardinia was given to 'Lubo', but after he refused it was passed on to another agent, whose identity remains a mystery. He thought about how to do it. He needed an excuse to smear some of the lethal gel onto Markov's flesh. Eventually, he came up with the idea of approaching Georgi on a crowded Sardinian beach, pretending to bump into him and, in the process, spilling the gel onto his skin. But when Georgi and his family arrived in Sardinia the weather was terrible and the beach was empty. There was no way to bump into him without it looking highly suspicious.

Plan B was to wait for Georgi to have a drink by himself in a hotel bar. The Bulgarian agent would then arrange for someone to make a call for Markov on the hotel telephone. The message would come through to the bar — *there's a call for you Mr Markov* — and Georgi would leave his drink unattended at the bar, giving the agent a chance to poison it.

But Georgi was wise to this. He had been warned by Lubo that there would be an attempt on his life in Sardinia. Rather than stay in a hotel, he had rented a private villa for his family. The second attempt on his life came to nothing.

This left the Bulgarians with only one option.

The ricin pellet.

Golubev flew to Sofia once more. This time, he brought with him a selection of tiny platinum pellets and, crucially, a device that could be used to fire them. He showed the Bulgarians how to operate it. They thanked him and asked him to stay in Sofia while they experimented with this new gadget.

The Bulgarians began by firing one of the ricin pellets into a horse. It died. But would the pellet work on a human? An unfortunate prisoner, who had recently been sentenced to death, was brought into a room in the Ministry of Interior and injected with one of the KGB's ricin pellets. According to Kalugin, who was not there, the pellet was fired using a gun disguised as an umbrella. 'The officer shot the poor prisoner with the umbrella and the fellow yelped as if stung by a bee. Apparently he was hysterical, realizing that his death sentence had just been carried out in a most unusual manner. But the poison wasn't released from the pellet and the prisoner remained in good health.'

Golubev returned to Moscow — furious, no doubt — and spoke to the scientists in Laboratory 12. The ricin pellet had not worked.

The scientists needed to sort this out. They got to work and soon had a new set of ricin pellets. Golubev returned to Sofia and handed them over to the Bulgarians, assuring them that the problem had been fixed. And that, according to Oleg Kalugin, was the end of the KGB's involvement in the attempt on Georgi Markov's life. He never found out who was chosen to carry out the attack or how the ricin pellets were transported to London.

The next time Stoyanov came to see Kalugin he presented him with a Browning hunting rifle. He did not say what the gift was for, but Kalugin felt that he did not need to. This was his way of thanking him for his help with the assassination in London.

Who had given the order for Georgi Markov's death? Kalugin was in no doubt. For him, the person ultimately responsible for his murder was Todor Zhivkov.

I looked again at the piece of paper that Todorov had given me with Zhivkov's address. I still wasn't sure what to do, and went for a walk around Sofia to clear my head. So many parts of the Umbrella Murder story could be traced back to where I was right now, to Sofia, and to the former dictator Todor Zhivkov. I thought about approaching Viktoria and breaking away from Franco to find Zhivkov, but that was unlikely to work because we needed a car and a camera. I had no choice. I would have to tell Franco about the piece of paper.

Later that day, Franco, Rikke and Viktoria returned to the hotel lobby, chatting about the interviews they had completed. One had been with a judge with insights into the Bulgarian intelligence service, and the internal strife in Bulgaria that had taken place after the fall of the wall. He felt that Georgi had remained loyal to the regime.

I walked straight over and told them that I had Zhivkov's address. Viktoria, our translator, was shocked. Until then, she had been the quiet one in the group. Suddenly, that changed. She thought it would be madness to drive to his house and try to arrange an interview. We must go about this in the proper way. We should write a letter to his address and wait for a formal response. We could not just turn up unannounced.

Franco felt otherwise. 'It's simple,' he said. 'We drive to his house.'

'OK,' Rikke said.

'When?' Viktoria asked.

'Now.'

So we piled into Franco's car and set out to find Number One.

18

ZHIVKOV

Todor Zhivkov had spent most of his life behind tall, fortified walls. During his thirty-five years as Bulgarian leader – a record among Eastern bloc dictators, for anyone who was keeping score, and Zhivkov certainly was – he could be found inside a palace, a government building or a military base, and always with armed guards near the entrance to keep undesirables out. His new home was similar – only this time, the men with weapons were there to keep him in.

Following the collapse of the communist regime in 1989, many Bulgarians wanted Zhivkov to answer for what he had done and his years of misrule – specifically, imprisoning and executing political opponents, denying citizens the right to a fair trial, stifling dissent, enforcing agricultural collectivisation, persecuting Bulgaria's Turkish minority and driving the country to the point of economic collapse. But almost none of these actions were specifically covered by Bulgarian law. There was no statute against being a brutal dictator. The prosecutors realised it would be easier to nail him for corruption, which is what they did.

Evidence was presented in court to show that Todor Zhivkov had pilfered vast sums of money on cars and entertainment, and that he built lavish homes for favoured officials and family members. Zhivkov's defence was, essentially, that this what every other head of state did. So if he was going to jail, then so should every other world leader, from the president of the United States to the queen of England.

The judge was not swayed. Zhivkov was found guilty and sentenced to seven years in jail. He was then allowed to serve his time under house arrest. All that anyone knew was that he was being held somewhere on the outskirts of the capital.

After half an hour of meandering through the suburbs of Sofia, with Franco stopping suddenly to wind down his window and ask for directions, or jerking the wheel to avoid a pothole, we arrived at the address I had for Zhivkov. It was a large building in a well-heeled suburb of Sofia, a few minutes' drive from the house in which Georgi Markov had spent his childhood. The house we were looking at was near the entrance to the Boyana complex, a gated compound filled with rolling lawns, rose bushes, and clusters of woodland, where most of the senior Communist Party officials had once lived. But Zhivkov was not allowed into this complex and was confined to the grounds of his villa.

We all stared at the gates to Zhivkov's villa, unsure what to do.

'Go on,' Franco said. 'Get out of the car and press the buzzer.'

'OK, OK,' I said, opening the car door. 'Viktoria, I need you to translate, though.'

Viktoria accompanied me up to the iron gate. I pressed the only button I could see and waited. Viktoria had not said a word since we arrived at the house and, as we waited for a response, I noticed that she had become unnaturally still. This was a very different experience for her. She had grown up in a world dominated by the presence of the man living behind that gate. The memories she had of her earliest years were decorated with portraits of him – on the sides of buildings, in offices, in her living room, in every school classroom that she ever attended. When she was allowed to watch television, his face was the one she was most likely to see. On the radio, his voice was everywhere. Viktoria had never met Todor Zhivkov but had come to know him so well that he felt like a revered member of her family.

Still no reply from the speaker. I began to think that nobody was at home when the gate began to open with a clanking sound. But before we could walk in, an angry-looking man stepped out. I recognized him at once. It was Vladimir Zhivkov, son of the country's deposed leader. He spoke in Bulgarian.

'He,' Viktoria translated, hesitantly, 'he wants to know what we are doing.'

'Tell him we would like to have an interview with his father.'

Viktoria thought for a bit before relaying this, which she did in a voice that was so quiet I struggled to hear what she was saying.

'He says that we can see him for $2,000.'

'No way,' Franco called out from behind me.

'Please tell him that we don't have that money,' I said.

Vladimir Zhivkov shrugged and walked away, and with a whirr, the gate began to close behind him.

I tried the buzzer again but no reply. I called over the wall and tried to persuade him to come back, but, again, nothing. I stood there for a while, trying to make sense of what had happened, before heading back to the car.

We had come so close. It was agonising to think that we had been just yards away from the man who might have ordered Georgi's murder, and that there was a chance he could have spoken to us. Franco was dejected. Viktoria was relieved. We were starting to reverse away from the complex when I noticed a movement ahead. The gate. It was opening again. Zhivkov's son had evidently changed his mind.

Franco did not wait for him to have second thoughts. Without any hesitation, he drove through the open gate into the grounds of Zhivkov's villa. Rikke got out her camera and began to film. We continued up the short drive and parked up next to the house.

Zhivkov's son came out of the house and walked up to the car. Once we had all got out, he said something to Viktoria. She looked to the ground, and then at me.

'He says that you and I can come in to see his father, but nobody else.'

'No Franco?'

'And no Rikke.'

Franco was furious. He told Viktoria that this was unacceptable. She passed this on but it had no effect. Vladimir Zhivkov had made up his mind. Viktoria and I were the only ones coming in. Franco and Rikke would have to stay in the car or else the interview was off. Franco eventually conceded defeat and stepped into the vehicle, slamming the door behind him. Viktoria and I followed Zhivkov's son up a small set of steps into the villa.

I had imagined that we would be shown into some kind of visitors' room, where we would wait as the great man readied himself for the interview. Instead, Zhivkov junior took us straight to the kitchen and pointed to an old man in thick reading glasses. He was sitting at a table, seemingly absorbed by the newspaper in front of him, but he looked up as we walked in.

It was Zhivkov. The man I had read about and seen so many times over the last few years — the unrepentant authoritarian and consummate totalitarian, a man once described as the dictator's dictator — and he was now giving us both a searching look. He was a shrivelled version of what I had expected to find. The topography of his face was dominated by deep wrinkles and his ears protruded from his head like gnarly branches. Here was a man who had clung on to power for decades. In some ways, I think I wanted to find him terrifying or repulsive. But instead, there was something utterly hopeless about the person in front of me. I understood something

Commuters on Waterloo Bridge in 1975 — the location, just three years later, of the attack on Georgi Markov.

The charismatic Georgi Markov.

The small pellet that killed Markov, found in his leg during the autopsy.

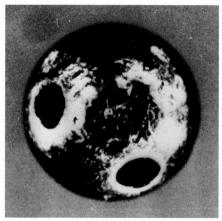

Bent Staalhøj and Franco Invernizzi at work, Bent filming while Franco directs. Together, they owned the company DokFilm.

Franco as I remember him: alive and interested.

Francesco Gullino photographed in Bulgaria with his car, in connection with the arrest that would completely change his life.

A very young Gullino (*left*), detained by the Bulgarian police. He escaped a prison sentence by agreeing to become a spy.

Gullino's house in Nærum on Egebækvej, north of Copenhagen. Eventually, he stopped wanting to live there alone and moved into Franco's house for a period.

Agent Piccadilly's attic room in Franco's house.

One of Scotland Yard's many folders with documents and summaries of the investigation into Markov's death. Despite many investigators taking on the case, Gullino was never charged or arrested for the murder.

At the beginning of the 1970s, Gullino worked for the company Mondial, based in Italy and Turkey. Mario Pagani was one of his aliases.

Gullino left behind calendars and notebooks in Denmark which tell of a busy working life and countless journeys. Around the time of the murder in September 1978, his calendar is empty for several months.

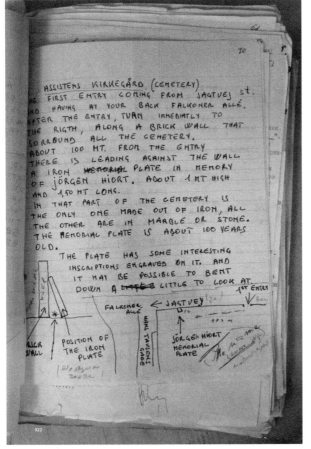

Agent Piccadilly made precise drawings of the places in Copenhagen that he used for signal posts and dead drops.

Gullino loved dogs and had several throughout his life.

A passport photograph of Gullino, alias Mario Pagani, alias Agent Piccadilly — and many other aliases.

Gullino arriving in Denmark from Hamburg in 1994 at Copenhagen Central Station. He travelled freely in and out of Denmark his whole life, even after the Danish state knew he was a spy.

Brandishing an umbrella, Gullino looks triumphant in this photograph from 2017. The picture helped us pinpoint his location.

Gullino in Wels, Austria, 2021. 'I'm just an old man waiting to die,' he said.

that an American scholar had written about Zhivkov mány years ago, when he had said that 'in a sense his greatest asset was precisely his mediocrity.'[1] He was not a monster, but he had been blinded by his desire to cling on to power.

Zhivkov's son indicated that this was where we could conduct our interview. But he would not allow us to film him, and no audio recording either. All we were able to do was ask questions and take notes. He made coffee for us and then left us alone with Number One.

Even though Todor Zhivkov could speak English – I knew this because I had seen footage of him doing so – he would only speak to us in Bulgarian. He began to talk to Viktoria in an angry, guttural voice. Viktoria fumbled with her papers and made notes. I sensed that if she had been asked to translate the words of almost anyone else in the world, no matter how powerful or disagreeable, she would have been fine. But being in the presence of Zhivkov was having a Pavlovian effect on her. She stared at the ground, before saying to me in a quiet voice.

'He is not happy,' she began. 'He says, "I need $2,000 now. My pension is pitiful and I need the money to travel and meet people. I'm lonely. I'll die of loneliness soon."'

I asked her to tell him that we did not have the money and anyway, as journalists, we never paid our sources. At first, Viktoria said nothing. Translating my negative response was, for her, like saying no to God. But at last, she managed it.

Zhivkov spoke irritably in response, but there was no question and Viktoria did not translate.

'Can you tell him that we would like to talk about the murder of Georgi Markov.'

'I won't answer any more questions about Georgi Markov,' Viktoria relayed back to me. 'And the assassination of the Pope. I've said enough about those topics. And why would we murder the Pope? He was the first Pope from a Slavic country!'

Zhivkov was talking about the 1981 attack on Pope John Paul II, in which the pontiff survived being shot four times by a young Turkish man. This attempted assassination had since spawned a family of conspiracy theories. The gunman was thought to have belonged to the Grey Wolves, a far-right group with links to Turkey and Italy, but he claimed to have been recruited by three Bulgarians. This led to a theory that the order for the Pope's assassination might have come from Moscow. This, in turn, produced a counter-theory that the CIA was behind the whole thing because they wanted to implicate the Soviet Union.

'We're not here to ask you about the Pope,' I said to Zhivkov directly. 'We only want to know about Georgi Markov. Do you think he could have been working for the British?'

Zhivkov forgot his earlier demand for money and began to speak. Soon Viktoria was struggling to keep up.

'He says, "How was I supposed to know if Markov was an agent or not? I was the leader of Bulgaria; I didn't meddle in the priorities of the ministries or the secret service. They could answer much better than I could."'

I turned to Viktoria. 'Can you ask him if he ordered Markov's murder?'

She gave me with a questioning glance, then looked at the floor for a long time. Nothing. Deep breath. Then she asked the question in Bulgarian.

'Why would we kill Markov?' Zhivkov replied. 'He was my friend! Before he went to the West, he actually came to say goodbye. I don't know why he left.'

I had never heard that Georgi went to say goodbye to Zhivkov before he left. If true, it was certainly not something that Georgi had included in his memoir. But the emotion underlying this response was interesting. Zhivkov had clearly thought of Georgi Markov as someone who was close to him, and as a man he could trust. Was it possible that Zhivkov had not ordered this killing? Perhaps one of his senior officials took it upon themselves to make this happen in the hope of gaining favour with Zhivkov. Markov had been attacked on 7 September, which happened to be Zhivkov's birthday. This might have been a coincidence, or the attack was intended as a gift for Number One. It would have been relatively easy for the minister of the interior to claim that Zhivkov had asked for this murder to take place, even if he had not. Or was the old man sitting across the table from me simply covering up the part he played in this murder?

'I don't understand why all of the secret service is going against me and the Communist Party now,' Zhivkov went on. 'In my thirty-five years as the leader, we didn't commit any political murders.'

Whether or not this was true, the communist militias controlled by Zhivkov in the years before he came to power were responsible for the deaths of thousands of his political opponents. Zhivkov followed up with a stream of complaints and rambling accusations. He was angry about his house arrest and the trial which had led to his being here, as well as the collapse of the Soviet Union, the state of Bulgaria today, and the level of crime and inflation in the country he had once ruled. Everything was scandalous, he told us. He would never have allowed any of this to happen during his time in charge.

Sometimes the former dictator would pause in the middle of a sentence to take in a faraway corner of his kitchen. In that moment, it seemed as if his mind was consumed by some distant panorama of the past, before something snapped him back to the kitchen and his unhappiness about the situation in which he found himself.

Zhivkov carried on like this for some time, urging us to believe that he had been right all along but the rest of the world was wrong. I realised after another hour or so that we were unlikely to learn anything new from him and that it was time to go. Viktoria and I packed up our things and made our way out to the car where Franco and Rikke were sitting in silence. I thanked Zhivkov's son and we began the drive back to our hotel. The following day, we began to make our way back to Denmark.

Had I gone far enough? This was the question I kept asking myself in the days after our return from Bulgaria. I was haunted by the idea that I should have stayed longer with Todor Zhivkov. Maybe there was some killer question that I had failed to ask, one that might have triggered a confession from him, a moment of humility or some hidden truth that would have changed my understanding of Gullino and the Umbrella Murder.

But no, I told myself, that was not the kind of man he was. Todor Zhivkov was not going to change his story, not at this stage of his life. He had spent so long barricaded behind a wall of lies that he had lost sight of the world beyond.

19
THE COFFEE CUP

Over the next few years, my life began to change. At DR, the Danish national broadcaster, I was promoted. I became an editor with a room full of people reporting to me and I was starting to make my own documentaries. This meant more responsibility as well as more days away from home. I covered the 1996 Olympics in Atlanta, the 1998 Winter Olympics in Japan in February, then travelled to Hawaii for the Ironman contest, and from there to Paris, where I led the DR coverage of the football World Cup. But everywhere I went, the Umbrella Murder stayed with me in the back of my mind.

I was spending more time away from my wife and young son than ever. On my way back from one of these trips, I bought an enormous toy pirate ship for our son, then aged four, and worried that he might not recognise me. That sounds crazy now, but I had seen so little of him over that summer that it felt possible. The constant travel was also adding to the distance between me and my wife.

When I was at home, I was still seeing Franco or carrying out more research into the Umbrella Murder story. I had tried to give less of myself to this, and to carve out parts of my life that were free from anything to do with Gullino, Markov and Bulgaria. It never seemed to work. Between the travel and my continuing obsession with the Umbrella Murder, I knew that something had to change.

In August of that year, our second son, Mikkel, was born. I needed to spend more time with my wife and our boys. This was going to mean fewer trips for work. And either I needed to keep going with Franco and bring this whole project to some kind of resolution by finishing the film and writing the book, or it was time to make a break.

A part of me was always going to be intrigued by who had killed Georgi Markov, and why Francesco Gullino, the prime suspect, had still not been prosecuted. But I had followed this path about as far as I willing to take it. I was beginning to worry that I was asking questions that could never be answered, and that there were too many details about this case that would forever be out of reach. Another part of the problem was my relationship with Franco. No matter how long I spent with him on this project, it was always going to be *his* investigation, *his* story, and *his* obsession. I felt as if I could spend the rest of my life working on this, but at the end of it all, with both of us as old men, I would still be the guy in the back seat, the son trying to help out the father.

Maybe this was where I had gone wrong. Without realising it, I had treated Franco with the same kind of deference and respect I usually reserved for my own father. Although I wouldn't say he was a disciplinarian, or that my childhood was unusual, the ultimate authority at home, when I was growing up, came from my dad. He was often away from home with work, so when he was around, my siblings and I were on our best behaviour. We all grew up with the idea that there was this older man in the house whose word was final, and whose authority we basically did not challenge. From the moment I met Franco, a man the same age as my father, I found myself not wanting to challenge him in the way I might have done if he was the same age as me.

A few months after the Bulgarian trip, I had gone to see Franco for one of our late morning coffees. He spoke about the papers that

Gullino had left behind in his house. Could I see them, I asked hopefully. No, Franco said, predictably. Not until he had finished with them. And here was the problem — Franco was never going to finish.

The nature of Franco's obsession was that he needed to keep the investigation going indefinitely. It reminded me of people in Sweden who become fixated by the mystery of who killed Olof Palme in 1986, the charismatic prime minister murdered in the street one night. Working out who could have done it remains a national preoccupation among Swedish people, to the extent that a new word recently appeared in the Swedish dictionary: *Palmessjukdom*, meaning 'Palme sickness', when you become obsessed with solving the mystery of who killed Olof Palme.

Franco seemed to be suffering from 'Gullino sickness'. His life had been taken over by the question of who his fellow Italian really was, and he appeared to be trapped in a world where nothing was as it seemed. Behind every truth he saw an alternate truth, a hidden reality that was waiting to be discovered. I had become more aware of this during our trip to Bulgaria. It was clear from the few interviews we did together that he was much less interested in the question of who had killed Georgi Markov than who might be controlling Gullino, and whether he could be linked to organised crime or another foreign intelligence agency. Put simply, Franco refused to believe that Gullino was just a Bulgarian intelligence agent. He was desperate to believe that there was more to it than that.

In Bulgaria, Franco had kept repeating his favourite question.

'You have to ask yourself,' he would begin. 'What is a right-wing fascist from Italy doing as a Bulgarian spy? Answer that, you've solved the mystery.' Franco's theory remained the same: that Gullino was an Italian agent of some sort and that he had been given instructions to infiltrate Bulgarian intelligence. He was never going to be prosecuted for the Umbrella Murder because the Italians had called in a favour from the Danes, the British, or both. That was his hypothesis.

But if there was evidence for any of this, Franco was keeping it to himself and had hidden it away in his house. Almost none of the people we had spoken to in Bulgaria believed any of Franco's theories. But that had no effect on him. In Franco's eyes, Francesco Gullino was capable of anything, and he, Franco, was the only one who had grasped this. He saw Gullino as an assassin, a double agent, and someone who would never go to jail because he was being protected by Italian intelligence and possibly British intelligence as well.

I had no idea if any of this could be true. Franco's strategy towards me was to reveal only a fraction of what he had found, and I could not tell if the material that he was keeping from me had any merit, or if it was pure speculation. Either way, this left me unable to finish the story myself. I had instead a vague sense that finding out everything about Francesco Gullino was more dangerous than I had initially thought. Some of Franco's ideas sounded far-fetched, but the people he was talking about were real and most were the kinds of individuals who did not take well to being investigated by an amateur filmmaker and a sports journalist.

What Franco wanted to do was a different kind of journalism. Although I had made some investigative television documentaries, such as one on sports doping in East Germany, none had left me with the feeling that I was putting my life in any kind of danger. Going after Gullino was completely different. It was a job for someone who was ready to put themselves in harm's way and I realised, at last, that I was not ready for that.

In the summer of 1998, at around the time Mikkel was born, I was again in Café Sebastopol with Franco. Same marble-topped table, same order, same everything. We had been talking for several hours about the Umbrella Murder (what else?) while I thought about how to tell him that I really had reached the end of the road with the investigation. I asked Franco, one last time, when I could meet Gullino.

'Didn't you see him?' Franco said, studying my eyes for a reaction. 'Gullino's been sitting behind us all this time. I had lunch with him before you came. When I said that you and I were going to meet, he said that he'd like to stay behind to take a look at you. He was just there.'

Franco pointed behind me.

I turned to see an empty table, and on it, a single coffee cup and saucer. The chair had been pushed out from the table, as if the occupant had left moments ago. As I stared at the coffee cup, I tried to make sense of what had just happened. Did this mean that Gullino was now aware of me? Had Franco told him that I was investigating his story? Because if he had, I might be in danger.

What really stayed with me from this exchange, however, was not so much the frustration I felt at being so close to meeting Gullino, but the look on Franco's face as he told me what had happened. He was elated. I had forgotten how much pleasure he seemed to take from taunting me like this and the feeling of power it clearly gave him.

It was time to leave Franco and his world behind. I needed to turn away from the darkness, the danger and all the unanswered questions. I told him that I was leaving the project. A part of me had hoped that as I said this, he would beg me to stay. But he did not. I felt sad that this was all coming to an end. Partly because we had failed to crack the case. I was also sad that I would no longer be seeing Franco. I was fond of him. Ours was not exactly a normal friendship – it had many moments of frostiness and a strange power dynamic – but it was still a friendship.

'I will keep going,' he said to me over coffee in Café Sebastopol. 'One day, you'll see what I have made.'

I had no notion at the time of the circumstances in which this would happen, or that when I saw what he had produced I would have a new death to investigate – Franco's own.

PART TWO

THE ARCHIVE

20

THE CALL

Twenty years later...

On an unseasonably cold day in March 2018, two Russian men began to walk down Wilton Road in Salisbury, southern England. There was snow on the ground and hardly anyone was out. The Russian visitors had come that day, they later explained, to admire Salisbury's historic cathedral and in particular its spire, knowing that it was the tallest in Britain. If anyone had stopped them to talk about their visit, they would, no doubt, have stressed that they were ordinary tourists, doing ordinary tourist things. After taking in the cathedral, they planned to see the nearby water meadows, some of the city's half-timbered buildings and the famous Charter Market, all of which would explain why they were on Wilton Road. There was one problem. They were walking in the wrong direction.

Salisbury has many attractions but the main draw if you worked for Russian military intelligence, as these two did, was that one of its residents was a sixty-six-year-old man called Sergei Skripal who had worked for Russian intelligence but was then recruited in the mid-1990s by Britain's secret intelligence service, better known as MI6, and worked for several years as a double agent codenamed 'Forthwith'. Skripal had provided MI6 with extremely valuable information about Russian military intelligence before he was uncovered, convicted and later sent to a high security jail deep inside Russia. As part of an international spy swap, in which ten Russian agents who had been arrested in the United States moved in the opposite direction, he was released and later embarked on a new life in the picturesque city of Salisbury.

The two Russian visitors did not take long to walk from the railway station to the home of Sergei Skripal, where they smeared a toxic substance onto the handle of his front door. Once they had finished, they made their way back to London and were soon on a flight to Moscow.

Later that day, Sergei Skripal and his daughter, Yulia, who was visiting from Moscow, went out for lunch. On their way home, they fell seriously ill and collapsed. The first passers-by thought they must be a pair of drug addicts. Both were sweating profusely, in spite of the cold, their pulses were weak and they were having trouble breathing. Someone decided to call an ambulance.

The paramedics realised right away that this was not a drugs overdose. They took the patients to the nearest hospital, where they were hooked up to ventilators and placed in medically induced comas. Samples of their blood were soon on their way to scientists in nearby Porton Down, where long ago Georgi Markov's flesh had been examined.

I was in Copenhagen when I heard that Sergei and Yulia Skripal had been poisoned. I remember feeling a mixture of shock and curiosity, as well as recognition. The outline of this story, in which innocent people had been poisoned on the streets of Britain, took me straight back to the Umbrella Murder. The similarities between these two attacks were overwhelming. Trained assassins had been sent into Britain with instructions to kill an individual who had fallen foul of a brutal regime. Both operations would have taken months to prepare and rehearse. Rather than stab the victim to death or shoot them in the street, the attackers had used an extremely rare and unusual poison, a toxin that had been tested inside a secretive Russian laboratory. It was even possible that the toxins used in these two separate attacks, separated by almost forty years, might have been developed in exactly the same laboratory inside Moscow. Both attacks would have relied on intelligence from other sources to reveal the target's whereabouts. There must also have been a sophisticated plan in place for how to smuggle the poison into the country, how to deliver it to the would-be assassins and how to get the assassins out of the country before they could be identified by the police.

The reaction from the doctors and scientists involved was eerily similar as well — victims rushed to hospital, unexplained symptoms, the involvement of Porton Down, a full-scale police investigation. Even the geography of these attacks had for a moment overlapped. The Russians tasked with killing Sergei Skripal had almost certainly crossed Waterloo Bridge with the poison in their bag on their way to catch a train to Salisbury.

I watched every report on the news and read every article. But none of them could answer the question that began to be asked in the British media, which was about the meaning of this attack. Was it a warning, in the sense that the attack was meant to be linked back to Moscow? Or had the operation gone wrong? The same question hung over the Umbrella Murder. Did those involved fail to cover their tracks or had they done just enough to let this attack serve as a deterrent to anyone else contemplating a similar course of action as the victim? The fact that the Russians who tried to kill the Skripals had used Novichok, an extremely rare nerve agent developed by Russian scientists during the Cold War, was interesting. There were other, more generic poisons they could have used. But they went for one that was always going to lead back to Moscow. In that case, this attack was probably meant to be a warning.

It had been twenty years since I had last spoken to Franco but the story of the Salisbury attack suddenly collapsed the time that had passed. In my mind, I was with him again, chatting away. I could picture his stubbly jaw, the intense and energetic way he had of speaking, the gold ring on his finger and the brown document folder he carried around with him everywhere.

But thinking of Franco, and the way we had been together, also brought into focus everything that had changed in my life since we last spoke. I was fifty-one now. I didn't think of myself as middle aged but, like it or not, that's what I had become. Since my last conversation with Franco, I had divorced my wife, moved house and remarried. I now had four sons and a daughter. When I thought back to the person I had been when I first met Franco, back in the 1990s, I struggled to recognise him.

I had also moved on in my job. After becoming a senior editor in the News Department at DR at a fairly young age — perhaps too young — I had moved in a different direction and decided to set up a television documentary company. I now had twenty-five people working for me. We made programmes about pretty much everything, from renovation projects, gardens and the Danish royal family, through to tales of missing persons, domestic abuse and examinations of the country's most notorious unsolved crimes. For me, this was a completely new way of working, one in which I felt as if I was only as good as the next idea I was able to come up with. I was always looking around for inspiration. The idea for one of our most successful television programmes had come from an advertisement I had seen on the side of a passing bus.

The work was busy, fun and unpredictable. But more recently, I had made the decision to scale things back. I wanted to have more time away from the office and was thinking about how to take on fewer projects each year. A new phase in my life seemed to be beckoning, a step towards retirement — when I heard about the attack in Salisbury and something inside me woke up.

Before I knew it, I was staying late at work and spending hours reading up on what had happened to Sergei Skripal and his daughter Yulia. There was something comforting, almost cosy, about being in the office after everyone else had gone home. I enjoyed looking out of the window to see that night had fallen. The only light in the room was from the lamp on my desk and everything was silent. All I could hear was the occasional splash of the cars outside as they drove through a slush of melting snow. It was just me and my computer, and the story of the Skripals. I couldn't tear myself away. My wife would message to ask when I was going to be home but no matter what time I told her, it was usually later. There was always one more article to read, another link to click, one more clue that might lead to the truth. Something was driving me on, but I couldn't work out what.

Then an idea formed. Perhaps I should give Franco a call. With the world gripped by the saga of the Salisbury attack, this would be the perfect time to pitch a documentary about Francesco Gullino and the Umbrella Murder. We could put the story to bed. I had contacts at each of the main Danish television stations and could easily find a home for this story. In all the years since we had last been in touch, had Franco found an ending to the story? Had he managed to squeeze Francesco Gullino into making some kind of confession? I knew that nothing had been published on the subject because I would have heard about it. But that didn't mean Franco had failed to make any progress. Perhaps he was close to finishing the film he had always wanted to make.

I looked up Franco's number, which was different to the one I had before. Clearly he had moved to another part of Copenhagen. I was about to make the call, but I couldn't do it. I kept putting it off, telling myself I would call him tomorrow. The piece of paper with his number sat on my desk for days. Staring at that note, I felt like a reformed alcoholic gazing at a bottle of vodka. I wanted to call that number and at the same time, I did not. It was the obvious thing to do, just as it was a terrible mistake. But ultimately, I realised that making the call was the only way to resolve something which had been quietly niggling away at me for the last twenty years.

One afternoon, with sun shining brightly into our office, I picked up the phone and punched in Franco's new number. I didn't know what I was going to say. As the telephone rang, I could imagine Franco in his house amid his mess, the piles of paper, the endless pots of coffee, his political pronouncements, Helene's infinite patience with him, his irritation with people who didn't understand him right away.

I was waiting for Franco's familiar voice — *si, e Franco* — when Helene, his wife, picked up.

'Hello Helene, it's Ulrik,' I start.

'Ulrik! My God. It's been so many years.' Her voice was sweet and welcoming. 'I expect you're calling to speak to Franco.'

'Yes.'

'Franco is dead,' she said calmly. 'He died, let me see, he died just over ten years ago.'

It took me a moment to register the shock hammering into me. Franco seemed indestructible, someone who would always be there and would somehow refuse to die, as if on principle. I struggled to imagine the scene at the other end of the line, or come to terms with the idea that Franco was never coming to the phone.

'I'm sorry to hear that,' I managed.

'Well, it's been a long time now. But it's funny you should call. I was trying to work out what to do with all his papers. You know, all his research. And I was about to call up the National Archive, to see if they would have it. But maybe you should take them instead.'

'Are there many?'

'Oh yes, boxes and boxes. And Franco kept telling me about how close he was to finishing his investigation. But then he died.'

'That's so sad.'

'It was sudden as well.'

'What do you mean?'

'His death came out of nowhere,' she went on.

'I'm sorry to ask, but how did he die?'

'So, we still don't really know. One day he was fine. No health problems. Then he became very ill and nobody at the hospital could tell what was wrong with him. He had a pacemaker but his heart was OK. That was not the problem. It was something else. They had him in intensive care. Then his condition became worse very quickly and, before we knew it, he was dead.'

As she described what had happened to Franco, I felt a strange sensation rising through my body: panic, mixed with an eerie sense of familiarity.

'Are you still there?' she said.

'Yes, sorry.'

'About Franco's papers,' Helene went on. 'If you like, you could come round and take a look. Maybe you'll understand what he was doing.'

21
HELENE

I went to see Helene the next day. She was living in an apartment in Vanløse, a pretty suburb of Copenhagen. As I made my way across town, I kept having to remind myself that Franco was not going to be there and that I would never see him again. The news of Franco's death was still catching up with me. That feeling was amplified, in some ways, by the recent death of my own father. These two men had been so close in age, had both lived through the Second World War and experienced many of the same hardships early in life. They also shared a certain forcefulness and vigour, each one used to getting his own way. Throughout my life, I had thought of them as belonging to the generation that was in charge, the one that was making the decisions that really mattered. It was strange to find myself adjusting to their absence, and the idea that I was now part of that older generation.

Helene welcomed me into her apartment and led me through to her living room. It had been twenty years since I'd last seen her but it didn't feel like that. She had lost none of her energy or presence. She went to the kitchen to make coffee while I hovered in the living room for a moment. Looking around me, I recognised furniture from her last home. Even if Franco had never set foot in this building, I could feel his presence and was half expecting him to come bounding in from another room.

'The film about Gullino was a huge part of his life,' Helene said as she handed me a cup of coffee, in a way that suggested she had been thinking about this since we spoke on the phone. 'It was a part of my life as well. That's why I couldn't throw away all of his material.'

'What happened to the film?' I asked. 'The last time I spoke to him was in 1998 and I remember him saying that he would keep going.'

Helene smiled. 'He kept going alright. He always kept going. I realised that he could not let this story go because he didn't want Gullino to get away with it. The problem was that he needed him to talk. He had to find a way to get Gullino on tape. But Gullino refused. Franco was sure he could talk him round one day, and he was still seeing him. He had that tiny tape recorder on him when they drove around together. But I think Gullino knew what was going on. He came from that world and was trained to spot that kind of thing. So he must have known that Franco was recording him.'

Helene went on to explain how Franco had tried to drum up interest in his Gullino film from various broadcasters and production companies. At first, there had been a lot of interest, Helene said, but all of them backed off once they encountered Franco's paranoia and it became clear that he was not willing to share with them everything he had found. At one stage, Franco was given a development grant of 40,000 DK by the Danish Film Institute to finish the research for the film and put together a script. If they liked what he had made, they would finance the production of the film.

But Franco couldn't get it all into a single script. He wanted this film to include *everything*. It was going to describe every plot, rumour and conspiracy that he had ever wanted to link to Gullino, as well as a blow-by-blow account of his own relationship with the alleged Umbrella Murderer. The Danish Film Institute suggested that Franco take a step back and let a more experienced director write a script. But Franco refused and the collaboration came to an end.

'Was that difficult for you?' I asked Helene. 'That he wasn't willing to work with others?'

'Sometimes it was, sure. It could be frustrating. I told him several times that he had enough material, and that he should go ahead and make the film with what he had. But he couldn't. I think this story is one that needs to get out there. People need to know about Gullino.'

'I never asked you before what you thought of him.'

'Who?'

'What you thought of Gullino.'

'I was on his side when he first came to us. When he talked about being interrogated by Scotland Yard and Danish intelligence, I felt cross! What the hell is going on? You can't do that. But that changed after he moved in. I could see that he was using Franco. He was asking him to do too much. Also, I was scared! Franco was finding out things about Gullino and I was worried. "He just has to get out of the house." That's what I said to Franco. "I don't want a murderer in here. He needs to go."'

'Where is Gullino now?'

Helene puffed out her cheeks. 'He could be anywhere. The last I heard from Franco was that he was in Hungary, or somewhere near there. But why is he not in jail? That is the question we have to answer.'

For the next hour, Helene talked more about the project and I began to realise the extent to which it had taken over both of their lives. Even their holidays related in some way to Franco's research for the film. Sometimes Franco would ask Helene to hold the camera as he recorded a piece in a location that was linked to Gullino's life. As we spoke that day, I sensed her desire to guard her husband's legacy. There may have been times when she thought he had gone too far but she never lost sight of why he was doing this. She loved his idealism and determination, and was reminded of it even now as we spoke about the film that he had tried so hard to make.

Once we had finished the pot of coffee, Helene took me up to the building's shared attic space and pointed at a wall of boxes.

'There we are,' she began, looking at them all with an air of resignation. 'Somewhere in those boxes is something valuable. But I can't deal with it right now,' she said, throwing her hands up in exhaustion.

'It's OK. We can come back to this later.'

'It would be nice if someone else was able to finish this story,' Helene said, gazing at the boxes, 'so that his work was not for nothing. I know Franco wanted this story to be told. He seemed to be so close when he died.'

'Was there anything unusual about his death?'

Helene paused for a moment.

'If we talk about his death now, then I might say that something suspicious occurred. I'm not sure if I want to do that right now.'

'I understand.'

'But what I can say is that he was not ill before it happened. Then one morning he woke up and said there was something wrong. He thought it must be his heart. The doctors examined him,' Helene went on. 'They carried out every test they could think of. Then the next day, they were ready to send him to another hospital, because they couldn't understand what was going on. Suddenly, his condition became worse and he died. I was in shock for a long time afterwards because it was so sudden.'

'Had anything happened to him in the days before he went to hospital?'

'Nothing, apart from the documentary.'

'What?'

'The documentary he was in. They showed it on television here in Denmark.'

Not long before his death, Franco had been contacted by John Hamilton, a British filmmaker, who was putting together a documentary about the Umbrella Murder. I knew from countless conversations with Franco that this had always been his greatest fear. He was petrified by the idea of someone beating him to it and producing a film about Gullino before he could finish his.

Hamilton had heard that Franco knew a lot about Gullino and he must have asked him if he was willing to be interviewed on camera. I could imagine Franco's dilemma. He would have been annoyed that this programme was going out before his film but he would have taken comfort from the fact that he had been asked to take part in it. At the same time, he must have been worried about Gullino finding out that he had participated in a programme like this, even if he was disguised.

One day in 2006, Franco was filmed speaking to John Hamilton about the Umbrella Murder. They stood together on Queen Louise's Bridge in Copenhagen. Efforts had clearly been made to disguise Franco. The camera was set up some distance away and Franco's face was blurred. Franco was recorded saying that Gullino was a dangerous man, someone to be wary of. 'He still lives here and comes and goes,' Franco said to Hamilton. 'He's a nomad.'

When he watched the documentary go out on television, Franco must have felt his heart sink. Despite the precautions to disguise him, his voice had not been dubbed by an actor. They had used the original audio. Even though Franco had been filmed from a distance, and had worn a large coat that day and a hat, it may well have been possible for those close to him to make out the familiar shape of Franco's upper body. The location may also have pointed to his true identity. Franco had been filmed just around the corner from Baggesensgade, the street on which he lived. The filmmakers had described Franco in the voiceover as a man who was 'very frightened and concerned not to be identified' and as someone who 'has known Gullino on and off for over fifteen years. They first met when Gullino owned a picture-framing business.'

'When did this documentary go out?' I asked Helene.

'I don't know. The day before. Something like that.'

'The day before what?'

'It went out on DR2 the day before Franco went to hospital. I think they watched it together.'

'What do you mean?'

'I can't remember, but I think Franco watched the programme with Gullino. But I don't want to talk about any of this now. I'm sorry. The person who knows more about all this is Bent,' Helene went on, hurrying her words. 'Bent Staalhøj. Talk to him. If you can find him. He has a lot of material. But I don't know if he's still alive.'

22
BENT

Ærø, June 2018

Early one summer's day, not long after speaking to Helene, I set out to meet Bent Staalhøj, who was indeed alive. I remembered Franco talking about Bent long ago, but I had never met him. He had recently retired from his job as a cinema projectionist and had moved to the small island of Ærø, in the South Funen archipelago, a place that could only be reached by boat. I was welcome to come and see him, he said on the phone. And yes, he went on, he had a load of Franco's stuff that I could go through.

I began by driving across Zealand to the island of Funen, and on to Svendborg, a small port, where I waited for the ferry to Ærø. Already, I could feel Copenhagen slip into the background of my mind. Everything around me seemed to move at a slower and more contented speed. The way people spoke was smoother than I was used to in the capital and more melodious, with the intonation rising towards the end of most sentences. I could see dinghies out to sea and families on small boats.

There was something nostalgic about all this, like stepping back in time. The people around here also seemed to be more open than in Copenhagen. On board the ferry, they were serving the traditional Smørrebrød of rye bread, mayonnaise, and prawns. After we arrived in Ærøskøbing, I drove the short distance to Marstal, the other town on the island, where I found Bent's house. I parked up, and knocked on the door.

Bent Staalhøj was a big, bald, middle-aged man with a booming voice.

'Welcome, welcome all the way from the capital,' he bellowed, giving me a meaty pat on the back as he beckoned me into his house. He later explained that his loud voice was not something he did on purpose — it went back to his childhood, and growing up with a mother who was partially deaf. Bent had also been a sailor for a few years, which added to his direct and rugged style of speaking.

Bent led me through to the kitchen and began to make coffee.

'You want to know about Franco, then?'

'Exactly. Helene suggested I come out to see you. I'm thinking of trying to finish Franco's film about Gullino.'

'Ha! I would pay to see that film. Even if he had lived for another hundred years, I don't think Franco would have found a way to end it.'

He paused to catch his breath, like he was gasping for air after a run.

'So, did you work with Franco on his film about Gullino?'

'All the time! I spent so many hours working with him on it. I even shot some of the footage. I remember, Franco asked me to film him meeting Gullino.'

He brought the coffee over to the table and sat down heavily opposite me.

'Franco and I go back a long way. At one time, we were like brothers. After I finished being a sailor, I began to make films. That's when I met Franco. I was filming protests and labour strikes, and I'd always see this Italian guy with a camera filming the same stuff. We got to know each other and we realised that our politics were the same. So, we thought, why not team up? Soon we had our own company.'

The memories were tumbling out of him now, one after the other, although not always in order. Bent spoke about the first films he had made with Franco and the pride he had in what they had done. Both men had set out to make films that exposed abuses of power by those in authority and the plight of anyone who had fallen on hard times.

One of Bent and Franco's best-known films was *Slaget om Byggeren*, or 'Battle of the Builder', which told the story of how the residents of Nørrebro – the neighbourhood where I had first met Franco – campaigned to prevent the demolition of a playground that they had built. The clashes with the police were so intense that a state of emergency was declared. Throughout the riots, Bent and Franco were there on the frontline with their cameras, recording everything and earning the trust of even the most violent activists.

Hearing Bent talk about the making of this film, I could feel Franco coming back to life in my mind. I had forgotten about his immense appetite for danger and risk. Maybe it came from the experience of shooting this particular film. Or maybe it had been there all along.

'Even I was worried when Franco told me about some of the things he was doing to find out more about Gullino.'

'Like what?' I asked.

'Oh my God, where to start. How about the press articles about Gullino? Back when he was living with Franco.'

I remembered some of this. In the summer of 1993, before I first met Franco, a news story had appeared on the front page of the respected Danish newspaper *Dagbladet Information* saying that Francesco Gullino had been questioned by Scotland Yard about the murder of Georgi Markov – although he was not actually named in that piece. Later that same day, the TV2 investigative television programme *Outlook*, which had the same parent company as *Dagbladet Information*, ran a long feature about Gullino. Again, they did not give his name. Just his initials: 'F. G.'

These reports were interesting because they had plenty of details about Gullino's life but no direct quotes. Everything in there was accurate. But they gave a watered-down version of the real story. Both pieces were said to be the work of a single Danish journalist, Ole Damkjær. I remember thinking at the time that Damkjær appeared to have just one source.

The story was picked up the next day by almost every other Danish media outlet and others around the world, including the *Guardian*, which named 'F. G.' as an Italian-born Dane called Francesco Gullino. After that, the secret was out. I read these articles in the library at work, thinking to myself that there was someone else out there leaking information about Gullino to the media. I began to understand why Franco was so worried. Clearly, I thought, he had a rival.

'Gullino was furious about those articles!' Bent told me. 'He could not believe that someone had sold the story to the media. He knew it was someone close to him. Apparently, he was shouting at the television as the TV2 programme went out.'

'He was doing what?'

'Shouting at the television.'

'How do you know that?'

'Because Franco told me. Franco was sitting next to him as he watched the programme.'

I tried to picture the two middle-aged Italians side-by-side on Franco's sofa as the programme went out.

'Gullino was convinced that Jørgen Jakobsen had leaked the story. You know, the lawyer. He was yelling, "You can't trust lawyers. They're all pigs." Jakobsen was a media louse, he said. A terrible person, someone who would do anything to be in the news. Gullino was very, very angry.' Bent was laughing at the memory of it. 'But Franco says to him, "Are you sure it's Jørgen Jakobsen?" And Gullino says, "Who the hell else is it going to be?"'

'Who did leak the story?'

'Franco!' Bent went on, his face creased up with mirth. 'It was Franco all along.'

I couldn't believe it. 'Why would he do that? I mean, that's a huge risk, isn't it?'

'I know.'

'If Gullino ever found out, then ...'

'But Franco was like that,' Bent went on.

He was right. Franco liked to fly close to the sun.

'I think the main reason that Franco went to the media was the deal they had made between themselves.'

'What deal?'

'Gullino had told Franco that he could make a film about his life once the story became public. Not before.'

It all began to make sense. Franco had leaked the story to the media so that Gullino would be compelled to be interviewed for his film. That was his plan. But something had gone wrong because Gullino never made the film with Franco; instead, his subject ran away.

'Vanished,' Bent went on. 'Franco had no idea where Gullino was. He went to Hungary, or somewhere like that. You know, Franco was frustrated by now. Really frustrated. He felt as if Gullino had not kept his side of their bargain. I said to Franco, "If Gullino won't give you what you need, then take it for yourself." Franco thought about this, then told me to come round to the house with a camera.'

The two men went to Gullino's room and filmed everything they could find in there. They were like detectives at the scene of a crime. They wanted to get everything on tape. I later saw the tape. Franco placed each item in front of a noticeboard while Bent captured it on film. At one point in the film Franco picks up Gullino's copies of *Mein Kampf*. '*Det var satans,*' you can hear one of them say in Danish, meaning, roughly, 'Bloody hell ...'

They also recorded the Mussolini calendar and a passport with Gullino's face but someone else's name. Then they went through the photographs he had taken of women, most of them naked and one draped in a Nazi swastika.

Once they had finished, Franco and Bent thought about ways they could film Gullino without his realising. They purchased the tiny recording devices that Franco could hide under his clothes. Bent spent some time rigging up a camera inside one of Franco's bags that he could operate using a remote control. The idea was that if Franco sat down with Gullino, he could put the bag on the table next to him, making sure it was pointed at him, and then press a button on a remote control in his pocket to start the recording.

'But Franco could never make it work,' Bent sighed. 'Another time, Franco calls me up. "Listen," he says, "Gullino has asked me to meet him off the train in Copenhagen. Let's record it. I want you to film me meeting him." I didn't know what to do! How do you film someone in a train station without them realising? There's nowhere to hide. So I thought of something else. I read in a book long ago about how the first people you see in a crowd are tourists, and it's always obvious that they're tourists. I thought to myself, *perhaps I can be one of them.* So I put on my brightest shirt and a big red hat. I went to the station and stood a short distance away from Franco with my camera. I've never felt so stupid. We waited. Then Gullino arrived and he saw me. I mean, everyone saw me. But I guess he thought I was just a tourist. I was moving my camera around, pretending to film the station. Sometimes I pointed the camera at him and I got some really nice shots of him. When they walked out to the car park, I followed them with the camera and recorded Gullino standing next to Franco as he put his bags into the car.'

Franco also started to record more of his conversations with Gullino on their occasional journeys around Europe. Listening to Bent describe these to me, I remembered Franco talking about these trips. They would always start with Gullino getting a call on his satellite phone, hanging up and telling Franco that he needed to be in

Germany, Austria or somewhere in Eastern Europe. Would Franco be able to drive him there?

Usually, the answer was yes. Franco saw these trips as an opportunity to gather more material and get closer to the truth about Gullino's secret life. On the first of these road trips, they took the ferry to Germany and spent the night in Lubeck. Over dinner in the hotel, Gullino talked to Franco at some length about *Mein Kampf* and what a great job he thought Hitler had done for the German economy. Gullino knew about Franco's left-wing outlook, and was looking for a reaction. But Franco kept his cool and what could have been an argument turned into one of those we'll-agree-to-disagree conversations that ended with one of them changing the subject.

Later that night, the two middle-aged Italian men went up to their shared room. Franco got into bed and was starting to drift off when he saw that Gullino had pulled out of his bag a small portable television. Half-asleep, Franco watched as his roommate fiddled around with the aerial until he had found what he was looking for: a German channel showing pornography. Franco pretended to be asleep, while the man believed to be responsible for the murder of Georgi Markov lay next to him watching people have sex.

Before leaving the hotel the next day, Franco rigged himself up with a microphone and began to record their conversation. They drove to an auction house in Hamburg. As they walked into the building, a female member of staff called out to them, 'Herr Gullino! How nice to see you.'

Franco was amazed. He followed Gullino as they were ushered into a private office and fussed over like a pair of big spenders who had just walked into a casino. Franco was bemused as he watched Gullino chat to the staff at the auction house about the sale of various pictures and the state of the art market. He wasn't entirely sure what happened in the next hour, as it was hard to follow, but later that morning they walked out of the auction house with 5,000 Deutsche Marks in an envelope and three framed pictures under their arms.

Although Franco was still piecing it all together, he could tell that the money Gullino had picked up was not his and these art deals probably had something to do with the calls he took on his satellite phone from his 'business' contact in Sicily. In other words, he was acting as an agent or a middle-man for someone else.

Franco recorded as much as he could, often wondering if Gullino had any idea that he was on tape. It was always hard to tell whether Gullino was having fun or being serious. One day, when they got to a petrol station and Franco went off to the bathroom, Gullino called out after him as he began to walk off: 'I guess you also need to change the batteries on the recorder!'

Was it a joke? Or was he aware of what was going on? There had always been this undercurrent of suspicion beneath the surface of their relationship. They liked each other but neither man really trusted the other. But Franco did not back off after this. If Gullino was onto him, then the fact that he was willing to joke about his recording their conversations meant that he did not mind. Nor did Franco want to stop. He had never been so close to figuring out who Gullino was.

On their way back to Copenhagen, Gullino pulled out his black satellite phone and made a call. Speaking in Italian, he told the person on the other end of the line that everything was fine and the trip had been a success.

'Who was that?' Franco asked.

'Nobody.'

'A friend, a colleague?'

'My friend in Palermo.'

That was all he would say on the subject, apart from one moment of possible candour when Gullino said to Franco: 'Here's something that almost nobody knows. I'm one of the biggest art forgers in Europe!'

Over the weeks that followed, Gullino asked Franco to become more involved in his art dealing. One day, a truck from Palermo arrived outside Franco's house. The driver unloaded a series of pictures and stored them in his basement while Franco cooked the driver some north Italian food – which he loved.

Franco's next task was to visit a bank and pick up some money that had been wired to Gullino's account earlier that day from a Swiss bank account. But Franco had not anticipated the size of the deposit – 490,000 Danish kroner. This was not a sum you could fit into your wallet. Once the bank tellers had counted it all, they fetched two large bin liners so that Franco could carry it out of the building. Franco left the bank both looking like a robber and feeling like one. He was not sure where this money had come from but he began to wonder if he was inadvertently part of some kind of money laundering operation.

Following Gullino's precise instructions, Franco drove the cash to an art gallery in Copenhagen, where he handed it over to the gallery owner. Once it had been counted, he was given a painting that had been set aside earlier. Franco loaded up the artwork into his truck. Next, he drove it to an Israeli art dealer who lived just outside Copenhagen.

Over the next few weeks, in the wake of Gullino's interrogation by Scotland Yard, Franco became involved in a number of similar transactions. First, a large sum of money was transferred to one of Gullino's bank accounts. Franco collected the cash from the bank and used it to buy an artwork on behalf of Gullino's 'friends' in Sicily. This was either sold at auction or purchased by another dealer.

But Gullino also dealt in forgeries. He had good relationships with several artists in Romania and Hungary who could produce dazzlingly good replicas of antique paintings. Gullino would mix these up with the genuine artworks that he was selling at auction and this allowed him to make some money for himself on the side. It also explained why he had so many dusty old frames in his collection – including those he had long ago begun to store in Franco's basement. These gave his fake paintings a veneer of truthfulness.

Franco was excited. He was starting to uncover another element to this mysterious man's life. Gullino appeared to be part of a money-laundering operation centred on Sicily. Perhaps he had a connection to the Mafia. Franco could not tell. But this helped him to understand why Gullino always seemed to have money in his pocket and almost nothing in the bank.

'Do you think Gullino knew that Franco was recording him?' I asked Bent, as we sat in his living room with its glorious views out to sea.

'He must have done. This man was trained as a spy. He knows how to work out if someone has a microphone.'

'But why didn't he say anything?'

'I think he liked having Franco around. Franco was useful for him and maybe he liked the company.'

'That sounds right.'

'You see, Gullino was a lonely man,' Bent added, a waver of compassion in his voice.

'Maybe that explains his trips to Karlovy Vary.'

Bent nodded.

On another trip, Franco had accompanied Gullino to Karlovy Vary, a small city in the Czech Republic. But there were no auction houses there. Karlovy Vary was where Gullino went to have fun. Franco watched as he found two local Roma women and paid them to pose for him and spend time with him. At one point, they went off to someone's house, presumably to have sex. But Franco could tell that Gullino was interested in more than that. He wanted to feel loved. He liked the idea that these women were his girlfriends and that they wanted to be with him, calling them his 'special friends'.

'I remember the story that Franco told me about that trip,' I said to Bent. 'Gullino had asked Franco to drive him and the two

Roma women to a wooded area outside town because he wanted to photograph them. Once Gullino was taking pictures, Franco got out his camera and started to film. But immediately, Gullino span round.'

'He told me the same story!' Bent said. 'I can show you the footage. You can see that he's filming Gullino, and on the tape you can hear Gullino call out. "You're not filming me, right?" Then Franco shouts back. "No, no." Then you can see the camera shift to the right and he zooms in on some ducks, and he yells over at Gullino, "I'm just filming the ducks here!"'

Bent laughed hard at the memory, and I felt a wave of nostalgia. I missed Franco. Most of all his fearlessness and his willingness to do things his own way.

I had been talking to Bent for a couple of hours when he suggested we head upstairs to see all of Franco's material. As we climbed the steps, Bent's breathing become heavier. Halfway up, he paused, gasping. Once he had righted himself, we carried on to the office he had set up for himself on the top floor.

One part of the room was taken up with piles of cardboard boxes.

'Here it is,' he said. 'Franco's very own archive.'

It was overwhelming to see all this material, mainly because there was so much of it. I peered into one of the open boxes and could see masses of letters, papers and Dictaphone tapes, as well as 16mm and 35mm film reels, among other things.

Bent began to pick out some of the papers that he thought might be interesting and was starting to make a pile of them for me to take when he stopped.

'Actually, you know what,' he began. 'Take it all. I won't be using it anymore.'

'Why not?'

'Well, if I'm honest, I don't have long left,' he said, still wheezing. 'I'll be dead soon. When I'm gone, all this will just end up in the bin. If you can make something out of this,' he waved at the boxes, 'if you can finish what Franco started, I'd feel much better about things.'

'That's really kind of you.'

'Franco was never going to finish the Gullino story. Never. But you might have a chance. Or perhaps I'm being unkind to Franco. If he hadn't taken part in that documentary, everything would be different.'

'You mean the one with the British guy? That went out the day before he went to hospital?'

'Right. If it wasn't for that, he would never have gone for the meal with Gullino.'

'*What?*'

'The meal with Gullino.'

'I don't know about this.'

'After the documentary went out, Gullino went for a meal with Franco. He was furious. He felt that Franco had betrayed him by going on camera. So they went out to Nordsjælland and ate at some restaurant there. The next day, Franco wakes up feeling terrible. After that, he goes to hospital. And a day or two later, he's dead.'

I felt as if everything at the outer edges of my vision had begun to spin, until parts of the world were buzzing and starting to press in on me. I could hardly believe what Bent had just said. The facts were straightforward. Gullino knew that Franco had betrayed him on television. He was angry and took Franco out for dinner. *Something* happened and less than twenty-four hours later, Franco was in hospital. Two days after that, he was pronounced dead.

I turned to Bent and asked the obvious question, the only question: did he think that Gullino might have poisoned Franco?

'I don't know. I try not to think about it too much. All I know is that it's a very, very mysterious death.'

I ferried the boxes out of Bent's studio and loaded them into my car. After saying goodbye to Bent, I set out again for Copenhagen.

On the drive back, one question burned through my mind: *Was Franco murdered?* I didn't want it to be true. It would be too much for Helene. She wanted peace in her life. The last thing she needed was to live with the idea that her husband had been killed.

Rather than take the boxes to my house, I drove to my office and stored them with the material I had taken from Helene's house.

The next day, I heard that Bent had had a serious heart attack. It happened less than twenty-four hours after I had left him. He had been out riding his tuk-tuk, and was found lying unconscious in a field. He was flown by helicopter to the nearest hospital and a team of surgeons saved his life.

There was something that Franco liked to say that used to annoy me, mainly because it sounded so superstitious. He told me that whenever the truth about Francesco Gullino was about to come out, there was death in the air. There was nothing suspicious about Bent's heart attack. But, at the same time, what had happened forced me to see what I was doing in a different light. It pushed me up against the fact that I might soon be the only one left to investigate Franco's death and tell the story of Francesco Gullino and the Umbrella Murder.

There had always been someone else to do it until then. Either it was the detectives from Scotland Yard, Franco, Helene, Bent or the person I had assumed was supplying the story to the Danish media – who was, I now knew, Franco. I realised that I was closer to this story than anyone else and that I might be the last one capable of piecing it together. If I didn't act on what I knew, then the truth about Gullino might disappear forever. Nobody would ever know what Franco had discovered. The man who was probably responsible for Georgi Markov's murder as well as Franco's would have got away with it.

23

THE BOX

As I walked into the office the next day, I could smell Franco's boxes long before I saw them. During the night, they had filled the space with a lingering aroma of damp and decay. What was meant to be the office of my youthful television production company smelled like a second-hand bookshop. I went to the room where I had left the boxes, eyeing them up as if preparing for a fight.

After so many years of not having enough material, I was in danger of having too much. Franco had put a lot of effort into keeping me in the dark about what he had discovered. But that was in the past. I had to keep reminding myself that going into Franco's material was less of a transgression than an act of friendship. I needed to go through his boxes to find out what Franco had discovered and to enter the alleyways of his mind. That was the only way to find out why Gullino might have wanted him dead.

I began to sort through the material. A lot of it was videotapes in different formats, seven in total, as well as reels of film, hard drives, floppy discs — all of which I would need to watch and look through — plus thousands of newspaper cuttings, notebooks, letters and drafts of different scripts. In among the files, I could also see Franco's old document folder. His faithful companion. Every time I caught sight of it, I felt a surprising pang of emotion. I thought about how this battered folder had come to symbolise Franco's solitary quest to find the truth about Gullino.

Opening the folder, I hoped to find some extraordinary piece of never-before-seen evidence, a crucial detail that he had kept to himself all this time that would prove to the world that Gullino had been the international superspy that Franco had always imagined him to be. But the folder was empty. It reminded me of the story Franco had once told me about his father, who had told his employees that he kept his secret recipe for gorgonzola locked in a cabinet, only for them to break in and find that it was empty. Franco's folder, all but lost among heaps of dusty papers and videotapes, seemed to have an inescapably tragic quality.

Then I came across a box that was immediately different to the others. I felt my heart beat a little faster as I realised that the handwriting I was trying to decipher was not Franco's. It was Gullino's. These were his belongings. He had left them in Franco's house and never came back for them. Among the documents were several passports, including his Danish one. It had been years since I had seen Gullino's handwriting. I tried to imagine what the Umbrella Murderer would have felt as he read these letters, most of them invoices and bills dated to the period in 1993 when he had been staying with Franco. Resignation? Anger? Or just indifference?

The first thing that became clear was just how bad Gullino's official financial situation had been when he moved in with Franco. Sparbank Vest wanted 9,000 DKK from him, at a crippling 22.7 per cent interest rate; BRF Kredit were after the 23,752 DKK he owed them; Auktionsverk in Stockholm demanded a repayment of 33,137 DKK; Danish Bank needed 42,500 DKK; auction house Julius Jæger was enquiring after an outstanding invoice for 15,223 German marks; Christie's in New York was short $23,930 from their latest dealing with Gullino and Christie's in London was owed £33,000. Everyone, it seemed, was demanding he repaid one debt or another. I went through letters from auction houses, framers, transport companies and art galleries, as well as those from debt collection agencies. Each of these letters came before Gullino was outed in the media, so none of them could have known that they were chasing the man alleged to have killed Markov.

In among Gullino's papers from this period, I even found an application for a name change. Although it had not been filled out, I was fascinated by the idea that Gullino had been thinking about ways to make himself disappear. Perhaps this was something he had since gone ahead with, which would make the job of finding him even harder.

Nestled at the bottom of this box I saw the two copies of *Mein Kampf* that Franco had once shown me when we had been sitting in his house. Next to these two books were his appointment diaries. Each one was made by a company called Mayland and had a spiral spine. It was strange to think of Francesco Gullino going out at the end of each year to buy a new diary, always the same brand, always the spiral, and how he must have taken some kind of comfort in the sense of continuity this gave him. The diaries had a page for each day and the hours were divided up into half-hour windows. As I began to flick through them, I noticed that the tops of these pages were still bound together by a light film of dust. They had not been touched for decades. I looked at them without much interest before I realised, with a jolt, that these diaries might cover the murder of Georgi Markov.

My fingers were trembling as I looked to see which years Franco had in the box. There were diaries for 1993, the year when Gullino lived with Franco, as well as 1989, 1986, 1987 ... And then I saw it — 1978. The year in which Georgi Markov was killed. Could Gullino have written down something that implicated him in the murder of Georgi Markov?

I knew I could flick straight to September, the month in which Markov was killed, but I decided I was going to pace myself. I started with January. On almost every day of the week there were names and words, but none of them looked suspicious. At this point, it seemed Gullino was busy setting up his new shop, Pi-Lo-Chum, meaning 'Spring Green Snail', which sold cheap Chinese clothes. His life was filled with meetings. On one day he had seven appointments. He was seeing wholesalers, builders, lawyers and tax accountants. In the evenings, I could see the names of women. Girlfriends? Business contacts? Sex workers?

I would get onto all that later. I kept going through Gullino's year. The intensity of his appointments showed no sign of letting up as spring gave into summer, and then I reached August 1978. Just like that, everything changed. The pages were blank. The same was true of September. Nothing. Not a single appointment. Nobody to see. It was as if Gullino had vacated his usual self, only to return to it later that year, in October, shortly after Georgi Markov had been laid to rest in a quiet graveyard in Dorset.

In the next box, I found an audio recording of Franco talking to Gullino. At one point the conversation suddenly moved on to Georgi Markov and the question of who could have been behind his murder.

'There are at least 800 different theories,' Franco said, as if to reassure Gullino.

'The most interesting theory,' Gullino replied, 'is that the story has nothing to it at all! Have you heard that one?'

'Yes, I have.'

'The Bulgarian they killed' – Markov – 'they tried to present him as an intellectual. In reality, he was just some fool who talked on the radio. Do you understand? The guy just died on his own. Probably from diarrhoea or colitis in the hospital.'

Franco laughed.

'They had to come up with something that could explain it. A James Bond-like operation. But look, Franco. A very *English* explanation. Have you ever thought that this story is strangely *English*? If it had been something the Bulgarians made up, they would have said it was an axe murder.'

I played this section of the tape back to myself repeatedly, to be sure that I had heard it correctly. It was an extraordinary clip. The prime suspect in the Umbrella Murder case was doing his best to put Franco off the scent. He was insisting that the British were behind this assassination, knowing, most likely, that this was precisely the kind of conspiracy theory Franco was bound to believe.

But the most interesting part of the conversation was the moment when Gullino dismissed and belittled Georgi Markov. He seemed to be irked by the idea that Markov had been a brave intellectual who stood up to a brutal dictator. In Gullino's mind, probably to assuage his feelings of guilt, he needed the victim of the Umbrella Murder to be nothing more than 'some fool who talked on the radio'.

Another one of the tapes was labelled 'Jakobsen'. I slotted it into the Dictaphone and pressed 'play'. The room was filled suddenly with the sound of my own voice. It's always strange to hear yourself in a recording, but unusual in a different way when it's a younger version of yourself that you're listening to. The recording was from 1994, when Franco and I had gone to meet Jørgen Jakobsen, the lawyer who had agreed to represent Gullino. I had no idea that Franco had been secretly recording our conversation.

'I understand you have interesting things to tell me,' I could hear Jakobsen say on the tape.

'Yes, perhaps,' came a voice in reply – my voice, the voice of younger Ulrik, a guy in his twenties who was clearly nervous and a little on edge. I felt protective of him, as if I wanted to go back in time to let him know that it was going to be alright. 'The person you represented in 1993,' the younger Ulrik went on, 'I have a lot of material about him. I'm considering making a documentary or writing a book.'

'My stance on the whole matter is that I won't say anything he doesn't approve of,' came Jakobsen's reply, stern and brusque. 'I won't approve of anything he doesn't know about. My stance on it is that I'm his defence attorney and I can't say anything if he objects.'

Jakobsen then called up his secretary.

'Can you check if there's a case in the filing system on ...' Jakobsen began. 'Oh, no, you can't. Can you find a case on a man named Galli, Gul ... Gullino? First name Francesco. I have a feeling he called himself something else.'

I knew that Gullino had a number of aliases, including, 'Mario Pagani', but had forgotten that he told Jakobsen about one of them. Next, I heard my voice again.

'Why was he actually never charged with anything?' I asked, sounding more confident than before.

'It was about Lockerbie,' he replied, as if to say *but surely you knew that already?*

I remembered the mixture of confusion and excitement I felt in that moment. What had Jakobsen meant? By 'Lockerbie', he was clearly referring to the horrific 1988 attack in which Libyan terrorists placed a bomb on board a Pan Am transatlantic flight. The plane had exploded over the Scottish village of Lockerbie, killing 259 people on board and 11 on the ground. What was Gullino's connection to this? I kept listening to the tape, hoping for an answer. But at that moment in the recording, and right through to the end, the conversation became impossible to make out. Franco must have shifted in his seat, as all I could hear was static. And yet, I had a vague memory of what Jakobsen had gone on to say. It was something like, 'they found out that he was one of their own'. After that, he shut down the conversation and showed us out of his office.

Could Gullino have been involved somehow in the Lockerbie bombing? Had he travelled to London again, ten years after going to murder Georgi Markov, and played some part in this clandestine operation? Did he run a safehouse, build the bomb, act as a courier?

I tried to piece it all together. I had to remember, first, that Jakobsen was not present during Gullino's interrogation. This line of his about Lockerbie was based on what he had heard from his client, Gullino, who was hardly the most reliable narrator. There was a chance that Gullino had simply invented this as a way of muddying the water.

The other thing that began to make sense of this was the historical context of the interrogation. Gullino had been questioned by Scotland Yard in 1993, at a time when the British were still trying hard to identify those responsible for the Lockerbie bombing. This savage attack was for them what the 9/11 attack on the World Trade Center would be the following decade for their counterparts in the USA. They were desperate to find out who was behind this and how they could have pulled it off, just as the American authorities poured themselves into catching the masterminds behind 9/11. Thousands of innocent people were questioned about their possible connection to the attack on the World Trade Center, without having any actual involvement in this plot, and in the same way Scotland Yard would cast a wide net in its attempts to solve the Lockerbie case. It was entirely normal that in an interview like this, several years after the attack, the British should be asking someone like Gullino about Lockerbie. It would have been strange if they had not. Even if it felt unlikely that Gullino could have been personally involved in this attack, he might have had some interesting information to pass on. Perhaps he had heard some rumours that were valuable to the British and was able to use these to give him leverage in the interview.

I remembered Franco's take on this in the days after that conversation with Jakobsen. He was convinced that Gullino had come to some kind of arrangement with Scotland Yard, and in exchange for information about Lockerbie they agreed to abandon their plans to charge him for the Markov murder. He thought there may have been other incidents that Gullino helped them with. When Franco heard that the 1981 attack on the Pope could have a Bulgarian connection, he wondered if Gullino provided them with information on this as well. But as was so often the case with Franco, there was no evidence. It was just speculation.

In another of Franco's boxes, I noticed a grubby white folder. Its plastic cover had stiffened with time, and it had an unpleasant smell, like vomit. I was about to put it down and come back to it later when I saw something inside that was astonishingly familiar — a page with my handwriting on it.

This was the folder Franco had kept for his dealings with me. I opened it up with a strange kind of reverence, not wanting to disturb whatever might be inside. Franco had kept notes from our conversations in Café Sebastopol and his house. He had also hung on to the agreement I had signed at the very start, in which I'd promised not to steal Franco's story and we had vowed to work together as a team.

The memory of signing that piece of paper came back to me more strongly than I had thought possible. It was hard to believe that I had written my name on this almost a quarter of a century ago, and that I was old enough now to have not just a past, but a history. Had I changed since then? I knew that I had, but was not yet sure how.

Even if Franco had refused to give me the exact details of what he was looking into and what he had found, he was always more talkative about the overall direction of his research. He was obsessed with Gullino's childhood and his Italian past: everything that happened in the years before he became a Bulgarian agent. Amid the landslide of papers and tapes, I could see that he kept returning to one story in particular.

Franco had written more than twenty versions of a text that he called 'The Italian Friend'. Sometimes it was in the style of a memoir of his time with Gullino. Other times it came out as the start of a historical novel in which he had dramatised Gullino's life in Italy. Most of the time, however, Franco had written it up as the script for a documentary.

Franco's account of Gullino's life began where you would expect, with his birth. In one version, he describes Gullino's mother dying in childbirth, but in others she dies several years later. Sometimes there were two sisters, other times three sisters and a brother. But the overall shape of this narrative was roughly the same: Francesco Gullino was born in the town of Bra, in north-western Italy, shortly after the end of the Second World War, and as a child, he saw little of his parents. According to Franco, Gullino's childhood had been tragic, and he had grown up without knowing what love was. His mother died when he was young and his father became an alcoholic and abandoned his children.

As a boy, probably at around the age of five, Gullino was sent to live with his aunt. Either she ran a brothel or she owned a bar located beneath a brothel, Franco could not make up his mind. Either way, Gullino grew up around men paying for sex. From an early age, he would have seen love as something you paid for and that other people experienced rather than him.

This helped to explain his attitude towards sex, and made it easier to understand his collection of pornographic photographs. It followed that a boy who had come of age inside a brothel, or right next to one, should feel no shame about paying for sex, and made sense of his paying women to show him affection by giving him what he called a 'girlfriend experience'. When Gullino was aged eleven, his aunt sent him to a boarding school. It was run by monks from the Salesian order, who took in orphans and children from impoverished families. He learned crafts that could be useful to him later in life and, alongside his academic studies, became a skilled wood carver. By the time he left school, Gullino was able to produce ornate picture frames.

Inside one of the boxes, I found a videotape with footage of his school. Franco had gone all the way to Italy and had set up his camera outside the main entrance to Gullino's old school. He had even tracked down one of the monks who had taught him all those years ago and persuaded him to be interviewed. The elderly cleric remembered a young Gullino as a student who enjoyed the stability of life in this monastic setting and someone who had excelled at school.

Perhaps part of the reason why Franco was always intrigued by this early period of Gullino's life was that it mirrored his own experience. Franco had also been sent away from his family to a strict Italian school. The two men often spoke about their experiences as boarders. In ways that they were still trying to understand, both seemed to have been shaped by the years they had spent inside these institutions.

Gullino's time at school also gave him his first taste of the black market. He would often tell Franco the story of how the monks at his school had secretly been in possession of the library, archives and official papers belonging to the Duchy of Savoy, a territory which had once been centred on Turin and included most of modern-day Piedmont, in north-western Italy. The monks were said to use this valuable collection as the school's own piggy bank. If they had a celebration coming up or a roof to repair, they would sell off some of these precious documents on the black market. When Gullino was in his last year, he accompanied two of the monks on a clandestine trip to meet an antiquities dealer and watched as they made a sale.

Right after leaving school, Gullino began to work in the same world. He lived in the Ventimiglia area, near the border between Italy and France, and was often seen out at local markets. He sold second-hand pictures, antiques and books. If he had the money, he would also buy objects that he felt were undervalued and for which he could find a buyer. Most of the time he sold to established antique dealers. He became known as someone who did not ask too many questions about the provenance of a piece if someone came to him with a valuable item they wanted to sell.

Up to this point in Franco's narrative, everything was straight-forward and clear. Most of his information appeared to have come from conversations that Franco had secretly recorded with Gullino. His narrative contained no wild leaps of the imagination and hardly any speculation. But in the years that followed, in the late 1960s, Franco's account of Gullino's life took on a different character.

It took me a long time to realise that Franco's aim in writing this script was not so much to present the history of this man's life. Instead, he wanted to produce a story that would confirm his theory – that Francesco Gullino had started out as an agent work-ing for the Italians, perhaps the British and the Americans as well, before being taken on by the Bulgarians. He was searching for gaps in Gullino's history that might conceal the moment when Gullino was recruited by an Italian case officer. That was what mattered to Franco more than anything else. But if Gullino really had been taken on by the Italians, they would have done everything possible to cover their tracks.

If some secret agents are blackmailed or coerced into working undercover, others agree to it partly because they have an underly-ing sympathy for the cause. Franco had no doubt that Gullino was a fascist, and that because of his political beliefs he would have wanted to work for Italian intelligence. But when did Gullino begin his drift to the right? Franco needed to answer this question. Probably at school, he decided. Franco was drawing on his own experiences here. At the religious school he had gone to, he remembered being sent out with his classmates to distribute leaflets that warned against the communist threat. He could imagine something similar happening to Gullino. He also speculated that Gullino was in search of a father figure and would have looked up to the monks and assimilated their traditional outlook on the world. Perhaps the experience of being surrounded by art and antiquities, high culture and valuable books, would have also drawn out this more conservative and right-wing outlook. Maybe the contrast to his life at home, next to the brothel, pushed him further in the same direction.

The political situation in Italy at that time could have also played a part in this. Gullino was enrolled at school at the start of a tumultuous period in Italian history later known as the *Anni di Piombo*, or 'Years of Lead'. The atmosphere in the country was unstable and tense. Those on the right, like the monks who taught Franco, were deeply worried – terrified, even – by the possibility of the Italian Communist Party achieving a popular victory. The Years of Lead were punctuated by horrific terrorist acts carried out by those on both sides of the political spectrum. A medley of anarchist and communist groups wanted to revolutionise Italian society, while an array of neo-fascist organisations, such as Ordine Nuovo and Avanguardia Nazionale, wanted the opposite and hoped for a return to how things had been under Mussolini.

Franco's theory was that Gullino must have joined one of these right-wing groups shortly after leaving school. He didn't have any proof for this. So he needed to find a possible point of connection, a moment that could provide a bridge between Gullino's story and the shadowy world of paramilitary neo-fascist groups.

Franco read everything he could, until at last he found it. The man at the heart of Franco's theory was a journalist and campaigner called Luigi Cavallo, who lived in Turin and had an interest in antique books. Gullino was always on the look-out for collectors. Although he did not live in Turin, he often came into the city to visit family members. Franco theorised that in the late 1960s, Gullino might have met Luigi Cavallo.

This excited Franco because Cavallo knew some of the most prominent figures on the Italian right, men like Edgardo Sogno, who was actively trying to prevent the rise of communism. Cavallo was also believed to have played some role within internal security at the FIAT factories in Turin. Gullino had friends who worked in one of those complexes. Was it possible that Cavallo had taken on Gullino as a spy inside one of these factories? Could he have ordered him to pass on details of who was involved in the industrial action and what they were saying?

But there is no record of Gullino ever having worked inside one of the FIAT factories. And the dates don't fit — if Cavallo had been involved in security at FIAT, it would have been in the 1950s, when Gullino was aged about ten. Yet another complication was that the strikes that Franco was writing about did not get going until much later, in the late 1960s, when Gullino was living elsewhere.

But I was beginning to see that details like this didn't matter to Franco. The coincidence of Gullino and Cavallo having been in the same city with an interest in common was just too compelling for him to ignore. Franco had established how he wanted the truth to look — all he needed were a few facts to back it up.

There was also a personal element to this part of Franco's narrative that seems to have blurred his historical vision. During the late 1960s, when the strikes at the FIAT factories in northern Italy began to be more intense and violent, Franco was living in Milan with his first wife and children. He filmed some of these protests. Not as a neutral observer, but as a supporter of the workers and the left-wing activists. He was proud to have been on their side. Was it possible that Gullino, his nemesis, could have been on the other side of this clash, working for the management? Even if the dates did not work, the thought of this made sense to him on a more emotional level. Franco was seduced by the symmetry of this idea, and the possibility that Gullino and he were forever on opposite sides of a deeper conflict, shadow boxing through time.

Franco had repeated the idea of a link between Gullino and Cavallo so many times that it became, in his accounts of Gullino's life, something that no longer needed to be bogged down with words like 'maybe' and 'perhaps'. With each new draft of 'The Italian Friend', the modifiers fell away. Gullino and Cavallo *must* have met, he reasoned, and if they did, then Gullino surely would have been taken on by one of the right-wing organisations that Cavallo had access to.

The best known of these was Gladio, a stay-behind organisation set up by NATO to act as an underground resistance movement in the event of a Soviet occupation of Western Europe. Perhaps Gullino attended the Gladio training camp in Sardinia, at Capo Marrargiu, and was one of several thousand young men who received training in basic intelligence-gathering and counterintelligence techniques.

'It's true,' Franco would always say to me, after he put forward one of his theories. He reacted to my looks of disbelief in the way that other people respond to encouragement. There was an expression I remember on his face in those moments. Come with me, he seemed to be saying. It's so obvious, so easy to understand – but only if you take that small leap of faith.

The next part of Franco's account of Gullino's life was easier to believe and was obviously based on conversations between the two of them. After starting out as an antiques dealer, Gullino had briefly gone into publishing. He found books that were out of copyright, including works on the occult and mysticism, then copied out the text and published them. He also put out an edition of the erotic novel *Emmanuelle*, about the sexual adventures of a French woman in Bangkok, which had come out in secret almost a decade earlier.

In addition to publishing books, Gullino claimed to have tried his hand at setting up a modelling agency. But, in truth, this may have been little more than an excuse for him to photograph vulnerable women. When Gullino travelled around Europe with Franco, he was always trying to set up meetings with escorts or sex workers, and often told them that he was a photographer with excellent connections. 'He liked to do what he called photographic studies of the women he was with,' Franco wrote. 'He asked them to pose in strange positions and photographed everything, while there was also sex involved.' This was natural for Gullino. He was used to seeing women exploited. He would always think of sex as something to seek out and buy.

After brief stints as a publisher and photographer, Gullino moved to Turkey in the late 1960s. By now he was in his early twenties. He soon had a job as a lorry driver, and, for the first time in his life, he had money and began to live more comfortably. Gullino's employer was an import-export company that was based in Turin with an office in Istanbul. He drove trucks through Greece, Turkey, Bulgaria and what was then Yugoslavia. Usually these were 'TIR' trucks, which stood for *Transports Internationaux Routiers*, a customs arrangement whereby goods were transported through multiple countries in sealed containers and could only be opened in the destination country. According to Franco, this was when Gullino began to smuggle, and soon he was moving small amounts of contraband across borders – as he tried to do in 1970 when arrested on the Bulgarian border.

But what was he doing in the months leading up to this moment? From everything Franco could find out, Gullino's life as a smuggler and lorry driver seemed to be going well. He later bragged to Franco about how he owned a Cadillac in Istanbul and would drive it around Turkey. The timing of this was interesting. At almost exactly the same time, in the country next door, Georgi Markov was driving a BMW around Sofia. Both vehicles drew admiring looks from passers-by. Both men enjoyed the attention.

But Franco never made that connection. He was only interested in Francesco Gullino and, in particular, the company that employed him during his time in Turkey.

In among the collection of Gullino's belongings that Franco had held on to, I found a tin decorated with a picture of three wide-eyed kittens. The lid was stiff but with a bit of effort it came away with a satisfying ring, a sound that reminded me right away of a metal box in which my grandfather used to keep his screws and nails. But Gullino's tin did not contain any ironmongery, just a jumble of business cards that he had picked up over the years. I sifted through them, handling each one as if I was an archaeologist and these were artefacts that might come apart in my hands. I noted down each of the names I could see. Perhaps one of these was an alias for his Bulgarian handler. I kept going until I found at the bottom of this tin a mass of business cards with Gullino's name on them and a logo that I had not seen before:

m◯ndial

The letters were in black, apart from the 'o', which was a yellow sun on a blue background. The business card stated that Gullino was a representative of this company, Mondial, based in Turin. This was the import-export company he had talked about. Only now did I understand why this was so important.

'Mondial Import-Export', to give it its official name, had been set up to trade leather goods within Europe, but the company was later alleged to have had a sideline in trafficking arms. During the 1970s, Mondial is rumoured to have supplied weapons and ammunition to customers in South Africa, Malawi, Angola and what was then Rhodesia. But the detail about Mondial that excited Franco so much, and I could understand why, was the identity of its owner, a man with connections to Ordine Nuovo, Italian for 'New Order'. This was the most notorious neo-fascist paramilitary group in Italy at the time. It had been set up in 1954 by Pino Rauti, who was also a partner in Mondial. There was no doubt that Ordine Nuovo and

Mondial had some kind of connection. Pino Rauti may have also had something to do with the Gladio training camp in Sardinia, and at the very least was an active figure within what Franco and others called 'the Black Army' — a catch-all term for the murky underworld of Italian neo-fascist groups, Masonic lodges, the Mafia and state officials who were willing to do whatever it might take to turn back the clock to what life had been like under Mussolini.

Ordine Nuovo, the extremist group with close ties to Gullino's employer, was a vital node within this network. The first time that most Italians heard about this group was after it had been linked to the bloody 1969 bombing of the Banca Nazionale dell'Agricoltura in Milan's Piazza Fontana. Seventeen people were killed and more than eighty injured. At first, the police investigated various left-wing groups as the possible perpetrators of this attack and singled out an anarchist called Giuseppe Pinelli. He was questioned by the police and died after falling from the fourth floor of the police station. The investigation into his highly suspicious death concluded that it was an accident and nobody was charged. Those on the left were furious. Three years later, the police officer thought to have been responsible for Pinelli's death was murdered by those seeking revenge.

Several years later, it emerged that the Piazza Fontana attack had been a 'false flag' operation carried out by members of Ordine Nuovo. They had gone to extraordinary lengths to make this look like an operation carried out by anarchists. What was their motivation? They wanted political instability. Their aim was to terrorise the country into thinking that the left was about to take over, and they hoped that this would create a nationwide desire for a stronger and more authoritarian form of government. What was so remarkable about this was the number of people who were in on the conspiracy and were willing to shield those responsible for the deaths. Evidence would later emerge to show that numerous state officials intervened to disrupt the investigation into this attack and protect the perpetrators. Some of them belonged to Propaganda Due, or P2, a masonic society with close ties to those on the extreme right, and to Ordine Nuovo.

Franco had long believed that Gullino was part of this spidery web of neo-fascist groups. Now he had something close to proof. The other connections he made were based on the kind of hopeful speculation that fell apart if you took a moment to inspect it. But Gullino's employment by Mondial was different. It was more substantial and suggested that Franco might have been onto something.

As I thought about it more, it made sense that Gullino might have wanted to join one of these neo-fascist organisations and become a foot-soldier in the Black Army. He had lost both of his parents at an early age. He may not have been an orphan but he grew up with a very fractured sense of family. He had a distant, sexualised idea of women. The first time he felt a powerful sense of belonging was probably at boarding school, so he was used to the idea of being part of an all-male group that was cloistered away from the rest of the world. Perhaps he also liked feeling that he was part of something larger, older and more significant than himself. In other words, Gullino's background made him perfectly suited to being recruited by a secretive right-wing group.

I still had masses of Franco's material to get through. I knew there could be something else in these boxes to suggest a connection between Gullino and one of these mysterious neo-fascist groups. There might also be evidence that Franco had stumbled upon information that he was not meant to have seen, a critical detail that was so sensitive it might have led to his death. Then again, the Mondial link might be the end of it. I simply could not tell. The timing of Franco's unexplained death so soon after seeing Gullino could still be nothing more than a bizarre coincidence.

After going through at least twenty versions of Franco's biography of Gullino, I began to watch each of the videotapes I could find in the boxes. This was going to take a long time. Most of the recordings were from Franco's earlier projects and had nothing to do with the Umbrella Murder.

It had been weeks since I had begun to wade through this stuff, and I was starting to lose hope, when I found a series of recordings that were at once different to any of the others and somehow stranger. In almost every other tape, Franco was an unseen presence. Either he was guiding the camera or speaking over the footage. But in this new set of tapes, Franco had put himself in front of the camera and presented himself as the detective. The case he was trying to solve was the same as it always had been: who was Francesco Gullino? At first, these tapes felt like a message which had been broken up and encrypted. In some of the footage I could see Franco sitting in his study. Then he was in Italy, either in Rome or Milan, it was hard to say. One tape showed him pacing outside an Italian court building, as if waiting to meet someone. Next, Franco was lying on a hotel bed, looking tired and disillusioned, like he was close to giving up. Helene sometimes appeared in the background of the shot and I guessed that she was often the one holding the camera. At times, Franco spoke directly to her, outlining his argument about who Gullino was and why he had never been prosecuted.

Other tapes showed Franco speaking in Italian on the phone. Although you could hear the other person's voice, it was not clear who he was talking to.

It was strange to watch Franco chatting away and to feel him come back to life again. He was just as I had remembered him, only sharper and more vivid. There was the half-smile I had carried in my memory, the same inward-facing laugh, the way he would nod as he listened, the occasional glances around the room as if he had forgotten something, and that enormous gold ring on his finger.

For a long time, I sat through this footage of him talking on the phone in Italian. Although I didn't understand what he was saying, it was clear from the look on his face that this was serious, and that the man on the other end of the line was important to him. Why had he chosen to record these conversations at all? Clearly, Franco attached some deep significance to them, but I was not sure what.

Then I found a tape that appeared to be a compilation of excerpts from these recordings. It was labelled 'Deep Throat', and was shorter than any other tape I had found in the boxes — just eighteen minutes and twenty-nine seconds. 'Deep Throat' contained footage of Franco on the phone and images of Gullino and his belongings, as well as library archive of protests in Italy during the 1970s. I felt as if I had found the thing I was looking for. I sent the tape off to be translated. While I was waiting to hear back from the translator, I found papers in another box that explained what these recordings were about and revealed the identity of 'Deep Throat'.

24

'DEEP THROAT'

Early in 2001, Franco wrote a letter to a man he had never met. He did this kind of thing a lot. Usually, the letters were addressed to famous figures and they never replied. This one was different. The man he was writing to was Guido Salvini and he was the Italian judge who had been tasked with investigating the Piazza Fontana attack. Salvini had devoted a large part of his life to this subject. He had conducted hundreds of interviews, and his investigation had broadened out to include more groups and a string of other attacks. He had mapped out the structure of some of these secret societies, including Gladio, the NATO-backed stay-behind network, and, after more than a decade looking into it all, Salvini had become an expert on the 'Black Army'. Salvini shared Franco's desire to know more about what had really happened during the 'Years of Lead'. The difference between them, however, was the access they had. Salvini was able to view the types of classified materials that Franco could only dream of being able to see.

In his letter to Salvini, Franco explained that he had some interesting and possibly incriminating information about one Francesco Gullino. He thought Gullino might have connections to Ordine Nuovo, the group that Salvini had been investigating, and would be happy to share what he had found.

Franco received a reply from Salvini. The judge said that he would be happy to meet. If there was one thing Franco wanted in life, beyond his urge to know the full truth about Gullino, it was to be taken seriously. He longed to be listened to and for people to react to his theories with something other than disdain or indifference. Salvini's reply must have felt like a victory. At last, someone was willing to listen to him. And not just anyone: Salvini knew what he was talking about. Perhaps he knew something about Gullino that he was not willing to put down on paper but was ready to share in person.

I could picture the excitement on Franco's face as he told Helene about what had happened, and how he needed to get to Milan as soon as possible to meet this important Italian judge. They were about to take a holiday anyway, so why not combine it with the meeting? Soon, Franco and Helene were on their way to Italy to see Salvini.

I asked Helene if she remembered this meeting. Although she couldn't recall every detail, she described a big courthouse in Milan. Or was it Bologna? She wasn't sure. But the abiding memory she had was that the Italian judge, Salvini, had offered to help her husband. He had said that if Franco wanted to learn more about this subject, he could take on one of the young paralegals working in his office and employ him as a paid researcher. This man's name was Andrea Speranzoni.

Franco got in touch with Speranzoni, explained his situation, and asked if he would be willing to work for him on a part-time basis. Speranzoni was bright, industrious and knowledgeable, and, by virtue of working for Salvini, he had access to the type of records that Franco longed to see. He agreed to help.

It was around this time that Franco received the grant from the Danish Film Institute to research his film, so, for once, he had some money to spend. Of course, there was a danger that Speranzoni would be unable to find anything, and that the money would run out before he could deliver any revelations about Francesco Gullino. But Franco was willing to take the risk. This was the best lead he had had in ages. He was closer to the truth than ever before. He drew up a contract of employment, Speranzoni signed it, and they got to work.

In the months that followed, Speranzoni would call up Franco from Milan to give him updates on his progress. Before each call, Franco set up a camera on a tripod and recorded the whole thing. Speranzoni was the man he had been talking to in those tapes I had seen – he was the figure Franco came to call 'Deep Throat', after the pseudonym of the source who exposed the Watergate scandal to journalists Bob Woodward and Carl Bernstein in the 1970s.

The early signs were promising. Speranzoni was clearly making some progress. He was getting close, he kept saying. Speranzoni always appeared to be on the verge of delivering something big, something that would blow the whole case open. As I went through the correspondence between them, I could feel Franco's excitement growing. Then he received from Speranzoni a cache of material: 500 pages from various criminal investigations into organisations such as Ordine Nuovo.

The documents were fascinating. They included lists of individuals who may have belonged to this group. I could imagine the manic speed with which Franco would have gone through these papers and the tension he must have felt as he looked for the name 'Gullino', only for that feeling to fade away as he reached the end. There was no reference to Francesco Gullino.

Not to worry. Speranzoni was soon back in touch to say that he had found a file on Franco himself. Again, this would have been thrilling for him and proof that he was on to something – *if I'm being watched, it's because of my interest in Gullino, which proves that he's one of them.*

But it turned out that Speranzoni had confused Franco with someone who had a similar-sounding name. There was no file on Franco.

Helene was under the impression that Franco never actually received anything substantial or useful from Speranzoni. It seemed that Franco had either run out of money before his researcher could find anything valuable or there was nothing to find. I was beginning to feel a similar sense of disappointment, when I heard back from the translator who had been going through the tape that had, for some reason, seemed particularly important. As I went through the transcript of this tape, I understood why Franco had made it. What he had put together was a compilation of the most revealing clips from his many hours of conversation with Speranzoni. This was the treasure I had been searching for.

In one of these excerpts, Speranzoni told Franco that he thought – but could not be sure – that documents about Francesco Gullino were now being removed from the records he had access to. In other words, Franco's interest in Gullino had triggered some kind of cover-up.

In another clip, Speranzoni warned Franco that the whole subject was extremely delicate. He then said something that left me confused. He explained to Franco that it was 'so delicate that you must avoid provoking crises between nation states'. What could he mean? Which countries was he referring to and why would his research provoke a crisis? I listened back to the original tape, from which this clip had been taken, in the hope of finding answers. But Speranzoni was maddeningly vague.

The next clip was fascinating. 'He is a protected person,' Speranzoni said, of Francesco Gullino. 'He is not just a fascist. He has always been protected.'

In another conversation, Speranzoni revealed that a judge he had recently spoken to described Gullino, the man alleged to have carried out the Umbrella Murder, as being 'still a protected person'. That word 'still' was hugely important. Not only did it suggest that Franco might have been onto something, but that Gullino was still alive and there were people who wanted to keep him safe. It followed that those same people would not welcome someone like Franco trying to make a film about him. Was it even possible that they could have played a part in his death?

According to Speranzoni, the judge who he had been speaking to was also told: 'You must only pursue the Bulgarian trail because there are no other trails.'

Again, what could this mean? It might have been a simple statement of fact. Perhaps there really were no other trails and Gullino had simply been taken on by Bulgarian intelligence as an undercover agent. Or else it was another coded warning, one more way of saying: stop looking into Gullino's Italian past.

That was not all. Franco had saved the best until the end. Andrea Speranzoni had also heard that Rosario Priore, one of the other magistrates investigating the Piazza Fontana bombing, was interested in Gullino. Although Speranzoni had only heard this second-hand, the rumour was that Priore referred to Gullino as 'a key person' and thought of him as someone who 'was protected by multiple intelligence agencies'. In another part of this tape, Speranzoni told Franco that there was one thing he should stress. He believed that it was a *quasi certezza*, 'a near certainty', that Gullino was *un funzionario dei servizi*, meaning 'an official working for the intelligence services'.

Was this it? After so many years of thinking that Franco might have imagined the whole thing, this was the first time I had heard someone who knew what they were talking about say that they believed Francesco Gullino had some kind of connection to Italian intelligence. Though he did not say what this link might be or which agency he was talking about. Nothing in Gullino's history suggested that he might have been a fully paid-up intelligence officer whose job was to run other agents and analyse their reports. It was much more likely that he was on the other side of the street, supplying information to a handler.

But if that had been the case, what was the arrangement? I was faced with a spectrum of possibilities. Right over at one end was the idea that Francesco Gullino had at one stage, in the late 1960s, been a casual informant passing on information about communist or socialist activities to someone who was — unbeknown to him — working for Italian intelligence. Maybe he was given specific jobs to do as well. Equally, it could have been even more basic than that. Gullino may have been involved in some nefarious Ordine Nuovo activity that a number of state officials wanted covered up. This would be enough to make Speranzoni think that Gullino was linked to Italian intelligence.

Another way of reading this was that Gullino was much closer to the James Bond figure Franco wanted him to be: a fully trained-up secret agent who was given instructions to penetrate Bulgarian intelligence. If something like that had really happened, it was possible that some of his intelligence might have been shared with other agencies, which could explain why Gullino had not been prosecuted for his alleged role in the Umbrella Murder or for his other espionage activities in Denmark. Gullino had, after all, spent two decades in Copenhagen as a Bulgarian intelligence agent. The Danish authorities had spoken to him and charged him with espionage, but that was it. As far as I could tell, they did not follow up with a major investigation. They just let the whole thing go.

Why?

Andrea Speranzoni's answer had been simple. 'He has always been protected,' he told Franco in another one of their conversations. 'He has been given freedom of movement because he has been useful in certain contexts.'

At several points in the 'Deep Throat' tape, Speranzoni was clearly warning Franco to back off.

'I repeat,' he said to Franco at one point, 'it is very delicate material. We must move very carefully, like dancing on tiptoe.'

Later, he gave his reaction to being told that Gullino might be protected. 'I think it's a warning not to dig and go astray,' he said.

At another point in this recording, Speranzoni urges caution again. 'I would ask you to be discreet. No one, absolutely no one must know.'

Even if Speranzoni was leading Franco on, even if he knew that he was never going to have first-hand access to material on Gullino and would always be going on rumours and conversations with others, he was evidently worried about some aspect of what they were doing. You could hear it in his voice. The underlying message of the 'Deep Throat' tape was simple: Francesco Gullino is still being protected in ways that we don't understand, and we should probably stop looking into this.

I knew Franco well enough to be confident that this would not have had the desired effect. Being told to back off was, for Franco, a form of encouragement. It meant that he was getting close to a valuable insight and made him want to dig harder.

'Franco did not care about his own life,' Bent had told me as he handed over the boxes. 'As long as he could get the truth out. That was all that mattered.'

Could Franco have been murdered because he was too close to the truth about Gullino? Had his appearance in the documentary played some part in his death? For the first time, it started to seem a realistic possibility. What I had found in Franco's boxes seemed to suggest that, at the very least, this was a possible explanation for what had happened. I began to circle back to the events leading up to Franco's death. If I was going to work this out, I had to piece together an account of what had happened to him in his final few days and look for any signs that he could have been poisoned. It reminded me of Jim Nevill starting his investigation into Georgi Markov's mysterious death. Here I was, forty years later, looking into another unexplained death involving the same suspect. But that's where the similarities ended. Nevill, of Scotland Yard, had access to some of the world's best forensic specialists and scientists, as well as a small army of seasoned detectives. I did not. It was just me. Me and Franco's material, and my two key witnesses, Helene and Bent.

It was not much. But it might be enough.

25

THE LAST SUPPER

What would Jim Nevill do? That's what I had to keep asking myself. Well, his first move had been to put together a timeline of all the events leading up to Georgi Markov's death. I figured that I should do the same. There were two fixed points in the chronology of Franco's death that I knew about already. One was Franco's admission to hospital. The other was the broadcast of the television documentary in which Franco went public and described Gullino as 'a dangerous man'.

Bent and Helene had conflicting memories of when this programme had gone out, but they both said that it was shortly before Franco's death. I searched online to find the exact time and date. This was crucial. If they had misremembered and it had, in fact, gone out the month before or the day after his admission to hospital, then that would blow a hole in the idea that Gullino or those protecting him could have had a hand in Franco's death.

I felt my heart sink as I saw that it had gone out in 2006, the year before Franco's mysterious death. Then I looked again. That was only the United Kingdom broadcast. It was not until the following year, 2007, that *Paraplymordet*, Danish for 'The Umbrella Murder', was shown in Denmark. More precisely, the programme had gone out on DR2 at 9.40pm on Tuesday 22 May 2007.

The other fixed point in the chronology was Franco's admission to hospital. Again, I needed to get this right and couldn't rely on anyone's memory. I contacted Helene to see if she had a report from the hospital about what had happened to Franco. She sent over a medical account and there, right at the top, was the detail I had been looking for. Franco was admitted to hospital complaining of 'sudden chest pain' at 12.30pm on Wednesday 23 May 2007. It was fourteen hours after the closing credits appeared on the television documentary.

But the final date in the chronology, and the most important one, was going to be much harder to pin down. This was the timing of the meal that Gullino and Franco had together. Bent and Helene both remembered it taking place shortly before he went to hospital. They had not spoken to each other for years so they were not just repeating what the other one had said. Both of them had told me that this meal had taken place *after* Gullino heard about the documentary and that Gullino was angry with Franco. This meal was a way of smoothing things out between them.

So what happened? Either Gullino called up Franco late on the night of the broadcast, at around ten o'clock, just after the closing credits, and had suggested they go for a drink or a meal. Or Gullino had heard about the documentary after it was broadcast in Britain and was reminded of it when it was scheduled to go out in Denmark. This seemed more likely. A programme like this being shown in Denmark could lead to a new criminal investigation into the Umbrella Murder. Franco might be a witness. It made sense both that Gullino would have known about it before it went out and that he would have been extremely annoyed.

Until then, I had not appreciated that the only other time there had been anything on television about Gullino's connection to the Umbrella Murder was back in the summer of 1993, after Franco went to the media with the story. Fourteen years later, Franco was a source for another programme on the same theme. Franco seemed to be the only person consistently telling the world about the connection between Gullino and the Umbrella Murder. It followed that if Gullino could silence him, he would be safe.

Helene had told me that Franco had gone for his final dinner with Gullino somewhere north of Copenhagen. This sounded plausible. Franco had once taken me to an Italian restaurant called 'Il Divino' in Strandvejen. Perhaps this was where he took Gullino.

When Franco came home that night he was nervous. From what Helene had said, it sounded as if Gullino was angry during this meal. Could Gullino have slipped something into his drink?

Gullino had both a motive and an opportunity. He also had form. By that I don't mean the murder of Georgi Markov, but that he was familiar with the notion of poisoning someone's food or drink. I would later speak to a Danish woman who had briefly been Gullino's girlfriend in the 1970s, before the Umbrella Murder, and who remembered how he was obsessed with a book called *Toxic Nature*, a complete guide to the natural poisons that could be found in the Amazon rainforest. I had also heard something in one of Franco's secret recordings of Gullino that gave me pause. The two men had been chatting amicably when Gullino said that of course the easiest way to kill anyone was by slipping arsenic into their coffee.

This proved nothing. But it did at least show that Francesco Gullino had given a certain amount of thought over the years to the practicalities of poisoning someone.

The morning after the documentary aired, Franco felt a sharp pain in his chest and neck. He decided not to call an ambulance as he didn't think it was all that serious. But Helene drove him to the nearest hospital anyway. The medics carried out an initial round of tests but could not work out what was going on. They found no sign of sepsis or blood clots. Nor was this likely to be liver or kidney disease. Franco was a seventy-one-year-old with a pacemaker and had recently been diagnosed as diabetic. But he was otherwise in good health. His blood pressure was a little higher than usual but nothing to worry about. Later that evening, they gave him nitroglycerin. Franco reacted badly to this, and looked pale and weak while his blood pressure began to drop. The doctors then put him in the Trendelenburg position, which meant tipping the foot of his bed up until his head was lower than his feet.

The thought of this reminded me of how Georgi Markov was placed in the opposite position, with his head above feet. At least, that's how one of his Bulgarian friends remembered it. Perhaps both men found themselves at one stage tipped upside down as their bodies struggled to fight two very different illnesses, which could both be linked back to the same individual.

Tipping Franco's bed up had the effect of improving his condition – or as one of the doctors wrote: 'the patient does not seem acutely affected.' Still, his chest pains had not gone away. Franco became more worried. At this point, they found a small tumour in his right kidney, which might have explained some of what was happening – but not everything. The doctors were not worried about the tumour and it was not about to kill him. As another doctor wrote later that night, 'the patient is unable to be diagnosed still.'

Even if the medical symptoms were entirely different, I couldn't help but notice some of the broader similarities to Georgi Markov's final days. Each man had gone to hospital with relatively mild symptoms only for his condition to become suddenly worse. The doctors looking after them were baffled. They had carried out tests and spoken to each other in increasingly panicked tones. Both patients had rallied for a moment before going into terminal decline.

When Franco woke up the next day, he felt worse. The pain in his chest was sharper and he had begun to vomit as well. The doctors kept coming up with possible diagnoses. But there was always some crucial detail that did not fit. At around lunchtime, his condition suddenly deteriorated. Franco's skin took on a bluish hue and he was struggling to breathe. He asked Helene to open the window. When she turned back to look at him, he had stopped breathing. She called for help. The medical staff carried out CPR. They put him on a ventilator and tried to bring him back to life, but were unable to do so. After ten minutes of this, they stopped and Franco was pronounced dead.

Helene was distraught. She could not understand what had happened. The whole thing had been so sudden. Franco had been fine and in good health, only to be snatched away from her. The doctors explained that they would need to take Franco's body away for an autopsy to work out what had happened. The doctors opened up his skull but found nothing that could explain his death. Their best guess was a pulmonary embolism that had progressed suddenly. They had a brief conversation about whether he could have been poisoned. But either they had not been told about Franco's meal with Francesco Gullino or they did not think it significant, as they concluded that there was no justification for a more detailed toxicological investigation. They did, however, contact the local police, in Bellahøj, after a conversation with Franco's children, and passed on their concerns. But the police decided not to open a criminal investigation into Franco's death. On his death certificate, the cause of his death was given simply as 'blood clot' – something that they had already ruled out.

I approached three doctors I knew from my neighbourhood and asked them about this case. I showed each of them the medical account of Franco's treatment. Each one agreed that the staff looking after Franco had taken the correct steps and did not miss anything obvious. The doctors and nurses had clearly put a lot of effort into finding out what could have been causing Franco's symptoms. There was no suggestion of medical negligence. But they also assured me that based on what had been written in the report, there was simply no way that Franco could have died from a blood clot.

The law requires you, as a doctor, to write something, so that's what they put. The tragedy here, in terms of being able to find out why he had died, was that listing a blood clot as the cause of death had removed the need for a detailed toxicological investigation or a forensic examination of his stomach.

If I'm honest, I had been hoping to find something in this medical account that would make sense of Franco's death. One detail that could burst the bubble of suspicion that had formed in my mind. I think a part of me wanted this episode to be a string of unlikely coincidences. But the more I learned, the harder it was to sustain that belief. It was pretty much impossible to dismiss the link between the timing of Franco's meal with Gullino and his unexplained death. Perhaps Franco really had been murdered by the man he had come so close to exposing.

Where did this leave me? I had a safe and comfortable life with my new wife, and two young kids to look after. Going after Gullino was going to be dangerous and uncertain. This man was toxic. What I had heard on the 'Deep Throat' tape left me in little doubt that he was a protected species, even if I was still in the dark about who or what was protecting him. The obvious thing to do was to leave him alone.

But if I didn't follow the path which was starting to present itself to me, then the truth about Gullino could die with him.

The Danish police were no longer looking for Gullino. Either they had made an agreement with him or they had just let him go. Scotland Yard had also tried to get him in court but had been unable to gather enough evidence. Then there was Franco, who had devoted part of his life to uncovering the truth about Gullino but had died before he could finish the job.

Whether it was down to a conspiracy, a lack of evidence, murder or lack of desire, I realised that nobody was pursuing

Gullino. Unless something changed, he was never going to have his comeuppance.

I knew what I had to do. I would go after the man behind the Umbrella Murder. Francesco Gullino must be in his early seventies by now. If he was still alive, I would locate him. Even if I was unable to find enough evidence to land him in jail, by exposing him to the world, I might be able to achieve some kind of justice for what had happened to Georgi Markov as well as Franco.

Now all I had to do was find him.

PART THREE

MANHUNT

26
THE TEAM

If I was going to do this, I needed help. I admired Franco in so many ways. His determination was contagious and the longer I had spent going through his boxes, the more I had come to love the renegade way in which he came at the world. But he had made mistakes in his pursuit of Gullino and, for me, the most obvious was his decision to do it alone. I didn't want to spend the next decade of my life on a solitary quest to find out the truth about the Umbrella Murderer. I wanted to be challenged and to see how other people would tell the story. If I was going to expose Francesco Gullino, I had to put together a team.

At my television production company, we often took on interns and young researchers to help out in the office. I had seen a lot of them over the years but there was one who had only just joined – Lukas – who really stood out. Lukas had a boyish, disarming smile and a gentle manner. But beneath that, as I had begun to find out, was an altogether different kind of person.

The first thing you noticed about Lukas was his memory. He only needed to skim through a text once to recall almost everything he had seen. He was able to point out the tiniest mistake that some-one might have made, because he had a brain that retained the sorts of details that the rest of us lose. But he was nice about it and when he made a correction, he did so with a bashful air, as if he recognised that it was unusual to have a memory as good as this.

He was also determined, and I had seen how his energy and purpose was rubbing off on some of the older journalists sitting next to him in our office. But what really set him apart, even in the few months that he had been with us, was his ability to find information. Lukas was, hands down, the best researcher I had ever worked with. He seemed to possess a dizzying knowledge of different directories, registers and databases, and, on top of that, he had a puzzle-solving brain. Once he had a question to answer – whether it was finding someone's contact details for an interview or identifying a face in a photograph – he would not stop until he had found it. A part of him seemed to be offended by the idea that he might not be able to track down a piece of information. In the office, we had started to call him the 'baby-faced assassin': if Lukas had you in his sights, he was going to find you.

Or had I overestimated him? Before telling Lukas about my idea for a film, I thought I would set him a small challenge. I knew that Gullino sometimes communicated with his Bulgarian case officer by leaving messages in a 'dead drop' – spy-speak for a hiding place known only to an agent and the case officer running them. Usually, the idea is that both will go to this location at regular intervals to check for a message. The dead drop used by Gullino and his Bulgarian case officer was situated behind the gravestone of a man called Jørgen Hjort, in Assistens cemetery in the Nørrebro district, here in Copenhagen, famous today for being the final resting place of Hans Christian Andersen, Niels Bohr and Søren Kierkegaard. But I had never visited this grave. The cemetery was huge, with thousands of graves, and I wasn't sure of its precise location.

I asked Lukas if he was free to talk in private. He looked apprehensive as we walked into one of the meeting rooms in the office. If the company was going through hard times, then a recent recruit like him was less likely to be kept on. He looked relieved as he realised that he was not being laid off. I told him instead about this gravestone. All I knew about its location, I said, was that it was close to the wall at the edge of the cemetery. I asked him if he might be able to find it and take a few photographs.

His face brightened. I was expecting him to ask a stream of questions – *Can you tell me more about the location of the grave? How do I get to the cemetery? Can you google it?* Instead, Lukas simply said that he would see what he could do and returned to his desk.

The next day, he came into the office as usual. I went over to see him.

'I found your gravestone,' he said, almost absent-mindedly. He pulled out his phone and showed me the photographs he had taken of it yesterday evening.

I was impressed. If I was going to track down Francesco Gullino, I needed Lukas on my team. We went to the meeting room for another conversation, in which I told him everything. The man we were going after was a trickster, a spy and a petty criminal. His only loyalty was to himself. I was confident that he was responsible for Georgi Markov's death and perhaps that of my friend Franco as well. He had links to Bulgarian intelligence and Italian intelligence, and probably the Mafia. My plan, I told Lukas, was to make a film exposing this individual for what he was.

It could be dangerous. Scratch that. It *would* be dangerous. But I needed his help. Was he in?

Lukas should have hesitated at this point, really. This was the moment to ask a few more questions or at least consider some of the reasons to say no. Instead, he looked as if he had just won a prize. Yes, he said, beaming. He wanted to be a part of this.

As I thought more about the kind of film that we were going to make, I realised that my own story would probably need to be a part of it. In other words, I might end up at one point in front of the camera rather than behind it. This made me think that we needed a director. Given how close I was to this material, the project would benefit from having someone else to shape the story and point out things that I might have missed. I knew from Franco, and from so many other projects I had worked on, that the temptation when telling your own story will always be to include everything, even when some of it doesn't serve the story you're trying to tell.

A few years ago, I had met a director called Frederik. He had started out at DR, like me, before leaving to make his own work. He had an impressive CV and had won several prestigious awards throughout his career. He was hugely talented and in demand: a celebrity in our world of Danish documentaries. Frederik was already working on another project for my company, but I still felt a rush of nerves as I walked into the café where we had agreed to meet and I began to tell him about the project.

As we talked, all my trepidation fell away. Frederik was ebullient and chatty, and as he fired off questions about Gullino, Franco and what we'd put together, his enthusiasm spurred me on. His reaction also allowed me to see things in the story that I had either forgotten about or overlooked. He was ambitious and creative, speaking excitedly about the range of this story – how it moved in time from the 1970s to the present, and took place in Britain, Bulgaria, Italy and Denmark – and how he liked the way it was a blend of true crime and espionage. But what really drew him in, he went on, was the enigmatic and oddly magnetic character at the heart of it – Francesco Gullino.

We kept going like this for several hours, until at last I asked him the question that I had been building up to all this time – would he be willing to come on board as our director?

Yes, he said. He was in.

For a moment, I thought that was it. Me, Lukas, Frederik. But we were going to need someone to film this. I had worked with a lot of different cameramen and -women over the years, but I knew right away who to ask.

Anders was a Swede who had begun to work for our company several years ago. He was someone who really cared about what he was doing, which wasn't always the case with people in his position. Anders went further than anyone else I had ever worked with in his pursuit of a particular shot, even if this meant driving for hours to get to the right location or waiting half the day until the conditions around him were just so. He was also calm when a situation became manic or out of control, as they sometimes did when filming a documentary project.

The other thing about Anders was that he had a way of making himself small and unobtrusive when we were filming interviews. Other cameramen and -women were louder and busier, and I had noticed the effect this could have on the person being interviewed, especially if they were about to talk about a difficult moment in their lives. But Anders was different. He could record footage almost without anyone noticing that he was there.

Anders listened carefully to my pitch and paused. I wasn't asking him to join the team on a permanent basis, but to be ready to help out as a freelancer each time we needed to shoot. His silence didn't worry me. That was his way. After a moment's reflection, he said that he was willing to become our cameraman. We wouldn't be shooting anything for a while, I warned him, but I was glad to have him on board.

27
LOOSE ENDS

In August 2020, despite the extra difficulties COVID-19 had thrown up, we made a proper start. We began by dividing up our investigation into three parts. First on the list was what we called 'the Italian connection': the idea that Gullino might have had, or continued to have, some sort of relationship with Italian intelligence. Perhaps he was being protected by the Italian government or he was linked to a shadowy neo-fascist group like Ordine Nuovo. The other question circling this part of his life was whether he really had been money laundering on behalf of his friends in Sicily, and if this was proof of a connection to the Mafia. Maybe they were the ones protecting him?

There were probably dozens of people out there who knew something about the truth of Francesco Gullino's connection to these different Italian groups, but only two of them were people we stood even the slightest chance of being able to put in front of a camera. One was Andrea Speranzoni, the researcher Franco had taken on who became the star of his 'Deep Throat' montage. The other was Guido Salvini, the Italian judge who had first introduced them and who seemed to know more than most about Francesco Gullino. We set about trying to track them down.

We quickly established that both men were still alive. In the years since his conversations with Franco, Speranzoni had become a distinguished lawyer and now had his own practice in Bologna. Salvini, meanwhile, was still a respected and well-known judge. I found an email address for him among Franco's papers and drafted a message to him. But I couldn't find anything for Speranzoni.

Lukas stepped in to help. Within minutes, he handed me a piece of paper with Speranzoni's telephone number. I picked up the phone and was about to dial the number when I paused.

So far, our investigation had been confined to the walls of this office and our team of four people. Making this call to Speranzoni would be the first time I told someone who might not be on our side about what we were hoping to do. It was like firing a flare in the middle of the night. I knew that Gullino, if he was out there, might see it. But there was no alternative. We could not creep up on him without his finding out about us. I made the call.

Speranzoni was busy, his secretary told me, but he would call me back. Later that day, I sent my email to Salvini, praising his fine work as a judge and asking about the possibility of an interview at some point in the future. Without going into too much detail about our investigation, I mentioned Franco's name. He would surely remember him. Now all we had to do was wait.

The second part of our investigation was closer to home. We needed to unravel the Danish thread in Gullino's story. For most people, what made Gullino interesting was the role he might have played in Georgi Markov's murder: the question of whether he had fired a ricin pellet into Markov's leg using an umbrella. Very little was ever said about his clandestine activities in Denmark, mainly because these remained cloaked in mystery.

But Francesco Gullino had spent a staggering two decades in Copenhagen as a fully-fledged Bulgarian spy. What had he been up to? Who was he spying on, what sort of intelligence was he passing on and, crucially, why had the Danish authorities never got round to arresting him and prosecuting him on the charge of espionage?

I remembered Franco saying that after Gullino was questioned back in 1993, he was told by a PET intelligence officer called Poul Erik Dinesen that he would be charged with espionage. When Gullino's lawyer wrote to the president of Copenhagen City Court, he said that his client had been charged under sections 107 and 108 of the Criminal Code. Gullino was told to appear in court some weeks later. But this appearance was later cancelled and that was the last of it. What had happened? Had Danish intelligence reached some kind of secret deal with Gullino?

I began by writing to PET, asking them why they had never formally charged Francesco Gullino. We then booked an appointment in the Rigsarkivet, the Danish national archive to see if there was a file on Gullino. Next, I arranged to see a contact of mine, someone who had once worked in PET and who might have good background information on this.

Of course, the people who knew exactly what had happened, and who were better informed than anyone else on this case, were Poul Erik Dinesen himself, who had first approached Gullino back in 1993 shortly before the interview with Bird and Kemp from Scotland Yard, and the police assistant Pia Birgitta Møller. Dinesen in particular had been present throughout that interview. If anyone could shed light on why Gullino was never prosecuted by the Danish authorities, it was him.

But how were we ever going to get hold of them? Were they still alive?

Pia turned out to be a dead end: we searched for her for a long time with no luck, and my sources within PET could not find or remember her. On to Dinesen. Lukas soon found an old website for the Haslev Video Club, a group which had been active back in the 1990s, when owning a video camera was new and exciting and had become a hobby. The chairman of this particular group had been one Poul Erik Dinesen. Could it be our man?

Lukas kept going with his research and found that the same Dinesen had been part of the local Lions Club, a charitable organisation that aims to provide humanitarian support around the world. On an archived website, he found photographs of various club meetings. One of these showed a man captioned as Dinesen shaking somebody's hand. He was in a suit and had thick black hair and sideburns. Yes, I thought to myself. That's got to be our man. It's hard to put my finger on what it was about him, but in that one picture he gave the impression of being someone who knew more than anyone else in that room. He looked like a spy.

I made a list of everyone with the surname Dinesen who lived in the vicinity of this video club. But as it was late, I decided to wait until the next day to call them up.

The third part of our investigation was broader and more open ended. We needed to go through Franco's papers again to see if there was anything about Gullino that I might have missed when I looked at them on my own. Had he worked for any other agencies? Were there more dark secrets in his past?

Franco's boxes were still stacked up in a corner of our office, filling the air with their aroma of decay. Lukas and I divided them between us and we started to go through them systematically. We agreed to make a note of every address and phone number we found that Gullino had left in Franco's house. For a moment, I thought about which of these write to or call, but the answer was obvious. All of them. I wanted us to follow up on every lead. Yes, I wanted to be quick, but it was also important to be thorough, and for all of us to arrive at the end of this journey knowing that there was nowhere left to go.

In the meantime, I couldn't help but start to feel a kind of watchfulness, one that reminded me of how I had felt when Franco had first brought me into this story decades earlier. I noticed that I was starting to become more on edge and doing things that at any other time I would have found ridiculous. On the subway each morning, I began scanning the faces around me to see if any were familiar. Then I started to vary my routes into work. After all, I told myself, if Gullino was protected – and it seemed that he might be – then it followed that there could be people who did not want our investigation to succeed or who, at the very least, would want to find out more about what we were doing.

My other worry was whether I was doing enough to keep the stack of boxes in our office safe. They represented our most precious resource. If we lost them, we lost our film. Once I'd had that thought, I became worried about the idea of leaving them unprotected in the office each night. I kept imagining me walking in one morning to find that they had all vanished. Leaving them where they were seemed reckless. A team of hardened burglars might be able to slip in at night and cart them off.

I decided to move the boxes. But where? A conventional storage unit did not feel secure and, besides, I would need regular access to fish out a particular tape or document. The longer I thought about it, the more obvious the answer became: I needed to store the boxes in my house.

This, of course, presented another problem. Last time I had gone after Francesco Gullino, I had shared everything with my wife at the time. My life at work and home had merged. But this time round, after I told my second wife about what I had begun to do, we agreed that I would do things differently by keeping the investigation out of the house. We both wanted our home to be a place that was free from Francesco Gullino and the Umbrella Murder.

But here I was, about to bring Franco's papers into my home. I told my wife that this was the only option and that they would not get in the way. Reluctantly, she agreed. So I moved the boxes from our office to my attic. The most precious papers, the ones that I treasured more than any others, I decided to hide in the secret compartment of a wooden desk that my grandfather had made many years ago. Yes, I had broken my own rule. But this was a temporary arrangement, I told my wife — and myself. Very soon, this would all be over.

Back in the office, Lukas and I began to cold-call the numbers we had found written down among Gullino's papers. Most were out of service. Either that, or someone would pick up who had never heard of the man we were investigating. It was laborious work. Sometimes, it took weeks to discover the identity of a particular name in Gullino's diary.

One of these names was 'Marianna'. We had no idea who she was. She could be his accountant, his mistress, his dentist, a sex worker he had met or an art dealer he had business dealings with. The number next to her name was no longer working. But Lukas found Marianna's surname and discovered her new number. He gave it a call. She picked up first time.

28

HANNE

Lukas explained to Marianna over the phone that he was researching a television documentary and was looking for anyone who might have known a man called Francesco Gullino. Oh yes, Marianna told him. She remembered him well. They had once owned a horse together. They'd kept it at a stable at Dyrehaven, outside Copenhagen. Absolutely, she went on, she was happy to talk on camera about him. Several days later, Frederik, our director, drove out to record the interview.

The interview with Marianna took place in a pretty, light-filled space with views out to lush countryside beyond. Marianna's description of Gullino had a similarly bucolic feel. She had fond memories of him as a skilful rider. He had, it transpired, a rare ability to control difficult and wild horses. They seemed to respond to something in him, an inner strength, and he was famous at the Dyrehaven stables for having this preternatural ability to tame horses that other people simply could not ride. He could, Marianna said, 'take the bad out of them'.

After an hour or so, the interview appeared to have run its course and Frederik thanked Marianna for her time. The conversation had been a success and this friend of Gullino's had given us an interesting new angle on the psychology of the man we were trying to understand. Then just as he was about to leave, she said that there was one thing she had forgotten to mention.

In January 1990, she explained, she received a phone call from the police in Copenhagen. They asked if she knew someone called Gullino. Yes, she said, Francesco Gullino. The police officer explained that they would like to talk to him. Marianna passed on his number and asked what this was about.

The police had contacted her in relation to a brutal murder that had taken place recently. Gullino's name had come up. The victim was called Hanne With. She was a twenty-three-year-old sex worker living in Copenhagen and had been found in the early hours of New Year's Day in a pool of blood in her Nørrebro apartment. Her throat had been cut with a kitchen knife. Her body had been stabbed repeatedly in what appeared to have been a vicious and sustained attack.

I remembered hearing about this murder after it happened, almost thirty years ago. The story was all over the news, mainly because of the shocking nature of this murder. Unknown to me back then, the police had found among Hanne's possessions a photograph of her riding a horse. On the back were the words: 'In Dyrehaven with Gullino'.

The police investigating the murder were extremely keen to speak to Gullino about what he might have been doing on the night of the attack and had contacted people who kept horses at Dyrehaven. This was why they got in touch with Marianna.

From the television documentaries I had made over the last decade, I had a few contacts at the police. I decided to call one of them to see if he was able to find out anything about the investigation into Hanne With's murder. Several days later, he came back to me. Although he would not tell me how he had found out, he knew what had happened.

Yes, he said, the police had spoken to Marianna. They had also called up Francesco Gullino, and asked him where he had been on New Year's Eve — the night of the murder. Gullino had said that he spent the night at a party with friends in Nærum. The names of his friends were Jens and Margit Hallin. The police then asked for Jens and Margit's contact details, so that they could be sure that his alibi checked out. Gullino gave them a telephone number and the officer thanked him for his time and hung up.

Later that day, the police called up the Hallins. The man who picked up the phone confirmed that Gullino had spent New Year's Eve with him. Everyone had had a great time at their party. Perhaps they had drunk too much. As far as he could remember, Gullino went home in the early hours, at the same time as everyone else. The police were happy with this. Gullino's alibi was fine, and they crossed him off their list of potential suspects.

The police officer I spoke to described this investigation into Hanne With's murder as 'massive', 'comprehensive' and 'really extensive'.[1] The police had interviewed more than 150 men in the weeks after the murder. But none of them were charged and this became one of Denmark's most notorious unsolved murders.

I had watched enough crime dramas to know that alibis are not always what they seem. On a whim, I decided to track down Jens Hallin, the man who had hosted the New Year's Eve party that Gullino attended on the night of the murder. I wanted to find out more about that party. Even if he could not remember anything about it – and not everyone can remember a party so long ago – he must have been one of Gullino's friends and might have some interesting memories of him.

It was fairly easy to get in touch with Hallin, and soon we were talking about the New Year's Eve party he had thrown back in 1989. To my surprise, he remembered it well. He even had photos from that night which he had recently put into an album. As he described it, he and his wife had thrown a small party for a handful of friends.

Then I asked him about when Gullino arrived.

Hallin sounded confused. What did I mean? Francesco Gullino never came to their party; he would remember a thing like that.

I asked him if he was sure.

Hallin said that he would check this with his wife and children. He would even look at the photographs he had of the party. Several hours later, Hallin called back. He had remembered it right. Gullino was not at their house on that night.

'But I don't understand,' I said. 'Why did you tell the police that he had been with you?'

'I did no such thing! The police never called me.'

'What?'

'The police did not call. Simple as that.'

I told Frederik and Lukas about the conversation. Gullino must have given the police the number for someone else and had told this person to play the part of Jens Hallin. He had also given him instructions to say that they had all been together on the night of New Year's Eve.

What was going on? According to my police contact, Francesco Gullino had paid for sex with Hanne With on numerous occasions. They had also seen each other for 'favour' exchanges. This was when Gullino paid sex workers to be with him in a non-sexual way – what he called a 'girlfriend experience'. When the police had asked Gullino about his relationship with the murder victim, he had said that he would sometimes drive her around in his car and on one occasion he had taken her out to the stables to ride his horse.

But why did Gullino lie to the police about where he had been on the night of her death? What was he trying to hide?

29

SALVINI

To my surprise, Judge Salvini wrote back. He was happy to be interviewed, he said in his email, but only if the conversation was in Italian.

Now we were starting to get somewhere. Salvini had an unparalleled understanding of the subterranean world that had produced Francesco Gullino, and the shadowy connections within the so-called 'Black Army' of right-wing groups, Freemasons, Mafiosi and state officials in Italy. If anyone could shed light on Gullino's past, it was Judge Salvini.

We agreed on a date for the interview and I contacted a translator I knew in Milan. Anders was unable to come, so I found another cameraman. A few days later, we were on a plane to Milan.

Salvini had said that we could film the interview in his office in the Milan courthouse. But I could tell from his email that something was wrong and it was not going to be straightforward.

'You do not have permission to get inside the offices with your camera,' he wrote. 'So I have to accompany you.'

I wasn't sure what this meant. All he would say was that on the day of the interview, he would be waiting for us at 12.30 sharp opposite one of the entrances to the main building.

On a cold February day, I went with our temporary cameraman to meet Charlotte, who had agreed to translate for us. She was a Danish journalist who had moved to Milan some years ago and had learned Italian. We met in a café close to the courthouse entrance. It was crowded inside, so we decided to sit outside, which gave me a chance to gaze up at the enormous building in which Salvini worked. It looked like a fortress — walls impossibly thick, windows set back from the street and armed guards at every entrance, scanning the street for the smallest sign of anything unusual. Everything about this building was a reminder of the enormous personal danger that Italian judges like Salvini faced as a result of their work.

I told Charlotte more about the man we were about to interview and what I was hoping to ask him about. I stressed that I was not going to ask about Francesco Gullino right at the start, but rather that this was where I was hoping to steer the conversation. She agreed that it was going to be delicate, and told me to be ready for anything.

After finishing our lunch we ordered coffees. We had just paid, when I heard a car race around the corner. We all looked up. With a cartoonish screech, a tiny Fiat came to a halt right next to our café. Inside was an agitated man in a suit and tie, who was gesturing at us.

We haven't done anything — was my first thought, before looking away. *Whoever this man is, he's got the wrong people.*

'My God,' said Charlotte. 'That's him. Salvini.'

I looked at the car again. The man inside was still frantically beckoning at us, only now his body language had an air of resignation. We quickly gathered up our things, left the café and walked towards the car.

'*Rapidamente, rapidamente!*' Salvini called out from the driver's seat. There was hardly enough room for us in the car but somehow we squeezed in. As soon as the doors had closed, the judge put his foot down. I remember thinking how ridiculous we must have looked, packed into this tiny vehicle. Salvini drove at speed down one side of the courthouse, scanning the street ahead of him. Looking around one last time, he turned sharply and steered the car into a tiny entrance to the courthouse. At the same time, he gestured for us to duck down into our seats. I threw myself down into the footwell as the tiny car drove down into an underground car park. Salvini parked up – still no explanation as to what was going on – and each of us climbed slowly out of the car. Charlotte and I exchanged looks. Salvini jumped out and ushered us, without a word, into a service lift.

He pressed a button and we ascended quietly through the centre of Milan's main courthouse until we reached Salvini's floor. The doors opened and he signalled for us to remain in the lift while he checked if the coast was clear. I watched him stride out into a long and echoing corridor. Everybody, it seemed, was having lunch. Salvini turned around and beckoned us into his office, diagonally across from the lift.

Once we had caught our breath, Charlotte, our translator, took control of the situation and began to speak to Salvini as if nothing at all unusual had just happened. A sense of calm descended. Soon we were talking in a relaxed way about Salvini's work over the last twenty years. I showered him with praise and compliments, while asking him increasingly probing questions about his investigations into the Years of Lead and the Gladio. We carried on like this for about twenty minutes, until I decided it was time to move on to the subject that had brought me here. I asked him about Franco and his former employee Andrea Speranzoni – the two men he had introduced to each other.

Everything changed. Salvini turned to Charlotte, and the two of them spoke in Italian for some time.

'He doesn't know who Franco is,' she told me.

OK, I thought. It had been almost twenty years since they had met, so that was understandable. I gave Charlotte a mass of details to help identify him. She translated. The judge continued to look confused, saying that he did not know a Franco from Denmark, until a different expression washed over his features.

'Ah, *si*,' he said.

He spoke to Charlotte in Italian.

'He had his wife with him, didn't he?' she translated.

'Yes, yes that's him,' I began, before formulating a follow-up question about Gullino and Speranzoni. But even before he heard the translation, I could sense something had changed. Salvini replied to Charlotte in short sharp phrases. She turned to me and said that the interview was now over.

I tried to salvage the situation but Salvini was already on his feet, indicating that we should gather our things and leave. He accompanied us to the lift and said we could make our own way out.

In the days that followed, I called Salvini several times. As soon as he recognised my voice, he slammed down the phone. What had happened? At the very least, this respected Italian judge felt that there was something about Franco that was embarrassing or dangerous and needed to be left alone. Thinking back to our meeting in Milan, I could not get out of my head the look on his face as he remembered who Franco was and how he had helped him. Perhaps he had simply realised that by putting him in touch with one of his assistants and encouraging them to work together he had crossed a line. Or maybe there was more to this. I remembered Speranzoni telling Franco in the 'Deep Throat' tape about how he had been warned off looking further into Gullino. Could Salvini have received a similar message?

I tried to contact Speranzoni many times but, like Salvini, he refused to speak. The Italian chapter in our investigation was coming to an end. I wasn't sure exactly what I had hoped for from our trip to Milan, but a part of me had dared to think that Salvini might tell us something in confidence once the camera was off which would hint at the idea that Gullino really had been working for Italian intelligence or he belonged to some shadowy neo-fascist organisation. But none of that happened. Maybe I was wrong to think that this ever going to happen . Even if Salvini had opened up, he was unlikely to give us the whole picture. The only person who could tell us everything about this part of Gullino's life was, after all, Gullino himself.

30
CLOSING THE CIRCLE

We had come a long way in our understanding of Francesco Gullino. But we still didn't know what he had been doing in Denmark for more than twenty years as a Bulgarian spy and why he was never charged.

I had already written to PET, asking them about their investigation into Gullino – but they wrote back to say that they had no comment. The response from the national archives was similar. Yes, they told us, they held files about Francesco Gullino and the Danish government's efforts to bring him to justice, but we were not permitted to see them.

My friend who had once worked at PET – let's call him 'Peter' – was a bit more helpful. Over coffee one day, he said that he didn't know anything about the Gullino case specifically but he could speak in more general terms about PET back in the early 1990s, around the time of the Scotland Yard interview. The point he made to me several times was that PET had been much smaller in those days than most people realised, and this meant they had to be extremely selective about which cases to pursue. They were often unable to go after a particular target simply because they did not have the resources. It was possible, he said, that they had wanted to investigate the Gullino case but did not have the manpower or money to do so.

Peter also explained that given their limited resources, they had to rely a lot on their international partners, such as MI6 in the United Kingdom and the CIA in the United States.

Did PET have a good relationship with Italian intelligence? Could a senior Italian intelligence officer have asked them to drop their investigation into Gullino, because he was one of theirs?

That kind of thing was not unheard of, Peter said, choosing his words carefully. The Danes had dealings with the Italians. But if we wanted to work out what had happened and why Gullino had never been prosecuted, we needed to ask ourselves the question: who benefitted? Put another way, who had the most to lose from Gullino standing up in a Danish court? The answer was obvious. The people whose reputation would suffer the most were those working for PET. The prospect of this experienced Bulgarian spy telling the world about how he had evaded Danish intelligence for two decades was going to be highly embarrassing for them. It was only natural that they might not want that to happen. As soon as they found out that Gullino had fled the country after his exposure in the media, the easiest thing to do was let this case go.

Franco had often talked to me with a feverish kind of intensity about a secret deal between PET and the Italians, the British, the Americans – or perhaps all three – but, talking to Peter, I began to question how likely that was.

Someone who could tell us a lot more about all this was Poul Erik Dinesen. Thanks to Lukas, I had a list of telephone numbers for Dinesens in the area where we thought he might be living. One afternoon, with Lukas sitting next to me, ready to press record if we got through to him, I picked up the phone and started to work my way through the list.

'Is Poul Erik at home?' I would ask.

No, came the answer, followed by apologies, confusion and talk of wrong numbers. Nobody knew a Poul Erik. We were coming to the end of the list when I dialled up one of the numbers and heard a woman say, 'What do you want with him?'

Lukas's face lit up.

'My name is Ulrik Skotte,' I said. 'I'm a journalist. I was wondering if I could speak to Poul Erik.'

She set off to find him. Cue clattering in the distance and murmuring, followed by a long pause, footsteps, a click and, finally, a voice thundering down the phone: 'Dinesen!'

I couldn't think of the last time I'd heard a voice with this kind of authority. It's him, I thought to myself, and he's made for television. A professional actor could not have uttered that word with more gravitas.

Feeling nervous, I introduced myself and explained that I was making a documentary about Francesco Gullino. I told him a little about what we had found so far, the connection to PET and to him, and asked if there was anything he could say about all this.

There was a silence, punctuated by the heavy sound of his breathing. Then he began.

'Under no circumstances will I speak without PET's permission.'

I tried again.

'I know exactly what you are looking for. And you won't get it from me!'

'So, what am I looking for?'

'You are already starting now,' he snapped. 'I am not going to tell you anything.'

That was that. Peter had warned me that Dinesen was very unlikely to speak to us. But in other films I'd made, I sometimes found that if we spoke in person this could change. Someone who was reluctant to speak over the phone might be willing to open up during a face-to-face meeting.

Not long after that brief phone call, I drove out to Dinesen's house with Lukas and Frederik. We pulled up outside the house, but agreed that it would be a mistake for all three of us to go to the door. Instead, I would go first to see if I could persuade the ageing spook to agree to be filmed.

Dinesen's wife opened the door. I explained who I was and she let me in, leading me through to the room where her husband was. He was much older than I had expected and extremely frail. I realised straight away that it would be wrong to film him in this condition. But I wanted to see if we could have a conversation.

I began to speak about the documentary we were starting to make and our interest in Francesco Gullino. His gaze remained fixed on a distant point. Occasionally, he blinked. But he would not meet my eye and I was not sure if he had registered my presence. I kept going like this for some time, talking about the attack on Waterloo Bridge in the hope that something in this would jog something his memory. Then I mentioned that Markov had died two days after he was poisoned.

Dinesen suddenly turned to me and held up four fingers.

Four days. That's what he seemed to be saying. Markov had died four days after the attack, not two.

He was right. It had been four days. Even at the very end of his life, with his mind starting to slow down, this former intelligence officer had not forgotten the innermost details of this case. But that was pretty much the only response I ever had from Poul Erik Dinesen. He told me that he would say no more. All I could think, as I thanked his wife and made my way back to the car, was that something about Francesco Gullino had made a deep impression on him. I felt as if the mention of this particular case had a powerful effect on him, and that he had become defensive. It's hard to interpret the way someone answers a question but I was struck by how he had refused to speak. Rather than just tell me he would not be interviewed, he had said to me before I left: 'I can't talk to you about that case.'

That case.

Would he have spoken about other cases? I don't know. But I felt that the story of Francesco Gullino had left a mark on him.

Driving home with Lukas and Frederik, we agreed that there was just one last thing to do before we tried to track down Gullino himself. We had been unable to find anyone who was willing to tell us why PET had let him go. But we might be able to discover more about what he had been doing in Copenhagen during his twenty years of undercover intelligence work. The 'Piccadilly' case files were in Sofia and I had heard from one of my contacts that if we came to Bulgaria, there might be a way to see them.

It was hot when Lukas, Frederik and I arrived in Sofia, late on a summer's evening. I could hardly believe how much had changed since I had last been here more than twenty years ago with Franco, Viktoria and Rikke. The city looked completely different. Huge blocks of concrete and glass had sprung up where before there had been nothing. Of course, I had changed as well. As we gathered up our bags and made our way out of the airport, I found it hard to recognise the young man I had been the last time I walked through this same building. That Ulrik seemed less sure of what he wanted, and someone more wary of the world than I felt now.

The next morning, we went to find a local historian called Christopher Nehring who had offered to help. He had told us to meet him outside the building that housed the Bulgarian security service archives. Christopher had got to know these archives well over the last few years and thought that, if we were lucky, we might be able to film in there. But he could not guarantee anything.

From the moment we met him outside the building, I could tell that he was on edge. We really might not be allowed to see the Piccadilly files, he stressed. It was all out of our control. We just had to hope for the best and make sure to follow any instructions we were given to the letter. One of these was to arrive on time. Seeing that we were ten minutes early for our 9am appointment,

I suggested knocking on the door to let those inside know that we were here.

'Absolutely not,' Christopher replied. 'We go in on the dot of nine.'

We all stared at our watches and phones, counting down the seconds. At last, it was time. Christopher knocked on the door.

A heavy-set man opened it and we were ushered in. It was like stepping into a time capsule. The tiny three-person lift, the walls decorated with lacquered wood, the thick carpet, the claustrophobic hush: everything was exactly how I imagined the 1950s.

We made our way up to the third floor, where our equipment was examined by another silent functionary, before following Christopher into a tiny room. It was stiflingly hot. He spoke in Bulgarian to the woman who controlled access to the room beyond and the material we hoped to see.

After a quiet discussion, Christopher turned to me and gave me a nod. Permission had been granted.

We moved through to the next room, this one even hotter than before. Several minutes later, a trolley appeared bearing the first of many boxes marked 'Piccadilly'.

The next eight hours passed by in a sweaty blur. Frederik and Lukas photographed and recorded everything they could. Christopher was translating, pointing us to the most interesting parts of the declassified material. It was almost overwhelming. In that one day, we saw all of the documents that Scotland Yard had shown to Gullino in their interrogation, as well as thousands of pages relating to his espionage activities in Denmark. It was everything we had come for and so much more.

Gullino's career as a spy in Denmark had begun, the papers confirmed, in 1973, when he arranged to meet his first Bulgarian handler, Colonel Micho Genkovski, in Copenhagen. Gullino received his instructions late at night on a state-of-the-art Sony ICF-7600 radio set supplied by his handler. He would tune in to a particular frequency at 11.30pm on the third and seventeenth day of each month. If he heard silence for the next ten minutes, then the message was *everything's fine, there's nothing for you to do*. If it was the sound of drums, then five days later he needed to be standing outside the Urania cinema in Vienna, a meeting place codenamed 'Veronika', to see his handler. If the radio played a particular aria from the Verdi opera *Aida* then Gullino was to meet the same man after five days by the entrance to Tivoli, in Copenhagen. Another tune from this opera and he had to pick up a message from the dead drop behind the grave in Assistens Cemetery — the headstone that I had sent Lukas to photograph. The files even contained a map and diagram that Gullino had drawn to show his handler precisely where secret material should be left in relation to the headstone.

According to the files, if Agent Piccadilly, alias Gullino, became nervous, or if he ever felt that he was in danger, his instructions were to leave the country and head to Sofia via Vienna — where he needed to call the number 87-12-25. On the last Saturday of every month, Gullino had to meet his handler at 6pm at the Round Tower in Copenhagen — a place I had walked past hundreds, possibly thousands of times — where they were to greet each other with a code.

'Do you know where to buy Japanese souvenirs in Copenhagen?' was the opening line.

The correct response was: 'No, but I know where to buy Chinese.'

In one of their meetings, in 1976, Gullino asked his handler about the possibility of moving to Britain. This was passed on to Sofia and the idea was approved. His handler then helped to set him up with a reason to visit London and Gullino worked on improving his English. In late 1977, he was summoned to Sofia for 'special training'. Part of this involved a polygraph test. His handlers wanted to make sure that he was entirely loyal. We'll never know what else this training involved but it is telling that he was looked after during this trip by one of the most senior figures in Bulgarian intelligence, the notorious Vasil Kotsev, director of the First Main Directorate of the Bulgarian intelligence service. This was extremely unusual. Very few Bulgarian agents ever met this man. Whatever this 'special training' involved – occurring at exactly the time that plans for killing Georgi Markov were taking shape – it was clearly important.

After that, Gullino's file went quiet. In June 1978, it recorded the fact that he received £2,000. There is also a reference to Gullino's cover story for being London, which was that he was looking to set up an importing business. Almost everything else from the year 1978 had been removed. The narrative only resumed after Markov's murder, when Gullino was suddenly being talked about by his handler in Sofia as a decorated and highly respected agent. The other change was that nobody was urging him to move to Britain any more. They were happy for him to stay in Copenhagen and do almost nothing. At times, it seemed as if their only concern for Agent Piccadilly, in the wake of Markov's murder, was if he was being paid enough.

After several years of lying low in Copenhagen, Gullino began to pass on scraps of information to his handler. I was intrigued to see this part of his file. It was part of the reason why we had come to Sofia. Perhaps Gullino had used his cover as an art dealer to befriend Danish government ministers and technological experts, and had found a way to steal national secrets on behalf of the Bulgarian regime. Maybe he had given them antiques with recording equipment hidden inside – or was he running his own circle of agents? He had been living in Denmark long enough to have taken on a team of 'sleeper' agents that could have infiltrated, let's say, the Danish civil service, and might now be in positions of power and influence.

Gullino told his handlers about his plans to recruit some of his friends as agents and almost everyone in his social circle appeared at one stage in one of his reports. A woman called Ulla, who had generously offered him a place to stay soon after he arrived in Copenhagen and had even invited him to her mother's house, featured in one. Ulla 'likes to live beyond her means', he told his handler, 'and her salary is therefore insufficient'. His handler had suggested using Ulla as a courier. Another person he told his handler about was Franco.

Seeing Franco's photograph in Gullino's file, on that hot summer's day in Sofia, my stomach knotted up and I found it hard to breathe. It was a black and white picture of Franco at an editing desk, working on a film. I found it odd to think of Gullino taking his picture and passing it on to his handler — that strange mixture of familiarity and betrayal. As I went through his file, I could see that Gullino had passed on to the Bulgarians just about everything he had been able to find out about Franco — his full name, the company he ran with Bent, what he knew of his finances and his relationships. At one point, his handler asked Gullino to persuade Franco to make a film about Turkey's oppression of its Kurdish minority, but Franco did not take the bait.

This added another layer to the complex relationship between these two men. They acted as if they were friends but beneath the surface both were spying on each other. Their political views were diametrically opposed. But they shared so much, had grown up in the same part of Italy and gone to similar schools. Each one seemed to be both fascinated and appalled by the other — two magnets attracting and repelling each other in equal measure. Stranger still was the idea that one of them might have taken the other's life.

Almost everyone who Gullino knew in Copenhagen, and told his handler about, was described to the Bulgarians as a potential agent. But the strangest thing about his time as a spy was that not one of them was actually recruited. Not Ulla, not Franco. Nobody. In one report, Gullino enthusiastically told his handler that he was about to ask an Italian diplomat if he might become a spy. But the man he had lined up decided to pull out of their meeting and the plan came to nothing.

Once, in the 1980s, Gullino was asked by his handler to seduce a Belgian woman in Brussels who was then working for NATO. The Bulgarians had been asked to do this by the KGB. Gullino accepted the task, but failed to find his target, let alone chat her up.

The most remarkable thing about Gullino's career as a Bulgarian spy in Denmark was how astonishingly little he achieved. There had been countless plans to recruit agents. All ended in failure. Gullino was so staggeringly unsuccessful during his time in Denmark that I began to wonder if that was the point. Perhaps he was just going through the motions by supplying his handler with a stream of low-grade information that was enough to justify his salary but never so much that it could land him in any trouble with the Danish police.

The impression I got from his Bulgarian file was that his handler was happy for this situation to continue given what he had done for them in London, in 1978, on Waterloo Bridge. In the years that followed, it seemed that he had all but retired from espionage and that the money he received each month was more like a pension than a salary.

One day, in the mid-1980s, according to his file, Gullino received a call from the Danish police. He must have thought for a moment that they were onto him. But no, they only wanted to inform him that, after living in Denmark for so many years, he was now eligible for Danish citizenship, an offer he happily accepted.

Copenhagen was sometimes referred to during the Cold War as the 'Nordic Casablanca'. I was starting to understand why. The combination of an intelligence service with such limited resources, our Danish wide-eyed naivety and semi-open borders made it a spy's paradise. During twenty years as a Bulgarian agent operating in Denmark, Francesco Gullino had not stolen any state secrets and at no point did he pose a genuine threat to Danish national security. But that was not the point. He had broken the law by working for the intelligence service of a foreign country and had never been properly investigated or prosecuted. Why?

There was a chance that those working for Danish intelligence had been asked by their Italian counterparts to turn a blind eye — that's certainly what Franco had believed. He also thought that the British were involved. But there was another explanation for all this. If Scotland Yard actually had enough evidence to prosecute Francesco Gullino for the murder of Georgi Markov back in 1993, then they might not have flown over to interview him in Denmark. The reason for coming to Copenhagen was to elicit from him some kind of confession from their suspect. Without that, they did not have a case. It was that simple. Although they had been shown copies of Bulgarian files and were certain that Gullino was the Bulgarian secret agent 'Piccadilly', they had nothing that could be produced in court to demonstrate beyond all reasonable doubt that this was the man who had killed Georgi Markov. The files were not enough. Their hope had been that Gullino would make a confession, but he had other ideas.

The Danish authorities were in a similar but slightly different situation. They were only interested in what Gullino might have done while living in Denmark, but they also needed original documents from Bulgaria. They could not go ahead with a prosecution based on the copies they had briefly been shown by the detectives from Scotland Yard. In the days after Bird and Kemp had spoken to Gullino, the Danish police asked their ambassador in Bulgaria to obtain the original Bulgarian documents about 'Piccadilly' — the ones that we were now looking at in Sofia.

The Danish ambassador did his best. He wrote to the relevant officials. No reply. He tried again, this time making the request through Interpol, the international organisation designed to facilitate cooperation between police forces. The Bulgarians said that the request had been addressed to the wrong department, so the

Danes tried again. Finally, in October 1993, the senior state prosecutor in Bulgaria, Ivan Tatarchev, said that the answer was no. The Bulgarian government would not hand over the 'Piccadilly' files. Without these, neither Scotland Yard nor the Danes could go ahead with a prosecution.

Four years later, the British foreign secretary, Malcolm Rifkind, brought up the subject of the Piccadilly files on a visit to Bulgaria. The following year, his successor, Robin Cook, did the same. Still, the Bulgarians refused to hand them over. Scotland Yard tried to obtain these files again in 2008. Again, no luck. More than a decade later, the Georgi Markov case was still open.

So Franco's theory that Gullino was being somehow protected by the British and the Danes did not add up. Why would they have gone to the trouble of trying to prosecute him at all? The most likely explanation for why Francesco Gullino was not charged by Scotland Yard for the Markov murder, or by the Danes for his work as a spy in Copenhagen, was that nobody had enough evidence. Although PET could have tried to interview Gullino's friends and build a case without the Bulgarian files, this was going to be hard. Much easier, they realised, to let this one go.

The only question that remained in my mind, strange as it might sound, was whether we might have made a mistake. How could we be *absolutely* sure that Gullino had been involved in the murder of Georgi Markov? We knew that the Bulgarian chief investigator, Bogdan Karayotov, had conducted many interviews with people connected to the Markov murder, before the trail led him to Gullino in Copenhagen in 1993 – a tremendous and persistent effort. In Sofia, we found a mass of interview notes Karyotov had put together. One man's testimony was of great interest: that of a former Bulgarian intelligence officer called Georgi Novev Georgieff, referred to in the notes as 'Novev'. He had made contact with Francesco Gullino while he was imprisoned in Bulgaria in the early

1970s following his arrest for smuggling and had played a part in recruiting the young Italian as an agent.

Karayotov interrogated Novev on several occasions in the early 1990s. In one of these conversations, he asked him: 'Do you have meetings with foreign agents here in Bulgaria?'

'Yes,' replied Novev, 'there was a young man. I was transferred to prison because I spoke a few languages. It must have been around 1970. I was to ascertain what this man was about.'

In another interview, Novev spoke more about this same man: 'I can't remember his name, only that he was from the northern part of Italy. I was to ascertain his contacts here in Bulgaria and the reason for his stay in our country. I think he had some trade going on. He drove through Bulgaria on his way to Turkey. He even showed me that he had bought some old watches.'

'Did you prepare him as an employee?' Karayotov asked.

By employee, Karayotov meant 'agent'.

'No, it wasn't my task. I was only to assess him and determine if he was suitable to become an employee.'

'Do you remember his agent name?'

'No.'

'Does the agent name "Piccadilly" ring any bells?'

'Now I remember, that was his agent name.'

This was all interesting but it was the next mention of Piccadilly that really caught our attention. Novev explained that the second time he had met Piccadilly was in Rome, in September 1978, in the days after the murder of Georgi Markov. His task was unusual. Rather than pass on a message to Piccadilly or have a conversation with him, his instructions were to observe this agent as he walked through St Peter's Square. If he showed up with the latest edition of the magazine *Newsweek* under his arm, it was a signal that the operation in London — the assassination of Georgi Markov — had succeeded.

'I saw him sitting in front of St Peter's,' Novev said. 'I walked past and that was it.'

'Who ordered this meeting?'

'The management.'

'Did you nod at each other during this meeting?'

'No, he sat there holding the magazine, which meant he was OK and that there were no problems.'

'Are you sure you saw Piccadilly at the meeting in Rome?'

'Yes, I'm sure.'

So there we had it: concrete proof that Piccadilly was involved in the operation even after the murder, and that the Bulgarian intelligence services were looking for confirmation of a job well done.

31

A FRESH LEAD

We had pushed as far as we could in our research into Gullino's life. All that was left to do now was to find him. But he could be anywhere. He could be dead. Finding out what had become of Gullino was going to be exceptionally difficult. If we were going to have any chance, we needed to start thinking more like him. When we found a door closed, we might have to clamber in through the window. It would take ingenuity as well as what one of my former bosses called *den yderste anstrengelse*, meaning 'the utmost effort'. We might also need a bit of luck.

We began by throwing around ideas for where in the world he could be. The whiteboard in our office was soon a jumble of interesting European destinations. Then came the wildcard option. Denmark — because it was the last place anyone would think to look. We had got almost nowhere and were starting to lose momentum when I heard my phone ring. It was an Austrian number that I did not recognise.

I picked up. A man introduced himself as a journalist working for one of Europe's largest magazines. He had heard that I was working on a story about Francesco Gullino.

My hackles went up. This guy could be anyone. I asked how he had heard about our investigation. But he would not say, which only put me more on edge. I had no idea who he was but felt that he must be a threat, and I should be careful about what I said.

Yes, I told him cautiously. I was part of a team working on a story that involved Francesco Gullino. *Keep it vague*, I thought to myself.

Well, he went on, he was also interested in this individual. He then ran through a list of murders and attempted murders that had taken place in Austria over the last fifteen years, and wondered out loud whether Gullino could have been connected to any of them. He wanted to know if I had evidence that could link him to some of these crimes.

I did not. But even as I said that, I was scrambling to rearrange my understanding of who Gullino was. Could he have been responsible for these murders as well as the others? I mean, it was possible. Wherever this man went, death seemed to follow.

Next, the journalist on the phone asked if I could confirm that Gullino was now living in Austria.

I felt a rush of excitement. Until the start of this call, we had been in the dark about where he was or if he was even alive. Our task was starting to come into focus. I mumbled something about how that sounded right.

The journalist — my new best friend — then asked if I knew anything about the secret network of former spies to which Gullino belonged. This was even more interesting.

'What do you mean?' I asked.

'It's made up of former agents from Eastern Europe who try to protect each other,' he began, before giving a lengthy description of this secretive network of ageing Eastern European agents. Franco had often talked about there being a group like this, that had been set up to keep people like Gullino out of jail and away from the media spotlight. But from the way Franco talked about this organisation, it sounded more like an urban myth than anything else and I hadn't really taken him seriously. Hearing the journalist on the phone describe this network in such definite terms forced me to think again.

After that phone call, our task of tracking him down had become both easier, in the sense that we had a vague sense of where he might be, and harder. Not only were there people trying to protect Gullino but now we had competition. I began to experience the same fear I had when making a television programme, only this time it was larger and more terrifying. My worry was that we might be beaten to it by someone else. I had premonitions of coming into work one morning, opening my emails, and reading about a new film by someone who had found Gullino, won him over and persuaded him to reveal everything on camera.

I was also starting to experience a paranoid fear of being followed. I had begun to use the back door to my office instead of the front. In traffic, I was in the habit of pulling over suddenly and waiting for at least ten cars to pass before I carried on with my journey. Up in my office, I wrote down the number plates of vehicles that had been parked in the street outside for more than a few hours. I wanted a record of everything, just in case. In case of what? I wasn't sure, but making these notes helped to keep my anxiety at bay.

A similar thing was happening at home. When I was around my wife and children, I was again finding it hard to be present. I would nod 'yes' to a question about completing a household chore but forget about it almost immediately. I missed vet appointments. The bins did not go out on time. Meals that I promised to make went uncooked.

I could sense my family's frustration, but all I could think about was an idea that had taken root in my mind – that I was about to get a call from Gullino himself. I kept running through the conversation we would have, although 'conversation' is a bit of a stretch. There was never any back-and-forth in the scenario that played out in my imagination. I never had a chance to earn his trust or work towards the more difficult questions I wanted to answer. Instead, in this interaction, he delivered different versions of the same message, something along the lines of — *you need to stop, stop now before you put yourself in danger.*

Then I'd come back to reality. Gullino was an expert in not being found and I might never speak to him. But, as Lukas had pointed out, with his usual optimism, it sounded as if the man we were after was at least alive and was living in Austria. So all we had to do was work out precisely where and then get to him before anyone else did.

32

CUMMINGS

Earlier in our research, someone had told us about a German documentary that came out in 2012 and included footage of Francesco Gullino. I wrote to the people who made it. For a while, I heard nothing, but then I got a message from the director, Klaus Dexel. He kindly put me in touch with one of the people who had helped him with the film, an American called Richard Cummings.

Cummings had a surprisingly long history with this story. Back in 1980, not long after Georgi Markov had been killed, he had been appointed head of security at Radio Free Europe, the radio station rumoured to have been run by the CIA, which had broadcast Markov's devastating attacks on the Bulgarian dictator Todor Zhivkov. Cummings remembered hearing about the murder but nobody told him much. He became interested in the subject and began to do his own research. More than thirty years later, at a very different stage in his life, he was approached by Dexel who asked for his help in tracking down the man thought to have been responsible for this murder.

The challenge that Cummings took on was essentially the same as ours. He had to find Gullino and get him in front of a camera. Cummings was an expert at locating people. But this was a more difficult assignment than usual. After Gullino had been exposed in 1993 – thanks to Franco – he appeared to have vanished. Cummings could find no trace of him, dead or alive, and was close to giving up. Then he found a clue.

In the early 2000s, police in Portugal had begun to investigate the theft of a painting entitled 'Salome' by the German artist Franz Stuck. It was thought to be worth more than $100,000. Their chief suspect was a Danish art dealer named Francesco Gullino. They put out an alert to border police across Europe and gave instructions for this individual to be stopped and for his vehicle to be searched.

Several days later, Gullino drove up to the German–Austrian border in his camper van, and was taken aside by the police. They searched the van and discovered an artwork that matched the description of the stolen painting by Franz Stuck. But Gullino protested that he had purchased it legally in Denmark and that this was simply a copy of the original 'Salome', hence the confusion. If an expert struggled to tell the difference between a copy and the real thing, the Austrian border police did not stand a chance. We may never know how the conversation played out between Gullino and the authorities, but he talked his way out of the situation and was allowed to carry on with his journey into Austria. Before he left, however, the border police made a note of his vehicle number plate and included it on their report. This was the document that Cummings had found. The number plate on Gullino's car indicated that he was at that time living in the Austrian city of Wels.

Klaus Dexel, the filmmaker that Cummings was working with, was soon on his way to Wels. He managed to find Gullino and record a short interview with him. Just like us, he had been hoping for a moment of contrition. Nothing beats the sight of a criminal break-ing down in tears on camera and making some kind of confession – because there's nothing more human than our innermost need for justice. But this was Gullino, master dissembler. He did not reveal a thing. Instead, he reacted to the questions by clowning around and playing the fool. He did everything he could to present himself to Dexel as a harmless old man, someone that nobody would ever suspect of having carried out an operation as sophisticated, brutal and ruthless as the Umbrella Murder.

Watching this short interview with Gullino was incredibly useful. It gave us a better sense of what to expect from him, if we were able to track him down. I pressed Cummings for more details on where in this Austrian city of Wels they had found him but he could not remember. We were going to have to work it out ourselves.

33
VALENTINA

The thing about Gullino, as Frederik, Lukas and I often reminded each other, was that he was more similar to us than we liked to admit. Yes, he was implicated in three murders and he appeared to have links to Bulgarian and Italian intelligence, and perhaps even the Mafia, as well as a weird predilection for women dressed up as Nazis. But to anyone who met him for the first time, Gullino would seem pretty normal. A normal guy who did normal things. Where would we start looking for a normal person like this? That was easy. Facebook.

There was a surprising number of people who went by the name 'Francesco Gullino' on Facebook, but only two who looked like they could be the man we were after. One had as a profile picture a photograph of an Italian city which Lukas identified as Bra, in northern Italy – where Gullino had grown up.

The other Francesco Gullino, or a second account belonging to the same person, claimed to be living in the little-known Czech town of Karlovy Vary. That name was immediately familiar to me. Franco had told me about the trip he had once taken to Karlovy Vary with Gullino, and that this was where the Umbrella Murderer liked to go to 'have fun' with his 'special friends', as he called them. Gullino had happy memories of Karlovy Vary, so it made sense that he might have moved there.

'Here's the other clue,' Lukas said, looking at his computer. I watched as he scrolled down through this Francesco Gullino account. The person behind it had posted dozens of photographs of umbrellas. I struggled to interpret this. Possibly we were looking at a spoof account, set up by someone who had heard about the notorious Francesco Gullino and thought it would be funny to impersonate him. But if that was true, how did they know about his connection to Karlovy Vary?

Was it coincidence that this little-known city was given as the account holder's address? An alternative explanation was so odd I found it hard to get my head around it — that this really was Gullino's account, and he was sitting at his computer posting pictures of umbrellas. Either he was laughing at the idea that he could have carried out this horrific murder because he was innocent, unlikely as it that might sound, or, more realistically, he was glorying in the fact that he had got away with it.

Lukas then showed me the profile picture for this account. It was of a dog. I remembered picking up in Franco's material that Gullino was a dog enthusiast and had owned at least three over the years. The first one was called 'Nike' because it had a birthmark resembling a Nike swoosh. Gullino had liked the name so much that he gave it to each of his next two dogs. It made sense that he might have used a picture of a dog for his Facebook profile.

In a digital sense, we might have found him. But locating his Facebook account meant nothing unless we could get him to talk. If we could do that, we might be able to persuade him to meet up. We needed some kind of disguise. Introducing ourselves as three Danish men who wanted to make a film about him — and by the way, did he know anything about the deaths of Franco, Georgi Markov and Hanne With? — was hardly going to work. He had no reason to speak to us. Silence was his superpower. We needed a daring strategy — something he wouldn't expect.

We decided to invent an imaginary person who possessed something that he wanted. We would try our hand at catfishing. What did Gullino like? Easy. He liked sex. Not just any kind of sex, we knew that he preferred being with a sex worker. Maybe we should pretend to be a local sex worker? That was probably not going to work. Nobody opens a message from someone they have never met who says they are desperate to have sex with them. We needed to be more subtle.

Lukas suggested we pose as an attractive Italian woman – attractive, but not too attractive – who wanted his help with something. Gullino knew a lot about the art market, so we could pretend to be someone looking for help in valuing an artwork that they owned. Lukas scoured the internet for a suitable picture and found an image of a youngish woman. It looked natural, like something a friend would take, and not a professional shot from a studio. Next, we needed to give her a name. Again, something enticing but not ridiculous. I liked the name Valentina. What was the Italian for beautiful? *Bella*. We settled on 'Valentina Abella'.

Next, Lukas set up Valentina's profile. He was careful to keep it private, so that Gullino would never know that she had no friends and had never posted anything on the internet. Once we had created Valentina Abella, we got to work on the message she was going to send Gullino.

'Hello Francesco!' we had Valentina begin (in Italian). 'I was just talking to Giorgio, and he told me a little about you. I'm looking for someone who can help me appraise a painting I inherited from my grandmother. I would be super grateful for your help. Maybe we can meet?'

Giorgio was one of Gullino's friends from Copenhagen.

Lukas then added a few emojis.

I hovered behind Lukas's desk as he pressed send and we waited for a reply. Minutes went by. Then hours. By the end of the following day, we had still not heard back from Gullino. Time for a different approach.

How else could we make contact with Gullino?

Lukas remembered something he had heard in one of Franco's secret recordings of Gullino. He was sure that at one point they had swapped email addresses. Over the next few days, Lukas patiently trawled through the tapes again. Because Franco's microphone was always hidden beneath his clothes, the quality of these recordings was often poor and the dialogue could be hard to follow. But, in the end, Lukas found what he had been looking for: a moment buried in a recording of a trip they had taken together in 2005, two years before Franco's death.

Lukas played it for me.

'Jump in!' I could hear Gullino call out to Franco in Italian. Once Franco had got in, he carried on: 'How are things going? You're not a day older, you look even better than before.'

'Not at all,' Franco had replied.

'Yes, you have become more beautiful. But you've got a bit of a belly.'

'I ...' Franco spluttered.

'The two of us don't look that good,' Gullino conceded. 'But you look better than me.'

'No,' Franco said, laughing and enjoying himself. 'It's always you that does well with women. It's you they want!'

'Well, how's it going?' Gullino tried again. 'What are you doing?'

They began to gossip. Franco talked about moving out of his house in Glostrup while Gullino listened and drove, interrupting sometimes to apologise for his dog farting. It was strange to hear these two chatting away so naturally, and to think that they both had such a long history of spying on one another.

Later, once they were more comfortable, Gullino talked about how long it had been since he had been in Denmark and how he barely recognised the roads. Then he touched on what had happened to him after he was named in the media, something they seem to have discussed several times before. Gullino still did not seem to think Franco had been responsible for this.

'I've had to go into hiding after all the accusations by the media,' Gullino said, sounding like the victim of a terrible injustice. 'People pointed fingers at me on the street.'

'Who do you intend to seek compensation from?' Franco asked.

'The Danish government. They prevented me from working. I had to flee to Transylvania for two years to find peace because they wanted to prosecute me everywhere for no reason.'

The two men carried on like this for a while. Once they had sat down in a bar, Franco offered to email Gullino some of the articles that he had collected about the Umbrella Murder. Gullino said that he'd like that and began to write down his email address. As he did so, he talked about why he had chosen this email address.

'So, "Nike", here, is my dog,' Gullino said.

'Ah,' Franco replied. 'Is that his name?'

'Nike1.tatibo@liwes.at,' Gullino went on. 'Yes, send me the details. I want to create documentation because one day, I'll have to claim compensation from someone.'

Lukas grinned at me.

We had his email address.

34
VALENTINA 2.0

I had never met Francesco Gullino and yet I knew more about him than I did about some of my closest friends. I could tell you about his tragic early life, his love of dogs and what he was like to live with, as well as the minutiae of his training as a secret agent and how he might have killed someone with a tiny, ricin-filled pellet. I was also getting a pretty clear sense of the kind of email that might draw him out. Our Facebook approach had failed. He had not been tempted out of his online cave by Valentina Abella. It was time to invent a slightly different Valentina.

For most of his adult life, Gullino had been in the business of buying and selling paintings. He was always looking out for an undervalued painting or the chance to meet either a wealthy collector or an expert forger. He was also interested in opportunities to sell off some of his inventory. None of us knew how active Gullino was at that moment as an art dealer. But thinking back to everything Franco had said about the number of pictures he'd once had in his home, and that he had been spoken to by the police in relation to a stolen painting, it was possible that wherever he was right now, he was surrounded by paintings that he wanted to sell.

Lukas and I got to work. Valentina, Version 2.0, was going to be someone who worked for an imaginary auction house in Vienna. We spent a long time thinking about the name of this venture, trawling through a list of respected Italian painters before we agreed to name it after the great Giambettino Cignaroli.

With that, Cignaroli's Auction House was born. Next, we needed a new surname for Valentina. Perhaps 'Abella' – *Valentina Beautiful* – had been too obvious. We agreed on Valentina Bianchi, and set up an email address in her name. In hindsight, we probably should not have used the name Valentina twice; it was an obvious red flag. But we didn't know any better.

'Dear Mr Gullino,' Valentina's email began. 'We are delighted to extend to you a cordial invitation to Cignaroli's Rococo Art Auction,' an event taking place later that year, which would 'showcase a captivating collection of artifacts and paintings hailing from eighteenth century Northern Italy, as well as remarkable works from Austria, France and Germany. To obtain a comprehensive catalogue detailing the entire array of artworks featured in this auction, please reply to this email with your full name and title.'

Was that enough to pull him in? Hard to say. One of the ways we could tip the odds in our favour was by creating a sense of urgency. Lukas added a line to Valentina's email about tickets being allocated 'on a first-come, first-served basis'.

'Should you have require any further information, please do not hesitate to contact our dedicated client representative, Valentina Bianchi. We eagerly anticipate your presence at this splendid occasion, where the finest examples of Rococo art await your admiration and acquisition.'

The message was ready to go. Our hope was that Gullino would respond and we could start a conversation, and that, along the way, he would reveal where he was living. He might even agree to a pre-auction meeting, giving us a chance to film him. But even if he did not reply, we might come away with a rough idea of where he was. I asked Lukas to install a tracker in the message that would give us the IP address of his device if he opened the message. This would not give us a precise location, but it might be enough for us to track him down.

Lukas pressed 'Send'.

I've never been a particularly patient kind of person and for the next hour I was unable to concentrate on anything else. I sat next to Lukas, asking him roughly every thirty seconds if the tracker had been activated.

It had not, and for the next few hours we heard nothing.

I tried to imagine Gullino's face as he read the subject-line of the email – 'Invitation to Cignaroli's Rococo Art Auction Vienna'.

Had we chosen the right name? Was 'Rococo' a mistake?

I could picture Gullino's nose wrinkling and the lips pursing as he thought about what to do.

Could it be a trap...? Should I open it?

Lukas received an alert. The email had been opened.

This was it!

I hovered behind Lukas as he inspected the IP address. I was desperate to find out if Gullino was in Wels or if he had moved away, perhaps to Karlovy Vary. I scanned Lukas's face for a reaction. But he just looked confused.

'It says he's in America.'

'What do you mean?'

'The IP address is for a US location.'

A completely different chapter in his past opened up before me. He might have a connection to US intelligence as well. Or had he changed his name and been sent on a mission to penetrate American society?

Just then, Lukas realised what had happened.

'He's not in America,' he said. 'The IP address is for Google headquarters. He's using an email provider that re-routes emails to Google. So, he's disguising his IP address.'

Gullino was alive. That was the good news. The bad news was that he was making himself almost impossible to find.

35
A GIANT PENIS

Sometimes the stories that bind us together are the ones without a definite ending. We are often drawn to questions that do not have a clear answer. Millions of Americans still pore over the murder of JFK as if it had only just happened. The equivalent in Bulgaria, we had come to realise, was the murder of Georgi Markov.

A bronze statue of Georgi Markov had recently been unveiled in Sofia. At the inauguration ceremony, in 2014, the new president of Bulgaria, Rosen Plevneliev, spoke about how Georgi's writing had 'spiritually liberated the Bulgarians even before the toppling of the communist regime'.[1] Over the years, Georgi Markov had continued to move closer to national sainthood, becoming an avatar of political bravery and artistic integrity. His death was also suffused with a certain tragedy: although he had escaped this communist state in a physical sense, he couldn't truly leave it behind politically or emotionally.

Many Bulgarians wanted to know who was responsible for his assassination and how it had happened. Most of them knew about the Umbrella Murder on Waterloo Bridge, and some had devoted themselves to finding out more about this case. They would share their insights on blogs and websites. In the early stages of our research, we had contacted some of these people to see if they knew anything about Gullino's whereabouts.

Nobody did, and it seemed unlikely that this would change. But then one of the individuals that we had contacted, a Bulgarian journalist, emailed me a photograph that I had never seen before. It had been taken recently, in 2017, and it was of Francesco Gullino.

I could see right away how much he had aged in the five years since he had participated in the documentary with Klaus Dexel. Another thing that stood out was the pose that Gullino had taken up. He was standing in front of a pink wall with a playful grin on his face. He was pointing at the person taking the picture with a huge umbrella.

Lukas, Frederik and I stared at this image as if in a trance. It was unlike anything we had seen. Similar to the Facebook profile that we thought was probably his, in which he had posted a stream of umbrella pictures, he seemed to be having fun with his notoriety. His expression as he stood there was both knowing and triumphant. But as I kept staring at this photograph, I became increasingly intrigued by the person we could not see: the photographer.

Whoever the person behind the camera was, they were in on the joke. Perhaps this photographer belonged to the network of former agents and had been tasked with protecting Gullino.

The photograph confirmed that Gullino had been alive as recently as 2017 and that at least one of the people in his circle knew that he was connected to the Umbrella Murder. So he was not a hermit. This was encouraging. Was there anything else we could glean from this picture? On the face of it, no. Then I remembered something I had learned several years ago, when I was making a very different kind of film.

At around the time that this photograph was taken, we had been filming a programme in collaboration with the Danish police. My idea had been to follow six different criminal cases right from the very start — the moment the emergency call came in to the police station — through to the charges being made and the accused standing trial for their alleged crimes. One of the cases we had focused on involved child pornography. While making this part of the documentary, we had met members of the specialist police unit that dealt with these types of crimes. After arresting the suspects, mostly middle-aged and married men, they would go through the pornographic material on their computers in the hope of working out where the abuse in these videos had taken place and eventually tracing those involved.

I remember asking the police how they managed to figure out where a particular video was shot. I had assumed they would use metadata from the digital files. Instead, they explained, they usually discovered clues in the footage itself. The members of this specialist unit had become experts at analysing imagery. They would spend hours looking at tiny details in these videos — anything from the shape of an electrical outlet in the background of a particular shot to a clothing label, the design of a piece of clothing, the haircut of those in the film, a crumpled note or a detail visible out of the window that might allow them to identify the location. Although it was rare to pinpoint the place where the abuse had happened, on several occasions, their hard work had taken them to the exact spot where the video was shot and they were able to rescue children who were being held in captivity.

I wondered if we could use the same approach to locate where this photograph of Gullino had been taken. The pink wall in the background was distinctively bright. There couldn't be that many walls in a city like Wels that were the same colour. Another detail that stood out was the window you could see up in one corner. There was something white behind it. Lukas zoomed in and we agreed that it was a lampshade. We could also see the edge of an ornamental carving that had been added to the building and looked somehow out of place and almost kitsch.

Lukas began to search through images of Wels for anything that resembled this wall. He went through pictures on Google Maps and anything he could find in the news. Over several days, he must have gone through hundreds of different images. He was beginning to think that the photograph could have been taken somewhere else – perhaps Karlovy Vary or some other central European location – when he saw the spot where the photograph had been taken. It had appeared for a few seconds in a news report.

In the same year that Gullino posed for the picture we had recently been sent, the people of Wels reacted with either shock or amusement to the appearance of a bizarre new artwork in their city. The person who had put it up was a local resident called Jürgen Hesz – someone who liked to tell everyone that he was a millionaire. The sculpture that Hesz had installed in his garden, in a spot where it would be seen by thousands of people, was a two-metre-tall rendering of an erect penis.

In the news story that followed, Hesz was shown at a press conference sitting next to the local mayor. He had decided to cover up his sculpture with a sheet of tarpaulin. 'I wanted to annoy people,' he told the journalists, looking a bit peeved about the whole thing. He had also wanted the tarpaulin that he used to cover it up to look like a condom, because that would be funny, he thought. But in the end he went for something less distinctive and had it printed with quotes from the work of Goethe and Nietzsche.[2]

In the footage accompanying this light-hearted news report, Hesz was shown standing outside his antiques store in Wels, a sprawling complex called Antik-Möbel-Hesz that he ran with his sister, Doris. At one point, you could see a section of the store's pink wall. It was the same one from the photograph of Gullino. If you paused the video, you could also see the ornamental carving and the window with a lamp in it.

Gullino had been photographed brandishing an umbrella outside an antiques shop that belonged to Jürgen Hesz. From the moment Lukas said that name, Hesz, it felt familiar. I went back into Franco's papers and searched until I had found what I was looking for.

Two of Franco's documents, dating back to the mid-1990s, showed that Gullino had not only bought artwork from Hesz, but supplied him with at least one artwork. These two had a business relationship.

We were getting somewhere. Lukas, Frederik and I went on a deep dive into the life of Jürgen Hesz. This was surprisingly easy, because Hesz appeared to be someone that craved attention, a colourful figure who enjoyed being a big fish in a small pond. We also had the idea of calling up other antiques dealers in Wels to ask them what they knew about Hesz. Some of them might have had dealings with either him or Gullino.

Most of the individuals we spoke to over the next few days were friendly and talkative right up to the point that we mentioned either man's name. It might have been coincidence, but saying either Hesz or Gullino seemed to have the effect of killing the conversation. We could not work out why.

One of the antiques dealers we spoke to responded to the name Hesz in a slightly different way and said that he would talk about him, but on the condition that we would never reveal his name. He said that he also knew Francesco Gullino and had last seen him in the flea market in Wels in 2019. I asked him if he had ever spotted Gullino in the company of Hesz. Yes, this man said. He was pretty sure they did business together and had heard that Gullino was the one who supplied Hesz with the two-metre-tall penis that had been in the news.

The next logical step was to contact Jürgen Hesz. But before doing that, there was one more lead to chase up. I had managed to find the contact details for Gullino's nephew, who was then living in Cyprus. I didn't expect much from this because Franco had told me that Gullino was estranged from his family. When I finally got through to his nephew, he confirmed that he had never even met his uncle. Did he know where he could be? No idea. But he agreed to put me in touch with his mother, Gullino's older sister.

When I spoke to Gullino's sister, she said that she had neither seen nor spoken to her brother for almost half a century. But several years ago, she had flown to Wels in the hope of seeing him again. I asked her about what had happened. She had gone to Antik-Möbel-Hesz and asked for Jürgen Hesz. She had been told that Hesz would know how to contact her brother. However, at the antiques shop, some men, who never gave their names, told her that it was not possible for her to see her brother. She was distraught, having come all that way, but they were adamant. One of them suggested that this was because Gullino was now suffering from dementia, and that he was in an old people's home and could not receive visitors.

Gullino's sister left Austria without seeing her brother and was convinced that he had all but lost his mind and did not have long to live.

As I finished that call, I felt a thump of disappointment, one that was heavier than anything I had experienced over the last few months. I tried to picture Gullino in a retirement home, staring out of a window, the light in his eyes gone.

Frederik and Lukas came over, and I told them about what I had just heard.

'We've left it too late,' I told them. 'She says he is in a home. He has dementia.'

'Are you sure?'

'That's what some of the people at Hesz's place said.'

'Did she actually see him in the home?'

'No. But it makes sense.'

'Wow.'

'I know.'

'That's it.'

'We were too slow.'

The energy in our group began to evaporate. Nobody needed to say what each of us had begun to think. It sounded as if Francesco Gullino, the would-be star of our film, had lost his mind. We were never going to be able to record any kind of showdown with him. After following this path as far as it would go, our quest had ended in failure.

36
THE END

I realised that the time had probably come to break up our team. I was sad about this, as I had come to enjoy working together. Over the months, Frederik had become the emotional heart of the group, the one who kept talking and ensured that things were always moving along. Lukas was always the most eager to prove himself, often coming up with new ideas. Anders was quieter and more reflective, reassuring us with his steady demeanour. Meanwhile, I was somewhere in the middle of all this, both inside the group and on the outside. Together, we clicked, and I knew that I would miss the camaraderie between us all. But there was something else I was feeling. What made my experience different to everyone else's was that I was more than an observer or investigator, I was part of the narrative itself. As much as I was trying to make a film, I was also revisiting parts of my life that I had long ago put away in the attic of my mind. The question that I kept returning to was whether I could have done things differently at the start. Had I been right to step away from this story in the late 1990s and part company with Franco? Should I have looked for him again sooner?

I had told myself at the time that the investigation was putting a strain on my marriage and there was no point carrying on. Why? Because Franco refused to let me see all the material he had. But there was more to it than that. Deep down, I had not wanted to follow Franco into the darkness. Was I afraid? Maybe. But in the years since, the world had changed and so had I. There was no longer anything to stop me from going after this man. I believed it would be dangerous, yes, but I was ready to face this and I had felt a need, like an unseen hand pushing me from behind, to follow this trail as far as it would go.

That night, I had a version of the dream that I had been having for months. It was roughly the same each time: I'm following a man through the red-light district of a city — I can't be sure where, Amsterdam perhaps. The man that I'm pursuing is slightly taller than me and walks a few steps ahead. I'm close to him, so close that I can almost reach out and touch him, but he remains beyond my fingertips. The street is busy and I keep being jostled out of the way. But each time this happens, I find a way to get back to him.

We carry on like this for a while, until I'm pushed out of the way again as he steps into the doorway of a building. He turns around and I can see who he is. It's a dark-haired man with a moustache, ratty teeth and a slightly pointed nose. It's Gullino. He smiles at me. Not a welcoming or friendly smile, but a knowing smile, a triumphant one.

Then I wake up.

Perhaps he was right, the Gullino I had seen in my dream. He had escaped.

I wasn't sure where this left me, but I knew I had to find a way to bring this whole thing to an end. Either I needed to find a way to let go of this story or I had to come at the problem in a different way. Could I find proof that Gullino had lost his mind? Was there a chance that Gullino's sister had been misled?

Once I was back in the office, I went to Lukas's desk and asked him to take another look at the German documentary featuring a short interview with Gullino. He had been standing in a street, somewhere in Wels. His home must have been somewhere nearby.

Lukas threw himself into this task with his usual intensity. For the rest of the day, I heard nothing from him. Usually, this was a good sign. Each time I looked over, I could see him glaring at his computer, moving rapidly between windows, typing in short bursts or shuttling his mouse around at speed. I went back to my office and got on with some other work. Several hours later, I heard a cry from Lukas.

'Found it!'

Frederik and I rushed over to Lukas's computer. He had located the spot where he thought the documentary had been filmed and, crucially, he had found an apartment just behind it that belonged to none other than Jürgen Hesz. It must be Gullino's home!

From what we could see online, the building looked as if it had been abandoned. Paint was peeling off the walls, the garden was overgrown and in the images we found there were no signs of life. I thought about what to do. We could go to this house in Wels to see if Gullino was there. This was what Danish journalists would call the 'rock'n'roll' option – when you approach your target without any clear plan and a willingness to roll with the punches (and sometimes there literally are punches). That's what Frederik wanted to do. We would turn up at this house and see what happened. If nobody was at home, we could ask his neighbours. They might know which old people's home he had been taken to and we could go there and try to speak to him. Even if he was now suffering from dementia, a final shot of him gazing out to the distance would give us the ending we needed.

The list of things that could go wrong with the 'rock'n'roll' option was long. Gullino might have people protecting him, probably the same people who had told his sister that she could not see him. Or he might refuse to open his door. The chances of us talking our way into an old people's home were somewhere between very small and zero. Nor were we likely to get much out of Jürgen Hesz. If we waited longer and were more cautious, we might be able to find out more about where he was. I gave us a 20 per cent chance of success. But as Frederik kept saying, that was at least a chance. He was right. We'd come this far. Any chance of success made it worthwhile.

We agreed that we would go to Austria.

On 22 June 2021, I met Lukas, Frederik and Anders at Copenhagen Airport. The atmosphere between us that day felt irresistibly different and new. All of the nervousness we might have felt on leaving our homes had transformed into a feverish, boyish excitement. This was it. The rock'n'roll option. Lukas was grinning enthusiastically. Frederik was speculating with his usual intensity about what was going to happen. *What if this ... What if that ...* Anders was being Anders – calm and watchful, the keel that kept us steady. The conversation continued to bounce along as we boarded the plane and flew towards Vienna.

37

WELS

The summer heat as we arrived in Austria was intense, and much warmer than it was in Copenhagen. As we walked out of the airport to collect our rental van, I could feel the heat all over my body as a prickly sensation. The air had a sultry taste to it that reminded me of holidays and heatwaves. Soon we were on our way to Wels. I was sitting next to Frederik in the front. Lukas was calling out directions from the back with Anders next to him. As we cruised through the Austrian countryside, the conversation became quieter and more sporadic, and I could feel the anticipation building between the four of us.

Several hours later, we arrived in Linz, close to Wels, where I had booked us into a hotel. Perhaps I was being unnecessarily cautious, borderline paranoid, but I didn't feel comfortable sleeping in the city that contained Gullino. We went to our rooms in the hotel in Linz and had a last-minute team meeting in which we ran through the different scenarios we might encounter in Wels.

One of these was to find Gullino at home, and for him to let us in and agree to an interview. That was the ideal outcome, but was almost certainly not going to happen. More likely, we would find that he had some kind of protection, someone living with him or a neighbour who had been given the job of making sure that no journalists came to see him. Another scenario was that our target had been moved to an old people's home. How were we going to find a way past the reception desk? One idea was that Lukas would dress up as a pizza delivery boy and we would try to get in that way. Either that, or we would improvise.

But we had to remember that this wasn't an elaborate game. The people we were dealing with were dangerous. We needed to be on guard. Nobody should accept drinks or food from anyone we met – especially Gullino himself. Frederik and I exchanged looks after I had said this. Had I gone too far? No, we agreed. We had a pretty good idea of what had happened to Franco and to Georgi Markov before him. Better to take no risks.

The final thing we agreed on was the most important: whatever happened in Wels, we must record everything. This last part of the trip was going to be the ending to our film. After that, we piled into the van and set out to find Francesco Gullino.

It was early afternoon when we arrived in Wels, and the streets seemed to have been abandoned. Everyone had moved indoors, drawn their curtains and closed their shutters to shelter from the heat. Outside in the sun, everything was quiet and still. Inside the van was a very different scene.

'Slow down, Frederik!' Lukas shouted.

'OK.'

'It's down here, I think.'

'I thought you said it was back there,' Anders added.

'It's somewhere around here,' Lukas said, his gaze flitting between his phone and the street we were on. We were all starting to sweat.

Then I saw Lukas's face light up.

'Stop!'

Frederik parked up.

'This is it.'

Lukas was looking at a three-storey building to the right. I checked the microphone hidden around my neck. It had a wireless transmitter that could send a signal to Anders's camera, so that even if we did not get the camera inside, I would be able to record whatever was said.

Once we were all ready, the four of us clambered out of the van and walked over to the building. Two cars were parked outside the building. Neither looked as if it had been driven in a while. In the boot of one, a Volkswagen Sharan, I could see frames and paintings. My heart began to pound against my chest. Could it be Gullino's?

The door to the apartment block was open. It gave onto a shared hallway where I saw four mailboxes. I went over to read the names. One was 'GULLINO'. All the nervousness I had felt until then fell away and a wave of calm concentration took over my body. This was it. The moment was coming.

I went outside to tell Frederik, Lukas and Anders. The news had a sobering effect on everyone. Without another word, Anders hoisted his camera up to his shoulder and followed me as I entered the block again. I walked up the stairs with Anders behind me. On the landing of the first floor, I saw two doors, including one, on the left, marked 'F. GULLINO'.

The door was thin and worn, and it shuddered as I knocked on it.

Nobody came to the door.

I knocked again, a little louder this time. Anders was still recording everything. It was strange to be in front of the camera like this, but strange in a way that gave me a new kind of confidence. I half-imagined that I was following a script and that everything I was doing had been plotted out already.

Still no reply from inside.

I kept knocking for a while before I noticed the bell by the side of the door. I pressed it. An electronic ditty sang out inside the apartment. I wasn't sure if I was imagining it but a few seconds later, I thought I could hear movement within. I put my ear to the door. Either it was movement, or the sound of a radio or television. Listening more carefully, I could make out the sound of an Italian man amid ripples of laughter and applause. I tried to picture Gullino watching a gameshow on television.

I knocked again and called out – 'Francesco!'

Then I heard a noise behind me. Gullino's neighbour's door had cracked open a little.

'*Guten Tag*,' I began.

The latch on the neighbour's door came off. I saw a small man with chalk-white hair appear.

'Yes?'

'I'm looking for Francesco,' I explained. 'Do you know if he's home?'

'Yes,' he replied. 'He's almost always home. But he doesn't hear well.'

I knocked again. The neighbour gently moved me out of the way and gave the door an almighty pounding, so hard that I thought it was about to come off its hinges.

'You have to keep going,' he shouted, hammering at the door. 'He's in there.'

Then he turned to look at Anders with his camera, as if he hadn't really taken him in before. He pointed at Gullino's door and whispered, as if it was a secret, '*Ich kenne seine Geschichte*'. I know his story.

With a smile on his face, he went back into his apartment.

Was this man about to sound the alarm? We had heard so much about Gullino being protected that it came to mind that people could have been given instructions to keep an eye on him, and pass on that four Scandinavians had turned up out of the blue with a film camera. We might not have long.

I walked around the building with Frederik to see if there was another way in. The street remained deserted and hot. Around the back of the building, I saw that the window to Gullino's kitchen was open. The sound of the Italian television was much easier to make out here. Beneath this open window, I could see a small porch. What if, I wondered, I got up onto that porch? There was a chance that I could then clamber into his kitchen. Sure, I'm a middle-aged man, not a parkour athlete, but it might be worth a try.

Frederik gave me a leg up and soon I was balancing on top of the porch. I could now peer into Gullino's kitchen. I had never seen anything like it. The stove was covered with unwashed pots and pans, and I noticed patches of mould on the walls, empty bottles and rubbish everywhere, as well as the occasional fly buzzing about lazily, as if spoilt for choice. This looked like an abandoned kitchen. Perhaps he had already left and had forgotten to turn off his television.

Should I try to jump in through the window? It was not too far. About a metre or so from where I was on top of the porch. There was a risk that I might fall. But the real danger was how Gullino would react to an intruder. It was entirely possible that he was armed. I caught myself in time. Jumping into Gullino's kitchen would be a mistake, I realised. I clambered down from the roof.

It had been two hours since we had arrived and we had tried almost everything. Then I realised that there was one last thing we had not done. I told Anders to follow me as I raced back into the building. This time, I tried the handle on Gullino's door. It opened. There was a chain that prevented it from opening further. But we could now see part of his hallway. Anders gave me a nudge.

'Umbrella!' he whispered, nodding at an umbrella stand in Gullino's hall that was stuffed with umbrellas.

'Ciao, Francesco,' I called into the apartment. This time, the sound of my voice reached into the rooms beyond and I heard something moving around out of sight.

'Hello,' came a faint and hoarse voice from within.

I looked through the crack in the door. There he was. Francesco Gullino was making his way towards me. He wore an unbuttoned shirt and a bucket hat, and was fiddling with his shorts as he shuffled towards the door.

I wasn't really sure what was happening, only that the next few minutes were going to be crucial. I had to get him talking. From the moment I caught sight of him, I started to talk at him almost non-stop, relaxed and casual, as if we were old friends who had been chatting away for the last few hours.

'I have talked to all your friends in Denmark that I could find,' I said, with all the familiarity I could manage.

At first, he just groaned. Perhaps he had lost his mind, I thought. Then he cleared his throat and tried again.

'Yeah, yeah,' he said, looking up at me. In that instant, I knew that he was all there.

'And I have some pictures to show you. I need to go back to Denmark very soon.'

'Are you flying?' he asked.

This was good. He was engaging with me.

'Yes,' I said. 'Can I come in?'

'Yes,' he replied, taking the chain off the door. 'But if you can,' he said, looking around him at the piles of belongings he had stacked up in the hallway.

'Sure, sure,' I said, as I moved into his apartment. 'No problem, I can.'

'Yes, I am sorry,' he said, moving a little to accommodate me. 'Come here.'

'I met Giorgio on the street, and Salvatore,' I said, as I moved further into his apartment, referring to two of his friends from Copenhagen.

'Giorgio! Salva!'

'Salvatore is very sick. Yes, he can't remember anything.'

'He can't remember?'

'Maybe you also remember Franco Invernizzi,' I went on.

'Yeah,' Gullino replied, nodding. 'You know all my friends.'

He smiled up at me, the same ratty grin I had seen so many times in photographs, on television and, more recently – now that I saw it, I recognised it with a startling intensity – in my dreams. I continued to edge into his apartment, and could hear Anders doing the same behind me. But now Gullino was blocking my path.

He looked past me at the camera.

It was a delicate moment. I felt as if everything hinged on this. If we were going to record this interview, he had to accept the presence of the camera. But the sight of Anders appeared to have put him off.

'And what are you doing, are you film...' he began. 'Filming me?'

'Yes, I said, trying to mirror his sing-song tone, 'because you are a very interesting person!'

'I am very interesting?'

I nodded, knowing that I needed to change the subject, to do something that would move us past this moment. Gullino was still blocking part of the hallway, either by accident or design. But there was a way past him if I was prepared to risk pulling a muscle. I took a huge lunge over the box that was to one side of him. It was too high, and I found myself stuck on top of it, balancing on my groin. Gullino looked at me with confusion. Pushing myself off the wall, I managed to scramble off the box and almost fell into his living room. As I did so, I beckoned at Anders to do the same.

'Excuse me,' Gullino said. 'OK. I'm sorry, can you enter?'

'Yeah, I can enter,' I said, trying to sound as if this was normal. Gullino seemed to accept this and was soon apologising for the mess everywhere.

'I didn't keep up very much,' he said, looking around him at the wasteland of cardboard boxes, clothing and stacks of dusty pictures.

From where I was, I could see on the wall in his kitchen a list of women's names that he had scrawled in black pen, with a price in Euros next to each one, ranging from 100 to 200. Presumably these were the local sex workers he paid to be with.

I gave Anders a nod, and he began to set up his camera for the interview. I then got out my phone and messaged Frederik and Lukas, who were still outside.

Come in now.

'You remember Ulla, and Salvatore,' I said to Gullino, as I typed, trying to distract him.

'I remember,' he replied, looking at Anders with a new curiosity. 'I see a gentleman next to you.'

'Yes, I have a cameraman. I would really like to talk to you.'

'What about?'

'I have so much to show you from Denmark!' I said, before reeling off the names of some of the other people we had spoken to. Then I showed him the calendars he had left in Franco's house, partly to prove our bona fides, but also to start bringing back memories of his time in Copenhagen. As he inspected them, I talked at speed about the time he had spent living with Franco and Helene. 'You told Franco that the Danish police and the English police contacted you and were interrogating you,' I went on. 'You said that to Franco and his wife.'

'Possible,' Gullino said, looking more thoughtful. 'So much time has passed.'

'Maybe we can talk a little bit and we can go out and have a beer later?'

'Yes. You want to sit here?' he gestured at a chair.

'I can sit here and maybe you have a chair somewhere.'

'You can sit there,' he said.

Anders had set himself up in a half-sitting, half-standing position with the camera wedged into his shoulder.

'I have so much to show you,' I went on, enthusiastically. 'I think you are a very interesting person and I only have one question for you, basically, because I would just like to know — who are you?'

It was at this point that I noticed a small change come over Gullino, as if at some level he had registered that something very unusual was about to begin and there might not be a way out of it. He was still on the armrest of his sofa. Lukas entered the room and set up a second camera but Gullino barely looked up. Instead, his gaze remained ahead of him and he seemed to be lost in thought. He then opened his mouth and quietly said to himself a solitary, exasperated word: 'Fuuuuuck.'

38
MEDALS

Gullino was perched on the edge of his sofa as Lukas walked up to him with a microphone that he wanted to clip onto his shirt. Gullino stood up, at which point his shorts fell down, and we saw that he was not wearing any underwear.

This moment seemed to stretch out into a space beyond time, where everything was still and nobody moved. Only a few days ago, I had reconciled myself to the idea that I might never find the Umbrella Murderer and had left it too late. Now I had two cameras on him and he was standing in front of me in just an open shirt and a hat, naked from the waist down.

Then it passed. Gullino gasped and reached to pull up his shorts. Once Gullino had sorted himself out, Lukas was able to attach a microphone to his shirt. I checked with Anders that the levels were OK and he had a good camera angle, and we began.

I started by showing Gullino some of the documents I had brought from Copenhagen – including his Danish passport and his notebooks. His expression changed as he saw these, he looked at once interested and serious, especially as he leafed through his passport.

'I wonder where you got it,' he said, half to himself.

'It was left in Copenhagen,' I replied. 'In Franco's house.'

'Hmmm. I think he took it.'

'Why?'

'He was once very curious about me.'

'Yes, he was. He was also recording you.'

'Probably, yes.'

'Do you remember that?'

'Vaguely, I think I remember something like that. But that was very many years ago.'

'Yes, but you and Franco were travelling around Europe, and he was recording you, when you were talking.'

'Uh-huh,' Gullino said, sounding nonplussed.

'And you were saying that Franco didn't understand what had happened to Markov, and he was too stupid to realise how big a case this was.'

Gullino went quiet.

'Francesco,' I began, 'I found you because I would really like to talk to you about your life. Do you remember Franco?'

'Yeah, is he still alive?'

'No. He is dead.'

Gullino looked at me, his eyes trying to read mine.

'God save his soul, or whatever you say.'

'He died many years ago,' I went on. 'You were one of the last people to see him alive. I talked to Franco's wife, Helene. Do you remember her?'

'Yeah, tall lady.'

'She said that you were watching the documentary together, where Franco was participating.'

'Yeah.'

'And in that documentary, Franco was talking about you. He was standing on a bridge in Copenhagen and he was saying that you were a very dangerous person, you were a nomad and you were working for the Bulgarian Secret Service, and you watched that documentary together.'

'No, I don't ...'

'Franco was very nervous, he was very scared that evening. And the next day, Franco got sick. Very sick, and came to hospital, and then he died two days later.'

'Oh,' Gullino said, with an exaggerated grimace. He looked as if he had heard something that was both shocking and funny. And at the same time — and this was what made this moment so strange — his body jerked up a little, as if he had been startled by the thought.

'He never finished his movie,' Gullino added.

'OK,' I said, unsure where to take this.

For the next few seconds, we eyeballed each other. There was a new look in his eyes, one that was suddenly more combative than before.

'Do you think I did it?' he asked.

I paused for a moment, and decided not to answer his question.

'I just want to know,' I said, 'do you remember your meeting?'

'No,' he said. 'I absolutely don't remember.'

'But do you remember that you saw the documentary together?'

'No.'

'Have you ever seen the documentary where Franco talks about you?'

'No.'

Three lies in ten seconds, I thought to myself.

'The next day,' I tried, 'he got very sick and died two days later.'

'No idea.'

Gullino was now in denial mode. If I mentioned a subject that he did not like, he would act ignorant, deny everything or change the subject. I recognised the way he would do this from the transcript of his interview with Scotland Yard.

I asked if he was a fascist or a communist.

Neither.

Had he once been part of Ordine Nuovo?

No.

Had he ever met his Bulgarian handler, Micho Genkovski?

No, never heard of him.

I showed him one of the reports he had written for Genkovski and asked what he made of it.

Forgery, he said.

Could he remember being interrogated by Bird and Kemp, the two British detectives?

No, he said. If that had happened, he had forgotten about it entirely.

At this point, Gullino raised his index finger in the air, keeping his eyes on it as he moved it around in a circle, before looking at me in a questioning way, as if to say — where are you going with this?

To be completely honest, at that precise moment in the conversation, I was not entirely sure. The heat in that room was making it hard to think. Nothing that I had tried so far had penetrated his defences, which made me think it was time to try something else.

'Did you go to Turkey and work for Mondial?' I asked.

'How do you find out that?' he asked, sounding indignant.

'When you worked for Mondial, you were driving to Turkey, Italy, Bulgaria.'

'Yes.'

'Can you tell me why you wanted to go to Denmark? Why not Sweden, Holland, France?'

'I had no particular reason to go there. It was a quiet, relaxed country.'

'And then you came to Denmark. Do you remember Assistens Kirkegarden, a cemetery?'

This was where Gullino and his handler had their dead drop.

'Yes, a cemetery.'

'You remember that, Assistens Kirkegarden.'

'It tells me something, the name, yes. What about it?'

'That was one of the places where you picked up your messages.'

'Oh!' he said, his face lighting up, as if he had been let in on a secret. 'Very interesting.'

'Yes! Come on, Francesco. Tell me your story. I mean, you know what I want to know. Please tell me your story.'

'Ask the police. They know better than me!'

'They don't know anything.'

'Oh?' he said. 'Why?'

'Because they have stopped investigating.'

'Ooof,' he chuckled.

Time for a different angle. I reached into the folder I had brought with me and, for a second time, showed him the passport he had left in Franco's house. Leaning forward, I opened it so that he could see what I was pointing at.

'Here are all the stamps in the passport,' I pointed to them one by one, 'and all the dates are the same dates that we can find in the Bulgarian archives, so we know you are going to meet Genkovski.'

'Maybe,' Gullino said, leafing through the passport with a new curiosity.

'We can see when you went to Cyprus to meet Genkovski in 1986.' I went on. 'There is a stamp in your passport saying Cyprus 1986.'

'Yeah.'

I needed to be more direct.

'Have you used your Danish passport to travel around to meet members of the Bulgarian Secret Service?'

'Can be ...' he stuttered. 'I, I, I ...'

'How can it be all the stamps are in your Danish passport when you go to meet the Bulgarian Secret Service?'

'I don't know if I met Genkovski, but I went to ...'

'You met Genkovski.'

'OK, I see,' he smiled. 'If you insist, if you insist.'

'Do you remember Genkovski?'

To my surprise, I could see that this question had landed differently.

'Still alive?' Gullino asked.

'No,' I said. 'He died some years ago, Genkovski. But he got very old.'

'He must be,' Gullino nodded. 'He must be very old.'

We were getting somewhere now. Gullino had acknowledged knowing something about the Bulgarian intelligence officer who had been his handler for decades. The thought of Genkovksi seemed to have put him in a more reflective place. I tried to imagine the bond he must have had with this man, and to guess at the trust, respect and intense camaraderie that must have existed between these two men.

'Did you like him?'

'Oh God,' Gullino laughed to himself, slipping back into his earlier frame of mind, batting off each question with a denial, a shrug or a joke.

'You know him.'

'I'm sorry,' he shrugged.

'Was he good to you?'

'I cannot say,' Gullino laughed sheepishly.

In the archives in Sofia, we had found in the Piccadilly file several photographs of Gullino. I leaned forward to show him one of them.

'This is from the Bulgarian archives,' I said. 'Is this your photo?'

'Yeah, it looks like me.'

Next, I showed him a photograph of two medals from his file.

'And these are the medals you received from the Bulgarian Secret Service?'

'Oooh, the medals! You have a very good documentation, if this is true, all of that!'

'But you can't remember?'

'No, they made so many fakes about me.'

'Who? Who made all the fakes?'

'I don't know, I don't know what kind of service, or what I did.'

The conversation drifted off again as he launched into a stream of denials before bringing it back suddenly to what we had been talking about.

'The medal,' Gullino said, almost to himself.

'What do you mean?' I asked, unsure if I had heard him correctly.

'The two medals.'

'You got two medals from the Bulgarian Secret Service. You remember that?'

'No,' he laughed. 'You are talking like a policeman right now. You keep repeating the same thing!'

'Yes, because I know!'

'Expecting, expecting that I will make a mistake,' Gullino said.

'Because I know that you know the truth and I am not a policeman. I just want the world to know the truth.'

'But why, what for?'

'Because we need to set the story straight. There are so many conspiracies out there. We need to get the story straight and you are the person who knows!'

'The last?'

'The last,' I agreed.

He whooped in mock celebration.

'So, please tell us.'

'Yes, I wish I could, really, because you are very kind and gentle. But that is all that I can.'

I paused to take stock. Gullino had *not* said that the case against him was an outrageous falsehood. He had *not* fumed at the thought of it, as any innocent person would. He had carefully parried each of my jabs, until now, as we were beginning to tire in the heat, when he hinted that while there was more he would like to tell us, he could not.

Then, without a prompt from any of us, he went back to the medals again.

'I got two medals, huh?' he chuckled. 'They gave me two medals.'

A look came over his face that I had not seen before. For the first time in our conversation he looked proud, like a boy who had just found out that he had done much better than expected in an exam.

'I must have done something very good!' he said.

'Do you know why they gave you the medals?'

'Yeah, you get a medal because somebody is doing something very good.'

'And what were you doing that was very good?'

'Somebody, they believe I did ...'

'What was that?'

'Boom!' he punched the air in front of him. 'With umbrella! Come on,' he said, and in that that wild moment he seemed to be irritated at the question, as if it was one that did not need to be asked. He had been given the medals because of the Umbrella Murder.

In the momentum of any interview, it's sometimes hard to recognise at the time the importance of something that has just been said. A particular word or phrase whose meaning you might only appreciate in full when you are no longer caught up in the cut-and-thrust of the conversation itself and you're able to listen back to it in a more detached way. It was later, when I played back the recording, that I saw what made this part of the interview so important: Francesco Gullino had acknowledged that Bulgarian intelligence had given him medals as a reward for the part he had played in the Umbrella Murder. He was careful with his language. He used the word *believe*. The Bulgarians awarded him these medals because they *believed* he was Markov's killer.

That moment was the furthest he would go. It was as if Gullino and I reached a silent compromise in the moments that followed. He had come as far as he possibly could towards a confession and I now understood why, for his own safety, he was unwilling to go further. I also accepted that I was not going to trick him into an admission that he did not want to make. If he said anything more, his life might be in danger. He had confessed without making an actual confession. We had reached the end of the road.

Finally, I showed him a picture of Hanne With, the sex worker he had known who was found dead in her flat on New Year's Day, 1990. Gullino had lied to the police about where he was that night.

'Do you know what happened to her?' I asked.

'She was killed,' Gullino said.

'Can you tell us what happened?'

'No, I only know from the newspapers what happened to her.'

We talked a little more about this but in the way he spoke about this I could see an absence of guilt. There was no fidgeting this time, no shrugs and no smirks. He did not seem to have been involved in this woman's death. In all likelihood, he had covered up his whereabouts on the night of her murder because he had in fact been seeing his Bulgarian handler.

Although I probed for more — talking about cancelling our flight home, coming back the next day, taking a walk — Gullino did not waver. As we neared the end of the conversation, I asked for his number. He looked surprised.

'Are you sure you don't have it?!' he said. 'You know about everything.'

'We know a lot, but not everything.'

Gullino read out his number and Lukas dialled it into his phone.

'Can you, can you call me?' he asked.

Lukas made the call and Gullino's phone rang.

Before we left, I asked Gullino for a photograph. Just me and him.

'But you took millions of me!'

'Yes, but with the two of us together.'

I went to stand beside him, closer than I had ever been — close enough to smell him and feel the presence of his body — and Lukas took the photograph.

Then the man behind the Umbrella Murder wished us a safe journey and we left his apartment.

AN END, AND A BEGINNING

Frederik, Lukas, Anders and I stepped out into the street and looked at each other. Our clothes were damp with sweat, we were exhausted, but none of that mattered. We fell into an embrace. Having convinced myself that Gullino had lost his mind and was living in a home, we had just taped a three-hour-long interview with him. The sound was good, the lighting was good. Everything was as I had hoped it would be. That night we went out for a drink to celebrate.

Even if we had not found a way to draw a straight confession out of Gullino, I no longer had any doubt that he was personally responsible for the deaths of Georgi Markov and my friend Franco.

For the last twenty-seven years of my life, I had been on the trail of a killer. Every time I had pictured him, there had been a cartoonish menace in his eyes. He had always been well-dressed in my imagination, sharp and potent, a man who exuded a sense of danger. Instead, we had discovered the shell of a man, someone living in squalor and all but cut off from the rest of the world. His life had been derailed. He'd been in hiding for so long, he no longer seemed to care about his surroundings, the world, or himself.

'I'm just an old man waiting to die,' he said to me at one point during our interview. His eyes looked sadder than usual, and in that moment it was as if every trace of artifice fell away and there was no longer any distance between us. The glint in his eyes had gone and I realised that this was what he looked like when he was telling the truth. Gullino was an old man waiting to die, and the saddest thing was that nobody cared. In many ways, this was a fitting end to the journey of his life. The path he had chosen had led him to this fetid flat with nobody close to him. Gullino may have avoided prison but he had ended up instead in a prison of his own making.

Four weeks later, on 26 July, Lukas saw a missed call on his phone. It was from Gullino. As we left his apartment, I had said that if he ever wanted to talk more he could just give Lukas a call. This must be it.

Lukas called him back immediately. But Gullino did not pick up. He tried again. Still nothing.

Three minutes later, Gullino called him again.

Lukas picked up.

'Hello?' he said, expecting to hear the old man's voice. 'Hello, Francesco?'

But Gullino said nothing.

Two weeks later, Francesco Gullino was found dead in his apartment.

A friend of Gullino's had become worried after not hearing from Gullino for some time, and had decided to drop by. When they found his corpse, the skin was blue and his flesh had begun to decompose. He had a blanket over his body and was lying next to the bed. Nobody could be sure how long he had been dead but it must have been a while.

We may never know how he died, or exactly when, but it is possible that the two calls Gullino made to Lukas that day were among the last ones he ever made.

Why did he call? What was he hoping to say? I like to think that Gullino might have been willing to make some kind of death-bed confession, and that a part of him was ready at last to unburden himself and to make peace with the story of his life. Francesco

Gullino left this world without anyone by his side, nobody to hold his hand or to offer some sense of comfort. As he took his last breath, he lacked the one thing he needed and had been searching for ever since his mother died and his father left him, and that was love.

I spent the next year working with Frederik, Lukas and Anders on our film about Gullino. We cut the material down into three hour-long episodes. The national broadcasters in Denmark, Norway and Sweden all bought the film, and in early 2023, it went out across Scandinavia.

I wasn't really sure what I wanted the reaction to be, but when it came, it felt transformative. In the days that followed, it was as if everyone I met had not only seen the film but entered into this secret part of my life, ranging from my ten-year-old son — who was now an expert on Gullino and the Umbrella Murder — to strangers who came up to me on the street and told me how much they had enjoyed the film. I had messages from journalists I had never met, and the story began to be reported internationally from those further afield. I hadn't understood until then just how many people around the world had heard about the Umbrella Murder, how they had hung onto a curiosity about exactly what might have happened and who could have been responsible. At times, I had lost sight of this being the most bizarre and enigmatic murder of the Cold War, one that many people found impossible to forget. For so many of us, the death of Markov had existed in a fictional universe. It was fantastical. Gullino had been an imaginary, mythic creature. Now he was real.

What I found most interesting and unexpected about the reaction to the film was how people responded to the story of Franco's death. I remember a waiter in a café coming over to me shortly after the broadcast of the final episode to say that he had seen the film and really wanted to know more about Franco's death. In the final cut, we had not explored this in as much detail as I would have liked. As I spoke to more people in the weeks that followed, I heard versions of the same thing. Everybody wanted to know more about what had happened to Franco. There was more to his story, I kept saying. So much more. Details that we hadn't been able to include the documentary, and more about the relationship between me and him. There were also things to say about Gullino that we had not been able to cover.

I had been hoping that the broadcast of the film would close this chapter in my life but it did not. If I was going to put this all behind me, and that had been my aim, I needed to tell the whole story, which is how I came to write the book that you're reading now.

As I write this, I'm sitting in the place where it all began, in Café Sebastopol, where I met Franco for the first time. The décor has changed in the thirty years since then, and of course, I have changed as well. Only now that I've finished writing this story can I feel the weight of it start to fade away.

The Umbrella Murder was the first story that I worked on as a journalist and it will probably be the last. I want to spend less time at a computer in the years ahead and do more with my hands – making things, building, painting, spending more time with my kids. This is something I've been thinking about for years. The desire has been there all this time but it's only now that I've put this story to bed that I am ready for a new beginning.

Sometimes, the best way to shake off a difficult memory from your past is to distract yourself. But that's not always possible. There are other times when to go forward we need first to take a step back and find a way to face down and confront the thing that's haunting us. To get past Gullino, I had to find him. Earlier in my life, I would have set out to do that by myself, but finally I realised that if I was going to track him down, I needed help.

The café is emptying out now and it's time to leave. Outside, I can see that it has begun to rain and some people are opening up their umbrellas. I've left mine at home. But that's OK. I don't think I'll be needing it anymore.

A NOTE ON
SOURCES

This book has been a long time coming and some of the research began more than thirty years ago, in 1994, as I began to scour the newspaper archives at DR, the Danish national broadcaster. But there was a limit to what I could learn about the Umbrella Murder from the public record. Most of the story contained in this book is based on other material.

Parts of the narrative are based on notes I made at the time about the conversations I was having with Franco. The growth of the internet helped, of course. And I have been aided by fellow researchers who I have come to know over the years. But most of this story is based on the treasure trove of material that Franco Invernizzi gathered during his life, including all the documents that Gullino left behind in his house. Also useful were the hundreds of hours of video tape and audio recordings that Franco bravely put together. My thanks to Franco's widow, Helene Invernizzi, and to Bent Staalhøj, his former collaborator, for letting me see this material. Without it, I don't think I would have been able to complete this project.

I have also benefitted from the research carried out by Andrea Speranzoni that was commissioned by Franco in the early 2000s and from the brilliant sleuthing of Lukas more than a decade later as we set out to find Gullino.

Usually at this point in a book, the author lets their readers know about which archives to visit in order to see the original material, so that they can, if they wish, delve deeper into the background of the story. Sadly, most of the material that I have been able to see is currently in storage and is not accessible to the public. Perhaps one day this will change and we can find a way to share more of Franco's material with the world.

REFERENCES

Prologue

1   Vladimir Bereanu and Kalin Todorov, *The Umbrella Murder* (Bury St Edmunds: TEL, 1994), p. 16

Chapter 2: An Unexplained Death

1   CID summary, May 1979
2   'Record of Interview: Francesco Gullino', 5 February 1993
3   Georgi Markov, *The Truth that Killed*, transl. Liliana Brisby (New York: Ticknor & Fields, 1984), p. vii
4   Anthony Tucker, 'German Warfare Theory on Murder of Defector', *Guardian*, 2 October 1978
5   Jack McEachran, 'Pin-Head Pellet of Death', *Daily Mirror*, 30 September 1978
6   Adrian Berry, 'Virus Theory', *Daily Telegraph*, 30 September 1978
7   Vladimir Bereanu and Kalin Todorov, *The Umbrella Murder* (Bury St Edmunds: TEL, 1994), p. 20
8   ibid, p. 20
9   Robert Trains, 'Has the Poison Brolly Killer Struck Again?', *Sun*, 3 October 1978

Chapter 4: Breakthrough

1   'Markov "Was on Hit Man's List"', *Daily Telegraph*, 27 October 1978
2   UK National Archives, FCO 28/3758
3   Michael Cockerill, 'Who Killed Georgi Markov?', *The Listener*, April 1979
4   John Miller, 'Bulgaria Complained to Britain Yesterday about the "Hullabaloo" over the Mysterious Death of Mr Georgi Markov', *Daily Telegraph*, 16 September 1978
5   'Man Quizzed Over Brolly Jab Murder', *Sun*, 19 August 1985

Chapter 8: 'A Pleasant Young Man'

1   Hristo Hristov, *The Double Life of Agent Piccadilly*, hristo-hristov.com, 2008, p. 15
2   ibid, p. 13
3   ibid, p. 16

Chapter 10: Laboratory No, 12

1   'Moscow ruled out', *Daily Mail*, 3 January 1979

Chapter 13: Georgi

1   Georgi Markov, *The Truth That Killed*, transl. Liliana Brisby (New York: Ticknor & Fields, 1984), p. 175
2   ibid
3   ibid
4   ibid, p. 176
5   Peter Todorov, 'The Discreet Dissident', *Trud*, 22 January 1998
6   Georgi Markov, *The Truth That Killed*, p. 18
7   ibid, p. 176
8   ibid, p. 177
9   ibid, p. 215
10 ibid, p. 9
11 ibid, p. 217
12 ibid, p. 221
13 ibid, p. 232
14 ibid, p. 233

Chapter 14: Todorov

1   Vladimir Bereanu and Kalin Todorov, *The Umbrella Murder* (Bury St Edmunds: TEL, 1994), pp. 76–8

Chapter 15: Dissent

1   ibid, p. 245
2   ibid , p. 241

3 ibid, p. 249
4 ibid, p. 219
5 ibid, p. 231
6 ibid, p. 236
7 ibid, p. 231
8 ibid, p. 253
9 ibid, p. 253
10 ibid, p. 262
11 Georgi Markov, Distant Reports about Bulgaria, p. 515, quoted in Hristo Hristov, *Kill the Wanderer*, hristo-hristov.com, 2005, pp. 84–5

Chapter 17: The Hunting Rifle

1 Oleg Kalugin, *The First Directorate* (New York: St. Martin's Press, 1994), p. 178
2 ibid, pp. 178–9
3 ibid, p. 179
4 ibid, p. 179
5 ibid, p. 179
6 ibid, p. 180

Chapter 18: Zhivkov

1 Myrna Oliver, 'Todor Zhivkov; Bulgarian Dictator, Kremlin Loyalist', *Los Angeles Times*, 7 August 1998

Chapter 28: Hanne

1 Author interview with Brian Belling

Chapter 35: A Giant Penis

1 David Charter, 'Bulgarian Honours Dissident Murdered on Waterloo Bridge', *The Times*, 12 November 2014
2 'Phallus Statue wurde eingehüllt', fotokerschi.at, 13 April 2017

ACKNOWLEDGEMENTS

The creation of this story has been a collective effort involving numerous individuals. Foremost among them is Franco, who will always be the central figure. Helene also, her invaluable assistance and patience serving as pillars throughout this journey. Allowing me access to Franco's materials and research reignited my pursuit of Francesco Gullino, and without the generous support of both Helene and Bent, none of this would have been possible.

Resurrecting the tale of Gullino and the Umbrella Murder required the dedication of a group committed to delving deep into the labyrinthine world of espionage. My heartfelt thanks go out to Anders Thomsen, Lukas Ouitre, and Frederik Bruun Madsen for their unwavering dedication and skill in bringing this story to life.

I extend my gratitude to those individuals who, for years, considered themselves friends of Gullino during his time in Denmark, and shared their personal anecdotes. Their experiences shed light on the hidden costs of the friendship, from surveillance to theft, to Gullino reporting information about them to the Bulgarian intelligence.

Engaging with an international narrative presents its challenges, yet it also offers invaluable opportunities. I am indebted to Richard Cummings and Christopher Nehring for generously sharing their insights into the parapolitical realm.

There are others, whose contributions remain unacknowledged by choice. Their anonymity is respected, yet their impact is deeply felt. I am particularly indebted to a perceptive and fearless Bulgarian whom I've known only through online correspondence for nearly three years. His meticulous analysis and openness have enriched both myself and the narrative. Similarly, a London-based individual has not only scrutinised the content of this book but has breathed life into its characters with unparalleled insight.

It is a rare privilege for a Dane to debut in a language other than their native tongue. I extend my heartfelt appreciation to the team at Penguin Random House for their boldness in allowing a Danish author to make his English debut. Special thanks to Linda Brusasco for facilitating this opportunity and to Jack Smyth for his exceptional design work.

INDEX

ABOUT THE AUTHOR

Ulrik Skotte is a Danish journalist who has been chasing the truth about the Umbrella Murder and the mysterious Agent Piccadilly for more than 25 years. He eventually managed to track down Piccadilly and met him face to face in an apartment in Austria in 2021. Shortly after, Piccadilly was found dead in the same apartment. Ulrik Skotte lives in Copenhagen and owns the TV company Doceye, which produces documentaries for the Scandinavian and European markets.